ECONOMIC ISSUES, PROBLEMS AND PERSPECTIVES

ECONOMICS OF WEALTH IN THE 21ST CENTURY

ECONOMIC ISSUES, PROBLEMS AND PERSPECTIVES

Additional books in this series can be found on Nova's website under the Series tab.

Additional E-books in this series can be found on Nova's website under the E-book tab.

ECONOMIC ISSUES, PROBLEMS AND PERSPECTIVES

ECONOMICS OF WEALTH IN THE 21ST CENTURY

JASON M. GONZALEZ
EDITOR

Nova Science Publishers, Inc.
New York

Copyright © 2011 by Nova Science Publishers, Inc.

All rights reserved. No part of this book may be reproduced, stored in a retrieval system or transmitted in any form or by any means: electronic, electrostatic, magnetic, tape, mechanical photocopying, recording or otherwise without the written permission of the Publisher.

For permission to use material from this book please contact us:
Telephone 631-231-7269; Fax 631-231-8175
Web Site: http://www.novapublishers.com

NOTICE TO THE READER

The Publisher has taken reasonable care in the preparation of this book, but makes no expressed or implied warranty of any kind and assumes no responsibility for any errors or omissions. No liability is assumed for incidental or consequential damages in connection with or arising out of information contained in this book. The Publisher shall not be liable for any special, consequential, or exemplary damages resulting, in whole or in part, from the readers' use of, or reliance upon, this material. Any parts of this book based on government reports are so indicated and copyright is claimed for those parts to the extent applicable to compilations of such works.

Independent verification should be sought for any data, advice or recommendations contained in this book. In addition, no responsibility is assumed by the publisher for any injury and/or damage to persons or property arising from any methods, products, instructions, ideas or otherwise contained in this publication.

This publication is designed to provide accurate and authoritative information with regard to the subject matter covered herein. It is sold with the clear understanding that the Publisher is not engaged in rendering legal or any other professional services. If legal or any other expert assistance is required, the services of a competent person should be sought. FROM A DECLARATION OF PARTICIPANTS JOINTLY ADOPTED BY A COMMITTEE OF THE AMERICAN BAR ASSOCIATION AND A COMMITTEE OF PUBLISHERS.

Additional color graphics may be available in the e-book version of this book.

LIBRARY OF CONGRESS CATALOGING-IN-PUBLICATION DATA

Economics of wealth in the 21st century / editor, Jason M. Gonzalez.
　　p. cm.
　Includes index.
　ISBN 978-1-61122-805-2 (hardcover)
　1. Wealth--United States--History--21st century. 2. Wealth--History--21st century. I. Gonzalez, Jason M.
　HC110.W4E26 2010
　330.1'6--dc22
　　　　　　　　　　　2010042630

Published by Nova Science Publishers, Inc. † New York

CONTENTS

Preface		vii
Chapter 1	Recent Trends in Household Wealth in the U.S.: Rising Debt and the Middle Class Squeeze *Edward N. Wolff*	1
Chapter 2	When the Market Does Not Deliver: An Inclusive Growth Experiment Falls Victim to Wealth Constraints *Roswitha M. King*	43
Chapter 3	Can We Explain Away the Black-White Wealth Gap? *Zhu Xiao Di and Yi Xu*	61
Chapter 4	Consilient Approaches to Modeling Wealth *Bernard C. Beaudreau*	71
Chapter 5	A Review of Modern Theories of Wealth Inequality *Claudio Campanale*	93
Chapter 6	Wealth Management *Klaus Hellwig*	113
Chapter 7	The Distribution of Wealth in the United States from 1983 to 2004: Inequality and Polarization *Conchita D'Ambrosio, Davide Fiaschi and Edward N. Wolff*	121
Index		145

PREFACE

Among the middle class, the debt-income ratio has reached its highest level in 24 years. Additionally, the racial and ethnic disparity in wealth holdings, after stabilizing during most of the 1990s, widened in the years between 1998 and 2001, but then narrowed during the early and mid 2000s. This book presents topical research in the study of the economics of wealth in the 21st century. Topics discussed include recent trends in household wealth in the U.S.; the black-white wealth gap and wealth management.

Chapter 1 – The author finds here that the early and mid 2000s (2001 to 2007) witnessed both exploding debt and a consequent "middle class squeeze." Median wealth grew briskly in the late 1990s and even faster in the 2000s. The inequality of net worth was up slightly during the 2000s. Indebtedness, which fell substantially during the late 1990s, skyrocketed in the early and mid 2000s. Among the middle class, the debt-income ratio reached its highest level in 24 years. The concentration of investment type assets generally remained as high in 2007 as during the previous two decades. The racial and ethnic disparity in wealth holdings, after stabilizing during most of the 1990s, widened in the years between 1998 and 2001, but then narrowed during the early and mid 2000s. Wealth also shifted in relative terms away from young households (particularly under age 45) and toward those in age group 55 to 74. Projections to July 2009 on the basis of changes in stock and housing prices indicate that median wealth plunged by 36 percent and there was a fairly steep rise in wealth inequality, with the Gini coefficient advancing from 0.834 to 0.865.

Chapter 2 - This paper explains one aspect of the challenges faced by regional development policy. At issue is a policy for the development and expansion of small and medium sized enterprises (SMEs). The causes and dynamics of difficulties with SME development policies are analyzed in a game theory framework, in which "policy failure" arises as an equilibrium phenomenon. The model results deliver a cautionary note: that indiscriminate application of market criteria may be counterproductive in an environment characterized by severe constraints on material wealth accumulation.

Chapter 3 - The racial gap in wealth in the U.S. is a large and persistent social issue, an important concern for both sociologists and public policy makers. Study after study has found this to be true: no one has found any set of factors that can explain it away. However, none of these studies used the data that best capture the total aggregate household wealth in the U.S. and therefore the real wealth gap between white and black households: the Federal Reserve's SCF data set. To reinvestigate this gap, therefore, the authors used the latest SCF data, collected in 2007. Their findings confirm that the black/white wealth gap cannot be explained away even using the best available data capturing household wealth.

Chapter 4 - With the productivity slowdown in the mid-1970's came a renewed interest in all questions pertaining to the wealth of nations (levels, growth, role of technology). Neglected for most of the 20th century, economic growth soon dominated and continues to dominate both the academic and public agendas. In time, new models and approaches were forthcoming. Examples include the Ak approach developed by Paul Romer (1987, 1990). While convincing, these models suffered from a number of shortcomings, not the least of which were weak fundamentals. Specifically, while most attributed variations in growth to technological change, little was known about technology per se. Some responded by modeling technological change (Aghion and Howitt 1998) while others called for a fundamental reexamination of the very way in which material processes were modeled in economics (Kummel et al. 1998, Beaudreau 1995, 1998, 1999). The upshot of the latter class of models is the belief that models of material processes in economics, like in all other physical sciences, should be consistent with the laws of physics, specifically classical mechanics and thermodynamics. This paper examines these models, historically, theoretically and empirically. They are shown to have a history that extends back in time to the 1920s and 1930s when physicists, engineers and economists alike proposed new approaches to understanding wealth, approaches that were consistent with basic physics.

Chapter 5 - Inequality in economic fortunes of different individuals is a popular topic both in the political debate and among academicians in different areas of the social sciences and especially in economics. Ultimately differences in individual well being will depend on their consumption level and variability. However, in so far as the availability of consumption is largely determined by the income and wealth of the households, inequality can be studied by focusing the analysis on the distribution of earnings, income and wealth in the society.

In this work the author will focus his attention on one particular dimension of inequality, that is, the inequality in wealth holdings among households. More specifically he will present a summary of the work done in the field of quantitative models that have attempted to explain the distribution of wealth that is observed in the data. Most literature in this field belongs to the class of incomplete market models sometimes referred to as Bewley models, from the author of the seminal work. In these models agents face a stream of random earnings.

Due to market incompleteness, earnings fluctuations cannot be insured so that accumulation of an asset is used to smooth consumption. Taking the process for earnings as exogenous these models analyze the endogenous response of wealth accumulation and wealth inequality. Prototypical examples are the models presented in Aiyagari (1994) which is cast in a dynastic framework and Huggett (1996) which is instead formulated in a life-cycle setting. These models have been able to generate the empirically observed relationship between consumption, earnings and wealth inequality; however they did so only in qualitative terms while quantitatively they grossly underestimate wealth concentration, especially at the top of the distribution. This failure has prompted a substantial amount of research that has extended the basic model to include features like heterogeneity in discount factors, bequest motives and entrepreneurial activity. The new features improved the ability of the model to match the data. Still explaining the large fortunes at the very top of the wealth distribution remains a hard task to accomplish. This work will review the main theories that have been proposed to explain wealth concentration.

The interest of studying wealth inequality arises from several factors. One is the key role that wealth plays as a resource that the household can use to finance its consumption. As such wealth inequality is a source of welfare inequality and for this reason considerations of equity make it an interesting topic to study. Beside that, several tax policies have effects on capital formation. In a world where capital is so unequally distributed, such effects are better analyzed if the authors have models that correctly capture the reasons for savings especially of the very wealthy. Finally, although most macroeconomics is currently based on representative agent models, there are many issues where heterogeneity is important for the aggregate behavior of the economy and once again models that capture this heterogeneity are needed to improve our understanding of macroeconomic phenomena. The final section of this essay will present some applications of models of wealth inequality to these issues.

The essay is organized as follows. In section 2, the author will briefly present the empirical evidence. In section 3 he will lay out the analytical framework of the incomplete market models, presenting the dynastic version and the life-cycle version of the model as well as some intermediate approaches that show features of both. In section 4 he will present the extensions to the basic layout that have been put forth in order to better match the wealth concentration observed in the data. In section 5 the author presents some alternative approaches. Finally, in section 6, the author presents some applications of the models presented in the previous sections.

Chapter 6 - Maximizing expected utility is the standard approach for the solution of multiperiod portfolio selection problems. However, the applicability of the approach is limited:

- It requires a multi-period utility function that reflects the time and risk preferences of the investor. Such a utility function can hardly be found.

- It requires a probability distribution of the multi-period portfolio cash flows which is difficult, if not impossible, to determine.

- The solution can be inefficient in the sense that the optimal portfolio may enable arbitrage.

- It is assumed that that the utility function does not depend upon the menu over which choice is being made. This, for example, has been criticized by Sen (1997).

As an alternative Hellwig (2004), Hellwig et al (2000), Korn (2000) and Selinka (2005) proposed a different approach where a portfolio is determined based on two conditions. First, the portfolio is required to be (intertemporal) efficient. Second, the valuation of the portfolio cash flows is required to support the growth preferences of the investor concerning the portfolio value. It is shown that under reasonable assumptions a portfolio exists where both conditions are satisfied. However, the approach poses a number of problems. First, the portfolio value is defined as discounted consumption after present consumption is realized. This excludes cases where present consumption is part of the decision problem. Second, theapproach rests on the assumption of a given multiperiod probability distribution that hardlyvcan be found. Finally, the solution does not exclude consumption to be negative. How to handle such situations remains open.

The aim of this paper is to solve these problems. In the next two sections the case is treated where the portfolio value is defined as discounted consumption before present consumption is realized (which will be denoted as ex ante valuation) while section four treats the case, where the portfolio value is defined as discounted consumption after present consumption has been realized (which will be denoted as ex post valuation). For both cases it is shown that a solution with a non negative consumption vector exists under reasonable assumptions. Finally, in section five it is shown that under relaxed growth conditions a solution exists under less restrictive assumptions.

Chapter 7 - Recent work has documented a rising degree of wealth inequality in the United States between 1983 and 1989 but little change from 1989 to 2004. In this paper, the authors compare the increase in the spread of the distribution with another dimension, polarization. Using alternative approaches proposed in the literature, the authors examine whether a similar pattern exists with regard to trends in wealth polarization over this period. Perhaps, our most notable finding is the huge increase in wealth polarization that occurred in the U.S. from 1983 to 2004, particularly from 1998 to 2004. In contrast, the Gini coefficient for household wealth shows an increase in wealth inequality from 1983 to 1989 but almost no change thereafter.

In: Economics of Wealth in the 21st Century
Editor: Jason M. Gonzalez

ISBN: 978-1-61122-805-2
©2011 Nova Science Publishers, Inc.

Chapter 1

RECENT TRENDS IN HOUSEHOLD WEALTH IN THE U.S.: RISING DEBT AND THE MIDDLE CLASS SQUEEZE

Edward N. Wolff
New York University, USA

ABSTRACT

I find here that the early and mid 2000s (2001 to 2007) witnessed both exploding debt and a consequent "middle class squeeze." Median wealth grew briskly in the late 1990s and even faster in the 2000s. The inequality of net worth was up slightly during the 2000s. Indebtedness, which fell substantially during the late 1990s, skyrocketed in the early and mid 2000s. Among the middle class, the debt-income ratio reached its highest level in 24 years. The concentration of investment type assets generally remained as high in 2007 as during the previous two decades. The racial and ethnic disparity in wealth holdings, after stabilizing during most of the 1990s, widened in the years between 1998 and 2001, but then narrowed during the early and mid 2000s. Wealth also shifted in relative terms away from young households (particularly under age 45) and toward those in age group 55 to 74. Projections to July 2009 on the basis of changes in stock and housing prices indicate that median wealth plunged by 36 percent and there was a fairly steep rise in wealth inequality, with the Gini coefficient advancing from 0.834 to 0.865.

Keywords: household wealth, inequality, racial inequality, portfolio composition

JEL Codes: D31, J15

1. INTRODUCTION

The 1990s witnessed some remarkable events. The stock market boomed. On the basis of the Standard & Poor (S&P) 500 index, stock prices surged 171 percent between 1989 and

2001. Stock ownership spread and by 2001 (as we shall see below) over half of U.S. households owned stock either directly or indirectly. Real wages, after stagnating for many years, finally grew in the late 1990s. According to BLS figures, real mean hourly earnings gained 8.3 percent between 1995 and 2001.[1]

However, 2001 saw a recession (albeit a short one). Moreover, the stock market peaked in 2000 and dropped steeply from 2000 to 2003 but recovered in 2004, so that between 2001 and 2004 the S&P 500 was down by only 5.3 percent in nominal terms but 12.0 percent in real terms.[2] Real wages rose very slowly from 2001 to 2004, with the BLS real mean hourly earnings up by only 1.5 percent, and median household income dropped in real terms by 1.5 percent.[3] On the other hand, housing prices rose steeply. The median sales price of existing one-family homes rose by 17.9 percent in real terms nationwide.[4] The other big story was household debt, particularly that of the middle class, which skyrocketed during these years, as we shall see below.

From 2004 to 2007, the stock market rebounded. The S&P 500 rose 31 percent in nominal terms and 19 percent in real terms. Over the period from 2001 to 2007, the S&P 500 was up 24 percent in nominal terms and 6 percent in real terms. Real wage remained stagnant, with the BLS real mean hourly earnings rising by only 1.0 percent. Median household income in real terms showed some growth over this period, rising by 3.2 percent. From 2001 to 2007 it gained 1.6 percent. From 2004 to 2007 housing prices slowed, with the median sales price of existing one-family nationwide advancing only 1.7 percent over these years in real terms. Over the years 2001 to 2007 real housing prices gained 18.8 percent.

Most studies have looked at the distribution of well-being or its change over time in terms of income. However, family wealth is also an indicator of well-being, independent of the direct financial income it provides. There are six reasons. First, owner-occupied housing provides services directly to their owner. Second, wealth is a source of consumption, independent of the direct money income it provides, because assets can be converted directly into cash and thus provide for immediate consumption needs. Third, the availability of financial assets can provide liquidity to a family in times of economic stress, such as occasioned by unemployment, sickness, or family break-up. Fourth, as the work of Conley (1999) has shown, wealth is found to affect household behavior over and above income. Fifth, as Spilerman (2000) has argued, wealth generated income does not require the same trade offs with leisure as earned income. Sixth, in a representative democracy, the distribution of power is often related to the distribution of wealth.

Previous work of mine (see Wolff, 1994, 1996, 1998, 2001, and 2002a), using the 1983, 1989, 1992, 1995, and 1998 Surveys of Consumer Finances, presented evidence of sharply

---

[1] These figures are based on the Bureau of Labor Statistics (BLS) hourly wage series. The source is Table B-47 of the Economic Report, available at
http://www.gpoaccess.gov/eop/tables09.html.
The BLS wage figures are converted to constant dollars on the basis of the Consumer Price Index (CPI-U).

[2] The source is Table B-96 of the Economic Report of the President, 2009, available at
http://www.gpoaccess.gov/eop/tables09.html. The Census Bureau uses the newer CPI-U-RS series to convert to constant dollars. However, for this period, there is virtually no difference between the CPI-U and the CPI-U-RS.

[3] The source is Table B-33 of the Economic Report of the President, 2009, available at
http://www.gpoaccess.gov/eop/tables09.html.

[4] The source is Table 935 of the 2009 Statistical Abstract, US Bureau of the Census, available at [http://www.census.gov/compendia/statab/].

increasing household wealth inequality between 1983 and 1989 followed by a modest rise between 1989 and 1998. Both mean and median wealth holdings climbed briskly during the 1983-1989 period. From 1989 to 1998, mean wealth continued to surge while median net worth rose at a rather anemic pace. Indeed, the only segment of the population that experienced large gains in wealth from 1983 to 1998 was the richest 20 percent of households. Moreover, despite the buoyant economy over the 1990s, overall indebtedness continued to rise among American families. Stocks and pensions accounts also rose as a share of total household wealth, with offsetting declines in bank deposits, investment real estate, and financial securities.

The ratio of mean wealth between African-American and white families was very low in 1983, at 0.19, and barely budged during the 1990s, though median wealth among African-American families did advance relative to white families. In 1983, the richest households were those headed by persons between 45 and 69 years of age, though between 1983 and 1989, wealth shifted away from this age group toward both younger and older age groups. However, the relative wealth holdings of both younger and older families fell between 1989 and 1998.

In this study, I update my earlier analysis on the ownership of household wealth to 2001, 2004, and 2007.[5] The next section, Section 2, discusses the measurement of household wealth and describes the data sources used for this study. Section 3 presents results on time trends in median and average wealth holdings, Section 4 on changes in the concentration of household wealth, and Section 5 on the composition of household wealth. Section 6 investigates changes in wealth holdings by race and ethnicity; and Section 7 reports on changes in the age-wealth profile. Section 8 provides details on stock ownership for different demographic groups. In Section 9 I provide a partial update of household wealth trends to 2009. A summary of results and concluding remarks are provided in Section 10.

I find here that the early and mid 2000s (2001 to 2007) witnessed exploding debt and a consequent "middle class squeeze." Median wealth grew briskly in the late 1990s and even faster in the 2000s. The inequality of net worth was also up slightly during the 2000s. Indebtedness, which fell substantially during the late 1990s, skyrocketed in the early and mid 2000s. Among the middle class, the debt-income ratio reached its highest level in 24 years. The concentration of investment type assets generally remained as high in 2007 as during the previous two decades. The racial and ethnic disparity in wealth holdings, after stabilizing during most of the 1990s, widened in the years between 1998 and 2001, but then narrowed during the early and mid 2000s. Wealth also shifted in relative terms away from young households (particularly under age 45) and toward those in age group 55 to 74.

2. DATA SOURCES AND METHODS

The data sources used for this study are the 1983, 1989, 1992, 1995, 1998, 2001, 2004, and 2007 Survey of Consumer Finances (SCF) conducted by the Federal Reserve Board. Each survey consists of a core representative sample combined with a high-income supplement. In 1983, for example, the supplement was drawn from the Internal Revenue Service's Statistics of Income data file. For the 1983 SCF, an income cut-off of $100,000 of adjusted gross

---

[5] See Wolff (2007) for an earlier update to 2004.

income was used as the criterion for inclusion in the supplemental sample. Individuals were randomly selected for the sample within pre-designated income strata. In later years, the high income supplement was selected as a list sample from statistical records (the Individual Tax File) derived from tax data by the Statistics of Income Division of the Internal Revenue Service (SOI). This second sample was designed to disproportionately select families that were likely to be relatively wealthy (see, for example, Kennickell, 2001, for a more extended discussion of the design of the list sample in the 2001 SCF). The advantage of the high-income supplement is that it provides a much "richer" sample of high income and therefore potentially very wealthy families. However, the presence of a high-income supplement creates some complications, because weights must be constructed to meld the high-income supplement with the core sample.[6] Several adjustments were also applied to the underlying SCF data in some years. See the Appendix for details.

The principal wealth concept used here is marketable wealth (or net worth), which is defined as the current value of all marketable or fungible assets less the current value of debts. Net worth is thus the difference in value between total assets and total liabilities or debt. Total assets are defined as the sum of: (1) the gross value of owner-occupied housing; (2) other real estate owned by the household; (3) cash and demand deposits; (4) time and savings deposits, certificates of deposit, and money market accounts; (5) government bonds, corporate bonds, foreign bonds, and other financial securities; (6) the cash surrender value of life insurance plans; (7) the cash surrender value of pension plans, including IRAs, Keogh, and 401(k) plans; (8) corporate stock and mutual funds; (9) net equity in unincorporated businesses; and (10) equity in trust funds. Total liabilities are the sum of: (1) mortgage debt, (2) consumer debt, including auto loans, and (3) other debt.

This measure reflects wealth as a store of value and therefore a source of potential consumption. I believe that this is the concept that best reflects the level of well-being associated with a family's holdings. Thus, only assets that can be readily converted to cash (that is, "fungible" ones) are included. As a result, consumer durables such as automobiles, televisions, furniture, household appliances, and the like, are excluded here, since these items are not easily marketed, with the possible exception of vehicles, or their resale value typically far understates the value of their consumption services to the household. Another justification for their exclusion is that this treatment is consistent with the national accounts, where purchase of vehicles is counted as expenditures, not savings. Also excluded is the value of future social security benefits the family may receive upon retirement (usually referred to as "social security wealth"), as well as the value of retirement benefits from private pension plans ("pension wealth"). Even though these funds are a source of future income to families, they are not in their direct control and cannot be marketed.[7]

I also use a more restricted concept of wealth, which I call "non-home wealth." This is defined as net worth minus net equity in owner-occupied housing (the primary residence only). Non-home wealth is a more liquid concept than marketable wealth, since one's home is difficult to convert into cash in the short term. Moreover, primary homes also serve a consumption purpose besides acting as a store of value. Non-home wealth thus reflects the

---

[6] For a discussion of some of the issues involved in developing these weights, see Kennickell and Woodburn (1992) for the 1989 SCF; Kennickell, McManus, and Woodburn (1996) for the 1992 SCF; Kennickell and Woodburn (1999) for the 1995 SCF, and Kennickell (2001) for the 2001 SCF.

[7] See Wolff (2002b) for estimates of social security and pension wealth.

resources that may be immediately available for consumption expenditure or various forms of investments.

I use the standard price deflator, the CPI-U, which the U.S. Bureau of Labor Statistics (BLS) has been computing since 1947, to deflate wealth values. The CPI-U has been criticized for overstating the rate of inflation. As a result, the BLS also provides an alternative consumer price series called the CPI-U-RS.[8] The CPI-U-RS series makes quality adjustments for housing units and consumer durables such as automobiles and personal computers and employs a geometric mean formula to account for consumer substitution within CPI item categories. As a result, the CPI-U-RS deflator is not subject to the same criticisms as the CPI-U series. Indeed, the Current Population survey (CPS) data are now normally deflated to constant dollars by the U.S. Bureau of the Census using the CPI-U-RS price index.

While the CPI-U-RS deflator incorporates quality and other adjustments, the adjustments are made only from 1978 to the present. The CPI-U index is used for years prior to 1978. The CPI-U-RS shows a much slower rate of inflation after 1973 than the CPI-U: 288 versus 238 percent. If we use the CPI-U-RS deflator, then constant dollar median family income would show a 22 percent growth between 1973 and 2000, in comparison to the 6 percent growth rate on the basis of the CPI-U deflator.

While the use of the CPI-U-RS will show a higher growth in real incomes (and wealth) since 1978, it is not clear that the degree of bias in the CPI has risen in recent years. If similar adjustments were made on the pre-1978 price data, it is possible that the inflation rate over the 1947-1978 period would be adjusted downward by a similar amount as the post-1978 inflation rate. Since my aggregate time-series data on wealth begin in 1922 and I have made calculations of household wealth trends on the basis of micro-data beginning in 1962, I have elected to use the CPI-U series to convert nominal values to real dollars to be consistent with my earlier work on the subject, since the CPI-U series is the only consumer price series that runs from 1922 to the present.[9]

3. MEDIAN WEALTH ROSE BRISKLY DURING THE 2000S

Table 1 documents a robust growth in wealth during the 1990s. Median wealth (the wealth of the household in the middle of the distribution) was 16 percent greater in 2001 than in 1989. After rising by 7 percent between 1983 and 1989, median wealth fell by 17 percent from 1989 to 1995 and then rose by 39 percent from 1995 to 2001. As a result, median wealth grew slightly faster between 1989 and 2001, 1.32 percent per year, than between 1983 and 1989, at 1.13 percent per year. However, between 2001 and 2004, median wealth *fell* by 0.7 percent, a result of the 2001 recession. Such a drop is not unprecedented. Indeed, it occurred during the last recession in 1992, when median wealth fell by a staggering 15 percent from 1989 to 1992. Indeed, it was not until 1998 that median wealth surpassed its previous high in 1989. However, from 2004 to 2007 there was a sharp recovery in median wealth, which grew by a sizeable 19.9 percent. Thus, over the 2001-2007 period it increased by 19.1 percent, even faster than during the 1990s (and 1980s).

---

[8] The "RS" stands for "research series."
[9] See, for example, Wolff (1987, 1994, and 2002a).

On the surface it seems rather surprising that median wealth fell from 2001 to 2004 when housing prices rose so rapidly and increased so fast from 2004 to 2007 when housing prices essentially stagnated. As shown in Section 5, houses comprise the majority of the wealth of middle class families (almost exactly two thirds of the gross assets of the middle three wealth quintiles). Just from the increase in housing prices alone, median net worth should have risen by about 11.8 percent between 2001 and 2004. (The decline in stock prices would have lowered median net worth by 0.9 percent, for a net gain of almost 11 percent over this period). The reason why median net worth failed to increase was the enormous increase of household debt of the middle class over these three years (see Section 5 below). The surge in median wealth from 2004 to 2007 is a bit of a mystery. The spike in stock prices accounted for only a small part of the increase (about 1.4 percentage points). There was also a slight decline in the debt to asset ratio of the middle three wealth quintiles (see Table 7). The remaining possibility is that middle class savings expanded over these years.

Table 1. Mean and Median Wealth and Income, 1983-2007 (In thousands, 2007 dollars)

Wealth Concept	1983	1989	1992	1995	1998	2001	2004	2007	1983-1989	1989-2001	2001-2007	1983-2007
A. Net Worth												
1. Median	69.5	74.3	63.4	62.1	77.2	86.1	85.5	102.5	7.0	15.8	19.1	47.5
2. Mean	270.4	309.8	301.2	278.3	343.8	445.1	472.5	536.1	14.6	43.7	20.4	98.2
3. Percent with net worth												
a. Zero or negative	15.5	17.9	18.0	18.5	18.0	17.6	17.0	18.6				
b. Less Than $5,000[a]	25.4	27.6	27.2	27.8	27.2	26.6	26.8	26.6				
c. Less Than $10,000[a]	29.7	31.8	31.2	31.9	30.3	30.1	29.9	30.0				
B. Non-home Wealth												
1. Median	15.0	17.7	14.9	13.5	22.7	27.2	20.0	23.5	18.0	53.4	-13.5	56.7
2. Mean	196.2	231.3	229.6	213.5	270.0	349.5	350.5	400.9	17.8	51.1	14.7	104.3
3. Percent with zero or negative non-home wealth	25.7	26.8	28.2	28.7	25.7	25.5	28.0	27.4				
C. Income[b]												
1. Median	43.5	48.3	45.3	46.4	49.5	49.4	48.7	50.2	11.2	2.3	1.6	15.5
2. Mean	52.9	61.1	57.4	61.1	66.0	68.1	66.4	67.6	15.5	11.6	-0.8	27.9

Source: own computations from the 1983, 1989, 1992, 1995, 1998, 2001, 2004, and 2007 Survey of Consumer Finances
a. Constant 1995 Dollars.
b. Source for household income data: U.S. Census of the Bureau, Current Populations Surveys, available on the Internet.

As shown in the third row of Panel A, the percentage of households with zero or negative net worth increased from 15.5 percent in 1983 to 17.9 percent in 1989 but fell off a bit to 17.6 percent in 2001 and then to 17.0 percent in 2004. However, this was followed by a sharp increase in 2007, to 18.6 percent, its highest level over the 24 years. On the other hand, the share of household with net worth less than $5,000 and less than $10,000 (both in 1995 dollars) declined somewhat between 1989 and 2007.

Mean net worth also showed a sharp increase from 1983 to 1989 followed by a rather precipitous decline from 1989 to 1995 and then, buoyed largely by rising stock prices, another surge in 2001 and then an additional rise in both 2004 and 2007. Overall, its 2007 value was almost double its value in 1983 and about three quarters larger than in 1989. Mean wealth grew quite a bit faster between 1989 and 2001, at 3.02 percent per year, than from 1983 to 1989, at 2.27 percent per year. There was then a slight increase in wealth growth from 2001 to 2007 to 3.10 percent per year. This modest acceleration was due largely to the rapid increase in housing prices of 18.8 percent in real terms over the six years counterbalanced by the reduced growth in stock prices between 2001 and 2007 in comparison to 1989 to 2001, and to the fact that housing comprised 28.2 percent and (total) stocks made up 24.5 percent of total assets in 2001. Another point of note is that mean wealth grew more about twice as fast as the median between 1983 and 2007, indicating widening inequality of wealth over these years.

Non-home wealth grew even faster than net worth during the 1990s. Median non-home wealth rose by 18 percent between 1983 and 1989, then plummeted by 24 percent from 1989 to 1995, and then surged over the next six years, for a net increase of 53 percent between 1989 and 2001. However, from 2001 to 2004, median non-home wealth plummeted once again – in this case, by 27 percent. Here, again, the reasons are falling stock prices and rising non-mortgage debt as a share of total assets. However, from 2004 to 2007 median non-home wealth recovered again and grew by 18 percent, reflecting the recovery of stock prices and the slight reduction in household debt. All in all, median non-home wealth fell by 14 percent from 2001 to 2007 but increased by 57 percent from 1983 to 2007, about 10 percentage points more than the gain in median net worth.

Between 1983 and 1995, the fraction of households with zero or negative non-home wealth expanded from 25.7 to 28.7 percent but then fell back to 25.5 percent in 2001 but then climbed again, to 28.0 percent in 2004 before falling slightly to 27.4 percent in 2007. Thus, the sharp decline in median non-home wealth from 2001 to 2007 reflected, in part, the growing non-mortgage debt of the bottom half of the distribution.

Mean non-home wealth, after increasing by 18 percent from 1983 to 1989, declined by 8 percent between 1989 and 1995, and then jumped after that, for a net gain of 51 percent between 1989 and 2001. From 2001 to 2004 there was virtually no change in mean non-home wealth but from 2004 to 2007 there was robust growth, with mean non-home wealth advancing by 14 percent, so that over the entire 1983-2007 period mean non-home wealth increased by 104 percent, slightly more than mean net worth. Increases were almost identical for median and mean non-home wealth from 1983 to 2001 but because of the sharp fall-off in median non-home wealth from 2001 to 2007 mean non-home wealth grew at about double the pace of median non-home wealth from 1983 to 2007. The bull market in stocks was largely responsible for the sharp growth in non-home wealth between 1995 and 2001, while the slow rise in stock prices coupled with rising indebtedness caused the slow growth in average non-home wealth from 2001 to 2007.

Median household income (based on Current Population Survey data), after gaining 11 percent between 1983 and 1989, grew by only 2.3 percent from 1989 to 2001, then dipped by 1.6 percent between 2001 and 2004, but gained 3.2 percent from 2004 to 2007, for a net change of 16 percent from 1983 to 2007. In contrast, mean income rose by 16 percent from 1983 to 1989, by another 12 percent from 1989 to 2001, then fell by 2.6 percent from 2001 to 2004 but gained 1.9 percent from 2004 to 2007, for a net change of -0.8 percent from 2001 to 2007 and a total change of 28 percent from 1983 to 2007. Between 1983 and 2007, mean income grew less than mean net worth (and non-home wealth), and median income grew at a much slower pace than median wealth.

In sum, while household income virtually stagnated for the average American household over the 1990s and 2000s, median net worth and especially median non-home wealth grew strongly over this period. In the 2000s, in particular, mean and median income changed very little while mean and median net worth grew strongly, as did mean non-home wealth, though median non-home wealth tumbled by 14 percent.

4. WEALTH INEQUALITY SHOWS A MODEST INCREASE OVER THE EARLY 2000S

The figures in Table 2 also show that wealth inequality, after rising steeply between 1983 and 1989, remained virtually unchanged from 1989 to 2007. The share of wealth held by the top 1 percent rose by 3.6 percentage points from 1983 to 1989 and the Gini coefficient increased from 0.80 to 0.83. Between 1989 and 2007, the share of the top percentile actually declined sharply, from 37.4 to 34.6 percent, though this was more than compensated for by an increase in the share of the next four percentiles. As a result, the share of the top five percent increased from 58.9 percent in 1989 to 61.8 percent in 2007, and the share of the top quintile rose from 83.5 to 85.0 percent. The share of the fourth and middle quintiles each declined by about a percentage point from 1989 to 2007, while that of the bottom 40 percent increased by almost one percentage point. Overall, the Gini coefficient was virtually unchanged -- 0.832 in 1989 and 0.834 in 2007.

Non-home wealth is even more concentrated than net worth, with the richest 1 percent (as ranked by non-home wealth) owning 43 percent of total household non-home wealth in 2007 (compared to 35 percent for net worth) and the top 20 percent owning 93 percent (compared to 85 percent for net worth). The inequality of non-home wealth shows a different time trend than net worth. The share of the top one percent gained 4.0 percentage points and the Gini coefficient increased from 0.89 to 0.93 between 1983 and 1989 – trends mirroring those of net worth. However, in the ensuing twelve years, from 1989 to 2001, the share of the richest one percent plummeted by seven percentage points, the share of the top five percent fell by three percentage points, and that of the top quintile by two percentage points. The share of the fourth quintile increased by 0.4 percentage points, the share of the middle quintile held its own, and that of the bottom two quintiles rose. As a result, the Gini coefficient fell from 0.93 in 1989 to 0.89 in 2001 and was actually slightly lower in 2001 than in 1983. However, the trend reversed between 2001 and 2007, with the share of the top percent rising by 3.0 percentage points, that of the top quintile up by 1.7 percentage points, and the shares of the third and four quintiles, and the bottom 40 percent all falling. As a result, the Gini coefficient rose from 0.89 in 2001 to 0.91 in 2007, still higher than in 1983 but lower than its peak value of 1989. The run-up in inequality in the 2000s is a reflection of the increase in the share of households with zero or negative non-home wealth.

The top 1 percent of families (as ranked by income on the basis of the SCF data) earned 21 percent of total household income in 2006 and the top 20 percent accounted for 61 percent --

large figures but lower than the corresponding wealth shares.[10] The time trend for income inequality also contrasts with those for net worth and non-home wealth inequality. Income inequality increased sharply between 1982 and 1988, with the Gini coefficient rising from 0.48 to 0.52 and the share of the top one percent from 12.8 to 16.6 percent. There was then very little change between 1988 and 1997. While the share of the top one percent remained at 16.6 percent of total income, the share of the next 19 percent increased by 0.6 percentage points and the share of the other quintiles lost, so that the Gini coefficient grew slightly, from 0.52 to 0.53.

Table 2. The Size Distribution of Wealth and Income, 1983-2007

Year	Gini Coefficient	Top 1.0%	Next 4.0%	Next 5.0%	Next 10.0%	Top 20.0%	4th 20.0%	3rd 20.0%	Bottom 40.0%	All
A. Net Worth										
1983	0.799	33.8	22.3	12.1	13.1	81.3	12.6	5.2	0.9	100.0
1989	0.832	37.4	21.6	11.6	13.0	83.5	12.3	4.8	-0.7	100.0
1992	0.823	37.2	22.8	11.8	12.0	83.8	11.5	4.4	0.4	100.0
1995	0.828	38.5	21.8	11.5	12.1	83.9	11.4	4.5	0.2	100.0
1998	0.822	38.1	21.3	11.5	12.5	83.4	11.9	4.5	0.2	100.0
2001	0.826	33.4	25.8	12.3	12.9	84.4	11.3	3.9	0.3	100.0
2004	0.829	34.3	24.6	12.3	13.4	84.7	11.3	3.8	0.2	100.0
2007	0.834	34.6	27.3	11.2	12.0	85.0	10.9	4.0	0.2	100.0
B. Non-home Wealth										
1983	0.893	42.9	25.1	12.3	11.0	91.3	7.9	1.7	-0.9	100.0
1989	0.926	46.9	23.9	11.6	11.0	93.4	7.4	1.7	-2.5	100.0
1992	0.903	45.6	25.0	11.5	10.2	92.3	7.3	1.5	-1.1	100.0
1995	0.914	47.2	24.6	11.2	10.1	93.0	6.9	1.4	-1.3	100.0
1998	0.893	47.3	21.0	11.4	11.2	90.9	8.3	1.9	-1.1	100.0
2001	0.888	39.7	27.8	12.3	11.4	91.3	7.8	1.7	-0.7	100.0
2004	0.902	42.2	26.7	12.0	11.6	92.5	7.3	1.2	-1.1	100.0
2007	0.908	42.7	29.3	10.9	10.1	93.0	6.8	1.3	-1.0	100.0
C. Income (SCF)										
1982	0.480	12.8	13.3	10.3	15.5	51.9	21.6	14.2	12.3	100.0
1988	0.521	16.6	13.3	10.4	15.2	55.6	20.6	13.2	10.7	100.0
1991	0.528	15.7	14.8	10.6	15.3	56.4	20.4	12.8	10.5	100.0
1994	0.518	14.4	14.5	10.4	15.9	55.1	20.6	13.6	10.7	100.0
1997	0.531	16.6	14.4	10.2	15.0	56.2	20.5	12.8	10.5	100.0
2000	0.562	20.0	15.2	10.0	13.5	58.6	19.0	12.3	10.1	100.0
2003	0.540	17.0	15.0	10.9	14.9	57.9	19.9	12.1	10.2	100.0
2006	0.574	21.3	15.9	9.9	14.3	61.4	17.8	11.1	9.6	100.0

Source: own computations from the 1983, 1989, 1992, 1995, 1998, 2001, 2004, and 2007 SCF.

For the computation of percentile shares of net worth, households are ranked according to their net worth; for percentile shares of non-home wealth, households are ranked according to their non-home wealth; and for percentile shares of income, households are ranked according to their income.

---

[10] It should be noted that the income in each survey year (say 2007) is for the preceding year (2006 in this case).

However, between 1997 and 2000, income inequality again surged, with the share of the top percentile rising by 3.4 percentage points, the shares of the other quintiles falling again, and the Gini index advancing from 0.53 to 0.56. As a result, the years from 1989 to 2001 saw almost the same degree of increase in income inequality as the 1983-1989 period.[11] The trend reversed between 2000 and 2003, with the Gini coefficient falling from 0.56 to 0.54 (though still above its 1997 level). The main change was a sharp decline in the share of the top one percent by 3 percentage points, reflecting a substantial downturn in realized capital gains. However, the trend reversed from 2003 to 2007. The share of the top one percent surged from 17.0 to 21.3 percent of total income, the share of the top quintile from 57.9 to 61.4 percent, the shares of the other quintiles fell, and the Gini coefficient rose sharply from 0.54 to 0.57. All in all, the 2000s witnessed a moderate increase in income inequality, a small rise in wealth inequality, and a significant jump in non-home wealth inequality.

Table 3. The Count of Millionaires and Multi-Millionaires, 1983-2007

Year	Total Number of Households (1,000s)	The Number of Households (in 1,000s) with Net Worth Equal to or Exceeding (in 1995$):		
		1 Million	5 Million	10 Million
1983	83,893	2,411	247.0	66.5
1989	93,009	3,024	296.6	64.9
1992	95,462	3,104	277.4	41.6
1995	99,101	3,015	474.1	190.4
1998	102,547	4,783	755.5	239.4
2001	106,494	5,892	1,067.8	338.4
2004	112,107	6,466	1,120.0	344.8
2007	116,120	7,274	1,466.8	464.2
% Change	38.4	201.7	493.8	598.3

Source: own computations from the 1983, 1989, 1992, 1995, 1998, 2001, 2004, and 2007 SCF.

It is somewhat surprising that net worth inequality did not decline from 2001 to 2004. The reason is that as shown in my previous work (Wolff, 2002a), wealth inequality is positively related to the ratio of stock prices to house prices. Between 2001 and 2004, that ratio (of the Standard & Poor 500 stock index to the median sales price of existing one-family homes) fell sharply from 8.1 to 6.1. The reason inequality did not fall is that household debt also mushroomed over these years (see Section 5 below). In fact, the inequality of gross assets did show a decline between 2001 to 2004, from a Gini coefficient of 0.774 to 0.767. It was only rising debt that led to a rise in overall net worth inequality. Likewise, from 2004 to 2007, we would have expected a larger rise in net worth inequality since income inequality was up sharply and the ratio of Standard & Poor 500 stock index to the median sales price of

---

[11] It should be noted that the SCF data show a much higher level of income inequality than the CPS data. In the year 2000, for example, the CPS data show a share of the top five percent of 22.1 percent and a Gini coefficient of 0.462. The difference is primarily due to three factors. First, the SCF oversamples the rich (as noted above), while the CPS is a representative sample. Second, the CPS data are top-coded (that is, there is an open-ended interval at the top, typically at $75,000 or $100,000), whereas the SCF data are not. Third, the income concepts differ between the two samples. In particular, the SCF income definition includes realized capital gains whereas the CPS definition does not. However, the CPS data also show a large increase of inequality between 1989 and 2000, with the share of the top five percent rising from 18.9 to 22.1 percent and the Gini coefficient from 0.431 to 0.462. Further analysis of the difference in income figures between the two surveys is beyond the scope of this paper.

existing one-family homes rose from 6.1 to 7.1. Again, the reasons are not apparent for the small rise in wealth inequality over these last three years.

Despite the relative stability in overall wealth inequality during the 1990s, there was a near explosion in the number of very rich households (see Table 3). The number of millionaires almost doubled between 1989 and 2001, the number of "penta-millionaires" ($5,000,000 or more) increased three and a half times, and the number of "deca-millionaires" ($10,000,000 or more) grew more than five-fold. Much of the growth occurred between 1995 and 2001 and was directly related to the surge in stock prices. The number of the very rich continued to increase between 2001 and 2007 at about the same pace, with the number of millionaires growing by 23 percent, the number of penta-millionaires by 37 percent, and the number of deca-millionaires by 37 percent as well.

Table 4. Mean Wealth Holdings and Income by Wealth or Income Class, 1983-2007
(In thousands, 2007 dollars)

Variable	Top 1.0%	Next 4.0%	Next 5.0%	Next 10.0%	Top 20.0%	4th 20.0%	3rd 20.0%	Bottom 40.0%	All
A. Net Worth									
1983	9,127	1,510	656.6	354.5	1,099.7	170.0	70.6	5.9	270.4
2007	18,529	3,656	1,201.3	641.9	2,278.9	291.0	106.0	2.2	536.1
% change	103.0	142.2	83.0	81.1	107.2	71.2	50.1	-62.9	98.2
% of gain[a]	35.4	32.3	10.3	10.8	88.8	9.1	2.7	-0.6	100.0
B. Non-home Wealth									
1983	7,870	1,152	450.3	201.8	837.4	72.5	15.6	-4.0	183.5
2007	17,116	2,936	874.4	404.1	1,863.6	135.7	26.0	-10.5	400.9
% change	117.5	154.8	94.2	100.2	122.5	87.3	66.6	159.6	118.5
% of gain[a]	42.5	32.8	9.8	9.3	94.4	5.8	1.0	-1.2	100.0
C. Income									
1982	786.4	203.2	126.2	94.7	158.8	66.3	43.3	18.9	61.2
2006	1,786.8	334.4	166.5	120.0	257.9	74.7	46.7	20.2	83.9
% change	127.2	64.6	32.0	26.7	62.3	12.7	7.7	7.1	37.1
% of gain[a]	44.1	23.1	8.9	11.2	87.3	7.4	2.9	2.4	100.0

Source: own computations from the 1983 and 2007 Survey of Consumer Finances.

For the computation of percentile shares of net worth, households are ranked according to their net worth; for percentile shares of non-home wealth, households are ranked according to their non-home wealth; and for percentile shares of income, households are ranked according to their income.

a. The computation is performed by dividing the total increase in wealth of a given group by the total increase of wealth for all households over the period, under the assumption that the number of households in each group remains unchanged over the period. It should be noted that the households found in a given group(such as the top quintile) may be different in each year.

Table 4 shows the absolute changes in wealth and income between 1983 and 2007. The results are even more striking. Over this period, the largest gains in relative terms were made by the wealthiest households. The top one percent saw their average wealth (in 2007 dollars) rise by over 9 million dollars or by 103 percent. The remaining part of the top quintile experienced increases from 81 to 142 percent and the fourth quintile by 71 percent. While the middle quintile gained 50 percent, the poorest 40 percent lost 63 percent! By 2007, their average wealth had fallen to $2,200.

Another way of viewing this phenomenon is afforded by calculating the proportion of the total increase in real household wealth between 1983 and 2007 accruing to different wealth groups. This is computed by dividing the increase in total wealth of each percentile group by the total increase in household wealth, while holding constant the number of households in that group. If a group's wealth share remains constant over time, then the percentage of the total wealth growth received by that group will equal its share of total wealth. If a group's share of total wealth increases (decreases) over time, then it will receive a percentage of the total wealth gain greater (less) than its share in either year. However, it should be noted that in these calculations, the households found in each group (say the top quintile) may be different in the two years.

The results indicate that the richest one percent received over one third of the total gain in marketable wealth over the period from 1983 to 2007. The next 4 percent also received about a third of the total gain and the next 15 percent about a fifth, so that the top quintile collectively accounted for 89 percent of the total growth in wealth, while the bottom 80 percent accounted for 11 percent.

The pattern of results is similar for non-home wealth. The average non-home wealth of the richest one percent more than doubled, that of the next richest four percent rose by over 150 percent, and that of the next richest 15 percent increased by about 97 percent. Altogether, the non-home wealth of the top quintile gained 123 percent. However, in the case of non-home wealth, the fourth and third quintiles also showed substantial gains, of 87 and 67 percent, respectively, though the bottom 40 percent showed negative growth. Of the total growth in non-home wealth between 1983 and 2007, 43 percent accrued to the top one percent and 94 percent to the top quintile, while the bottom 80 percent collectively accounted for only 6 percent.

A similar calculation using income data reveals that the greatest gains in real income over the period from 1982 to 2006 were made by households in the top one percent of the income distribution, who saw their incomes grow by 127 percent. Mean incomes increased by almost two-thirds for the next 4 percent and by about a third for the next highest 5 percent and by 27 percent for the next highest ten percent. Groups in the bottom 80 percent of the income distribution all experienced 13 percent or less real growth in income. Of the total growth in real income between 1982 and 2006, 44 percent accrued to the top one percent and 87 percent to the top quintile, with remaining 13 percent distributed among the bottom 80 percent.

These results indicate rather dramatically that despite the relative stability of inequality of net worth and the slight decline of non-home wealth inequality during the 1990s and early 2000s, the growth in the economy during the period from 1983 to 2007 was concentrated in a surprisingly small part of the population -- the top 20 percent and particularly the top one percent.

5. STOCKS REMAIN HIGHLY CONCENTRATED IN THE HANDS OF THE RICH

The portfolio composition of household wealth shows the forms in which households save. In 2007, owner-occupied housing was the most important household asset in the breakdown shown in Table 5, accounting for 33 percent of total assets. However, net home equity -- the value of the house minus any outstanding mortgage -- amounted to only 21 percent of total assets. Real estate, other than owner-occupied housing, comprised 11 percent, and business equity another 20 percent.

Demand deposits, time deposits, money market funds, CDs, and the cash surrender value of life insurance made up 7 percent and pension accounts 12 percent. Bonds and other financial securities amounted to 2 percent; corporate stock, including mutual funds, to 12 percent; and trust equity to 2 percent. Debt as a proportion of gross assets was 15 percent, and the debt-equity ratio (the ratio of total household debt to net worth) was 0.18.

There have been some notable changes in the composition of household wealth over the period between 1983 and 2007. The first is the steep rise in the share of gross housing wealth in total assets. After fluctuating between 28.2 and 30.4 percent from 1983 to 2001, the ratio jumped to 33.5 percent in 2004 and then declined slightly to 32.8 percent in 2007. There are two factors behind this. The first is the rise in the homeownership rate. According to the SCF data, the homeownership rate, after falling from 63.4 percent in 1983 to 62.8 percent in 1989, picked up to 67.7 percent in 2001 and then to 69.1 percent in 2004 before falling slightly to 68.6 percent in 2007. The second is the sharp rise in housing prices, noted above. Between 2001 and 2004, the median house price for existing one-family homes rose by 17.9 percent in real terms. The rise in housing prices by itself would have caused the share of housing in total assets to rise by 5.05 percentage points, compared to the actual increase of 5.2 percentage points.[12]

A second and related trend is that net equity in owner-occupied housing (the difference between the market value and outstanding mortgages on the property), after falling almost continuously from 23.8 percent in 1983 to 18.2 percent in 1998, picked up to 18.8 percent in 2001, 21.8 percent in 2004, and then 21.4 percent in 2007. The difference between the two series (gross versus net housing values as a share of total assets) is attributable to the changing magnitude of mortgage debt on homeowner's property, which increased from 21 percent in 1983 to 37 percent in 1998, fell back to 33 percent in 2001, and then rose again to 35 percent in 2004 and 2007. Moreover, mortgage debt on principal residence climbed from 9.4 to 11.4 percent of total assets between 2001 and 2007. The fact that net home equity as a proportion of assets increased between 2001 and 2007 reflected the strong gains in real estate values over these years.

Third, overall indebtedness first increased, with the debt-equity ratio leaping from 15.1 percent in 1983 to 19.4 percent in 1995, before falling off to 17.6 percent in 1998 and 14.3 percent in 2001. However, it jumped to 18.4 percent in 2004, close to its previous 1992 high, though it fell off slightly to 18.1 percent in 2007. Likewise, the ratio of debt to total income first surged from 68 percent in 1983 to 91 percent in 1995, leveled off in 1998, then declined to 81 percent in 2001, then skyrocketed to 115 percent in 2004 and 119 percent in 2007, its

---

[12] As noted above, housing prices were essentially flat from 2004 to 2007.

high for this period. If mortgage debt on principal residence is excluded, then the ratio of other debt to total assets fell off from 6.8 percent in 1983 to 3.1 percent in 2001 but then rose to 3.9 percent in both 2004 and 2007. One implication is that over the 1990s and 2000s families used tax-sheltered mortgages and home equity loans rather than consumer loans and other forms of consumer debt to finance consumption.

Table 5. Composition of Total Household Wealth, 1983 - 2007 (Percent of gross assets)

Wealth component	1983	1989	1992	1995	1998	2001	2004	2007
Principal residence (gross value)	30.1	30.2	29.8	30.4	29.0	28.2	33.5	32.8
Other real estate (gross value)[a]	14.9	14.0	14.7	11.0	10.0	9.8	11.5	11.3
Unincorporated business equity[b]	18.8	17.2	17.7	17.9	17.7	17.2	17.1	20.1
Liquid assets[c]	17.4	17.5	12.2	10.0	9.6	8.8	7.3	6.6
Pension accounts[d]	1.5	2.9	7.2	9.0	11.6	12.3	11.8	12.1
Financial securities[e]	4.2	3.4	5.1	3.8	1.8	2.3	2.1	1.5
Corporate stock and mutual funds	9.0	6.9	8.1	11.9	14.8	14.8	11.9	11.8
Net equity in personal trusts	2.6	3.1	2.7	3.2	3.8	4.8	2.9	2.3
Miscellaneous assets[f]	1.3	4.9	2.5	2.8	1.8	1.8	1.8	1.7
Total	100.0	100.0	100.0	100.0	100.0	100.0	100.0	100.0
Debt on principal residence	6.3	8.6	9.8	11.0	10.7	9.4	11.6	11.4
All other debt[g]	6.8	6.4	6.0	5.3	4.2	3.1	3.9	3.9
Total debt	13.1	15.0	15.7	16.3	15.0	12.5	15.5	15.3
Memo (selected ratios in percent):								
Debt / equity ratio	15.1	17.6	18.7	19.4	17.6	14.3	18.4	18.1
Debt / income ratio	68.4	87.6	88.8	91.3	90.9	81.1	115.0	118.7
Net home equity / total assets[h]	23.8	21.6	20.1	19.5	18.2	18.8	21.8	21.4
Principal residence debt / house value	20.9	28.6	32.7	36.0	37.0	33.4	34.8	34.9
Stocks, directly or indirectly owned / total assets[i]	11.3	10.2	13.7	16.8	22.6	24.5	17.5	16.8

Source: own computations from the 1983, 1989, 1992, 1995, 1998, 2001, 2004, and 2007 SCF.

a. In 2001, 2004, and 2007, this equals the gross value of other residential real estate plus the net equity in non-residential real estate.
b. Net equity in unincorporated farm and non-farm businesses and closely-held corporations.
c. Checking accounts, savings accounts, time deposits, money market funds, certificates of deposits, and the cash surrender value of life insurance.
d. IRAs, Keogh plans, 401(k) plans, the accumulated value of defined contribution pension plans, and other retirement accounts.
e. Corporate bonds, government bonds (including savings bonds), open-market paper, and notes.
f. Gold and other precious metals, royalties, jewelry, antiques, furs, loans to friends and relatives, future contracts, and miscellaneous assets.
g. Mortgage debt on all real property except principal residence; credit card, installment, and other consumer debt.
h. Ratio of gross value of principal residence less mortgage debt on principal residence to total assets.
i. Includes direct ownership of stock shares and indirect ownership through mutual funds, trusts, and IRAs, Keogh plans, 401(k) plans, and other retirement accounts

A fourth change is that pension accounts rose from 1.5 to 12.1 percent of total assets from 1983 to 2007. This increase largely offset the decline in the share of liquid assets in total assets, from 17.4 to 6.6 percent, so that it is reasonable to conclude that households have to a large extent substituted tax-deferred pension accounts for taxable savings deposits.

Fifth, the proportion of total assets in the form of other (non-home) real estate fell off sharply, from 15 percent in 1983 to 10 percent in 2001, but then increased to 11.3 percent in

2007. The change from 2001 to 2007 (particularly 2001 to 2004) to a large extent reflected rising real estate prices. Financial securities fell from 4.2 to 1.5 percent of total assets between 1983 and 2007. Unincorporated business equity fell slightly as a share of gross wealth over the years 1983 to 2004 but then surged to 20.1 percent in 2007. The share of corporate stock and mutual funds in total assets rose rather briskly from 9.0 in 1983 to 14.8 percent in 1998, stayed at 14.8 percent in 2001, and then plummeted to 11.8 percent in 2007. If we include the value of stocks indirectly owned through mutual funds, trusts, IRAs, 401(k) plans, and other retirement accounts, then the value of total stocks owned as a share of total assets more than doubled from 11.3 percent in 1983 to 24.5 percent in 2001 and then tumbled to 16.8 percent in 2007. The rise during the 1990s reflected the bull market in corporate equities as well as increased stock ownership, while the decline in the 2000s was a result of the relatively small rise in the stock market over this period (particularly relative to housing prices) as well as a drop in stock ownership (see Table 13b below). The change in stock prices by itself would have caused the share of total stocks in assets to fall by 2.9 percentage points between 2001 and 2004, compared to the actual decline of 7.0 percentage points. Most of the decline in the share of stocks in total assets was due to sales of stocks and withdrawals from stock funds.[13]

A. Portfolio Composition by Wealth Class

The tabulation in Table 5 provides a picture of the average holdings of all families in the economy, but there are marked class differences in how middle-class families and the rich invest their wealth. As shown in Table 6, the richest one percent of households (as ranked by wealth) invested over three quarters of their savings in investment real estate, businesses, corporate stock, and financial securities in 2007. Corporate stocks, either directly owned by the households or indirectly owned through mutual funds, trust accounts, or various pension accounts, comprised 21 percent by themselves. Housing accounted for only 10 percent of their wealth (and net equity in housing 9 percent), liquid assets another 5 percent, and pension accounts another 6 percent. Their ratio of debt to net worth was only 3 percent, their ratio of debt to income was 39 percent, and the ratio of mortgage debt to house value was 15 percent.

Among the next richest 19 percent of U.S. households, housing comprised 32 percent of their total assets (and net home equity 24 percent), liquid assets 7 percent, and pension assets 16 percent. Forty-four percent of their assets took the form of investment assets -- real estate, business equity, stocks, and bonds -- and 19 percent was in the form of stocks directly or indirectly owned. Debt amounted to 12 percent of their net worth and 110 percent of their income, and the ratio of mortgage debt to house value was 26 percent.

In contrast, almost two thirds of the wealth of the middle three quintiles of households was invested in their own home in 2007. However, home equity amounted to only 35 percent of total assets, a reflection of their large mortgage debt. Another 21 percent went into monetary savings of one form or another and pension accounts. Together housing, liquid assets, and pension assets accounted for 86 percent of the total assets of the middle class. The remainder was about evenly split among non-home real estate, business equity, and various financial securities and corporate stock. Stocks directly or indirectly owned amounted to only

---

[13] However, the rebound in the stock market from 2004 to 2007 would have raised the stock share to 20.8 percent by itself. This was probably offset by increases in asset prices of other assets.

7 percent of their total assets. The ratio of debt to net worth was 61 percent, substantially higher than for the richest 20 percent, and their ratio of debt to income was 157 percent, also much higher than the top quintile. Finally, their mortgage debt amounted to almost half the value of their principal residences.

Table 6. Composition of Household Wealth by Wealth Class, 2007
(Percent of gross assets)

Asset	All Households	Top One Percent	Next 19 Percent	Middle 3 Quintiles
Principal residence	32.8	10.2	31.8	65.1
Liquid assets (bank deposits, money market funds, and cash surrender value of life insurance)	6.6	4.5	7.3	7.8
Pension accounts	12.1	5.8	15.9	12.9
Corporate stock, financial securities, mutual funds, and personal trusts	15.5	25.2	15.0	3.6
Unincorporated business equity other real estate	31.3	52.3	28.5	9.3
Miscellaneous assets	1.7	2.0	1.6	1.3
Total assets	100.0	100.0	100.0	100.0
Memo (selected ratios in percent):				
Debt / equity ratio	18.1	2.8	12.1	61.1
Debt / income ratio	118.7	39.4	109.8	156.7
Net home equity / total assets[a]	21.4	8.7	23.6	34.8
Principal residence debt / house value	34.9	15.2	25.6	46.6
All stocks / total assets[b]	16.8	21.4	18.6	7.0
Ownership Rates (Percent)				
Principal residence	68.6	98.8	96.0	76.9
Mobile home	4.1	0.0	0.3	6.0
Other real estate	19.0	76.0	48.0	14.7
Vacation homes	6.5	37.4	16.7	4.9
Pension assets	52.6	87.7	81.1	53.4
Unincorporated business	12.0	73.8	29.7	8.8
Corporate stock, financial securities[c], mutual funds, and personal trusts	27.8	85.3	63.4	23.1
Stocks, directly or indirectly owned[b]	49.1	92.6	85.5	47.8
(1) $5,000 or more	36.3	89.7	82.2	31.8
(2) $10,000 or more	31.6	89.1	78.4	26.0

Source: own computations from the 2007 SCF. Households are classified into wealth class according to their net worth. Brackets for 2007 are:

Top one percent: Net worth of $8,232,000 or more.
Next 19 percent: Net worth between $473,000 and $8,232,000.
Quintiles 2 through 4: Net worth between $200 and $473,000.
Also, see notes to Table 5.
a. Ratio of gross value of principal residence less mortgage debt on principal residence to total assets.
b. Includes direct ownership of stock shares and indirect ownership through mutual funds, trusts, and IRAs, Keogh plans, 401(k) plans, and other retirement accounts
c. Financial securities exclude U.S. government savings bonds in this tabulation.

Almost all households among the top 20 percent of wealth holders owned their own home, in comparison to 77 percent of households in the middle three quintiles. Though this homeownership rate looks large, 6 percent of households in the middle three quintiles reported having a mobile home as their primary residence. Over three-quarters of very rich households (in the top percentile) owned some other form of real estate (37 percent owned a vacation home), compared to 48 percent of rich households (those in the next 19 percent of the distribution) and only 15 percent of households in the middle 60 percent. Eighty-eight percent of the very rich owned some form of pension asset, compared to 81 percent of the rich and 53 percent of the middle. A somewhat startling 74 percent of the very rich reported owning their own business. The comparable figures are 30 percent among the rich and only 9 percent of the middle class.

Among the very rich, 85 percent held corporate stock, mutual funds, financial securities or a trust fund, in comparison to 63 percent of the rich and 23 percent of the middle. Ninety-three percent of the very rich reported owning stock either directly or indirectly, compared to 86 percent of the rich and 48 percent of the middle. If we exclude small holdings of stock, then the ownership rates drop off sharply among the middle three quintiles, from 48 percent to 32 percent for stocks worth $5,000 or more and to 26 percent for stocks worth $10,000 or more.

The rather staggering debt level of the middle class in 2007 raises the question of whether this is a recent phenomenon or whether it has been going on for some time. The overall debt-equity ratio in 2007 was still below its peak value in 1995, while the overall debt-income ratio has been generally trending upward since 1983 and actually took a big jump from 2001 to 2004.

Table 7 compares the wealth composition of the three wealth classes in 1983 and 2007. There is remarkable stability in the composition of wealth by wealth class between 1983 and 2001. The most notable exception is a substitution of pension assets for liquid assets -- a transition that occurred for all three wealth classes but that was particularly marked for percentiles 80-99 and for the middle three quintiles. The debt-equity ratio actually fell for the top one percent from 1983 and 2007, as did the debt-income ratio. The debt-income ratio increased slightly for the next 19 percent, while the debt-income ratio rose sharply, from 73 to 110 percent.

Table 7. Composition of Household Wealth by Wealth Class, 1983 and 2007
(Percent of gross assets)

Component	Top One Percent 1983	Top One Percent 2007	Next 19 Percent 1983	Next 19 Percent 2007	Middle 3 Quintiles 1983	Middle 3 Quintiles 2007
Principal residence	8.1	10.2	29.1	31.8	61.6	65.1
Liquid assets (bank deposits, money market funds, and cash surrender value of life insurance)	8.5	4.5	21.4	7.3	21.4	7.8
Pension accounts	0.9	5.8	2.0	15.9	1.2	12.9
Corporate stock, financial securities, mutual funds, and personal trusts	29.5	25.2	13.0	15.0	3.1	3.6
Unincorporated business equity other real estate	52.0	52.3	32.8	28.5	11.4	9.3
Miscellaneous assets	1.0	2.0	1.6	1.6	1.3	1.3
Total assets	100.0	100.0	100.0	100.0	100.0	100.0
Memo:						
Debt / equity ratio	5.9	2.8	10.9	12.1	37.4	61.1
Debt / income ratio	86.8	39.4	72.8	109.8	66.9	156.7

Note: own computations from the 1983 and 2007 Survey of Consumer Finances. Also, see notes to Table 5.

Table 8. Composition of Household Wealth of the Middle Three Wealth Quintiles, 1983-2007 (Percent of gross assets)

Asset	1983	1989	1998	2001	2004	2007
Principal residence	61.6	61.7	59.8	59.2	66.1	65.1
Liquid assets (bank deposits, money market funds, and cash surrender value of life insurance)	21.4	18.6	11.8	12.1	8.5	7.8
Pension accounts	1.2	3.8	12.3	12.7	12.0	12.9
Corporate stock, financial securities, mutual funds, and personal trusts	3.1	3.5	5.5	6.2	4.2	3.6
Unincorporated business equity other real estate	11.4	9.4	8.8	8.5	7.9	9.3
Miscellaneous assets	1.3	2.9	1.8	1.2	1.4	1.3
Total assets	100.0	100.0	100.0	100.0	100.0	100.0
Memo (selected ratios in percent):						
Debt / equity ratio	37.4	41.7	51.3	46.4	61.6	61.1
Debt / income ratio	66.9	83.0	101.6	100.3	141.2	156.7
Net home equity / total assets[a]	43.8	39.2	33.3	33.8	34.7	34.8
Principal residence debt / house value	28.8	36.5	44.4	42.9	47.6	46.6
All stocks / total assets[b]	2.4	3.3	11.2	12.6	7.5	7.0
Ownership Rates (Percent)						
Principal residence	71.6	71.5	73.3	75.9	78.2	76.9
Other real estate	15.4	15.5	13.7	13.2	13.6	14.7
Pension assets	12.2	27.3	48.5	52.9	51.4	53.4
Unincorporated business	8.5	8.4	8.5	7.9	8.1	8.8
Corporate stock, financial securities [c] mutual funds, and personal trusts,	21.6	24.2	26.7	27.5	27.1	23.1

Source: own computations from the Survey of Consumer Finances. Households are classified into wealth class according to their net worth. Also, see notes to Table 5.
a. Ratio of gross value of principal residence less mortgage debt on principal residence to total assets.
b. Includes direct ownership of stock shares and indirect ownership through mutual funds,
Trusts, and IRAs, Keogh plans, 401(k) plans, and other retirement accounts
c. Financial securities exclude U.S. government savings bonds in this tabulation.

Table 8 shows the wealth composition for the middle three wealth quintiles from 1983 to 2007. Perhaps, the noteworthy finding here is that changes in the asset portfolio composition of the middle class basically paralleled those of all households. Houses as a share of total assets remained virtually unchanged from 1983 to 2001 but then increased in 2004, largely a reflection of rising house prices. Pension accounts rose as a share of total assets by almost 12 percentage points (and the proportion of households with a pension account surged by 41 percentage points) from 1983 to 2007 while liquid assets declined as a share by 14 percentage points. This set of changes paralleled that of all households. The share of investment assets in total assets rose by 3 percentage points from 1983 to 2001 and then fell by 2.6 percentage points in 2007, reflecting the stagnation of stock prices. The share of all stocks in total assets mushroomed from 2.4 percent in 1983 to 12.6 percent in 2001 and then fell off to 7.0 percent in 2007 as stock prices stagnated.

Changes in debt, however, were much more dramatic. There was a sharp rise in the debt-equity ratio of the middle class from 37 percent in 1983 to 61 percent in 2007, with most of the increase occurring between 2001 and 2004. The rise was much steeper than for all households. The debt to income ratio skyrocketed over this period, more than doubling. Here, too, much of the increase happened between 2001 and 2004. Moreover, the increase was much steeper than for all households. In fact, in 1983, the debt to income ratio was about the same for middle class as for all households but by 2007 the ratio was much larger. As for all households, net home equity as a percentage of total assets fell for the middle class from 1983 to 2007 and mortgage debt as a proportion of house value rose.

B. Concentration of Assets by Asset Type

Table 9. The Percent of Total Assets Held by Wealth Class, 2007

| Asset Type | Top 1.0% | Next 9.0% | Bottom 90.0% | All | \multicolumn{8}{c}{Share of Top 10 %} |
					1983	1989	1992	1995	1998	2001	2004	2007
A. Investment assets												
Stocks & mutual funds	49.3	40.1	10.6	100.0	90.4	86.0	86.3	88.4	85.1	84.5	85.4	89.4
Financial securities	60.6	37.9	1.5	100.0	82.9	87.1	91.3	89.8	84.1	88.7	87.9	98.5
Trusts	38.9	40.5	20.6	100.0	95.4	87.9	87.9	88.5	90.8	86.7	81.5	79.4
Business equity	62.4	30.9	6.7	100.0	89.9	89.8	91.0	91.7	91.7	89.6	90.3	93.3
Non-home real estate	28.3	48.6	23.1	100.0	76.3	79.6	83.0	78.7	74.9	78.5	79.4	76.9
Total for group	49.7	38.1	12.2	100.0	85.6	85.7	87.6	87.5	86.2	85.5	85.6	87.8
Stocks, directly or indirectly owned[a]	38.3	42.9	18.8	100.0	89.7	80.8	78.7	81.9	78.7	76.9	78.8	81.2
B. Housing, liquid assets, pension assets, and debt												
Principal residence	9.4	29.2	61.5	100.0	34.2	34.0	36.0	31.7	35.2	37.0	38.0	38.5
Deposits[b]	20.2	37.5	42.3	100.0	52.9	61.5	59.7	62.3	51.0	57.2	60.9	57.7
Life insurance	22.0	32.9	45.1	100.0	33.6	44.6	45.0	44.9	52.8	46.0	57.3	54.9
Pension accounts[c]	14.4	44.8	40.8	100.0	67.5	50.5	62.3	62.3	59.8	60.4	58.3	59.2
Total for group	12.0	33.8	54.2	100.0	41.0	43.9	45.2	42.5	44.0	45.9	45.7	45.8
Total debt	5.4	21.3	73.4	100.0	31.8	29.4	37.5	28.3	27.0	25.9	27.0	26.6

Source: own computations from the Survey of Consumer Finances.
Households are classified into wealth class according to their net worth. Brackets for 2007 are:
Top one percent: Net worth of $8,232,000 or more.
Next 9 percent: Net worth between $883,800 and $8,232,000.
Bottom 90 Percent: Net worth less than $883,800.
a. Includes direct ownership of stock shares and indirect ownership through mutual funds, trusts, and IRAs, Keogh plans, 401(k) plans, and other retirement accounts
b. Includes demand deposits, savings deposits, time deposits, money market funds, and certificates of deposit.
c. IRAs, Keogh plans, 401(k) plans, the accumulated value of defined contribution pension plans, and other retirement accounts.

Another way to portray differences between middle class households and the rich is to compute the share of total assets of different types held by each group (see Table 9). In 2007 the richest one percent of households held about half of all outstanding stock, financial securities, trust equity, and business equity, and 28 percent of non-home real estate. The top 10 percent of families as a group accounted for about 85 to 90 percent of stock shares, bonds, trusts, business equity, and non-home real estate. Moreover, despite the fact that 49 percent of households owned stock shares either directly or indirectly through mutual funds, trusts, or various pension accounts, the richest 10 percent of households accounted for 81 percent of the total value of these stocks, somewhat less than its 89 percent share of directly owned stocks and mutual funds.

In contrast, owner-occupied housing, deposits, life insurance, and pension accounts were more evenly distributed among households. The bottom 90 percent of households accounted for 62 percent of the value of owner-occupied housing, 42 percent of deposits and 45 percent of life insurance cash value, and 41 percent of the value of pension accounts. Debt was the most evenly distributed component of household wealth, with the bottom 90 percent of households responsible for 73 percent of total indebtedness.

There was relatively little change between 1983 and 2007 in the concentration of asset ownership, with three exceptions. First, the share of total stocks and mutual funds held by the richest 10 percent of households declined from 90 to 85 percent from 1983 to 2004 but then rose back to 89 percent in 2007, while their share of stocks directly or indirectly owned fell from 90 percent in 1983 to 79 percent in 2004 but then rose slightly to 81 percent in 2007. Second, the proportion of total pension accounts held by the top 10 percent fell from 68 percent in 1983 to 51 percent in 1989, reflecting the growing use of IRAs by middle income families, and then rebounded to 59 percent in 2007 from the expansion of 401(k) plans and their adoption by high income earners. Third, the share of total debt held by the top 10 percent also fell from 32 to 27 percent between 1983 and 2007.

C. The "Middle Class Squeeze"

Nowhere is the middle class squeeze more vividly demonstrated than in their rising debt. As noted above, the ratio of debt to net worth of the middle three wealth quintiles rose from 37 percent in 1983 to 46 percent in 2001 and then jumped to 61 percent in 2007. Correspondingly, their debt to income rose from 67 percent in 1983 to 100 percent in 2001 and then zoomed up to 157 percent in 2007! This new debt took two major forms. First, because housing prices went up over these years, families were able to borrow against the now enhanced value of their homes by refinancing their mortgages and by taking out home equity loans (lines of credit secured by their home). In fact, mortgage debt on owner-occupied housing (principal residence only) climbed from 29 percent in 1983 to 47 percent in 2007, and home equity as a share of total assets actually fell from 44 to 35 percent over these years. Second, because of their increased availability, families ran up huge debt on their credit cards.

Where did the borrowing go? Some have asserted that it went to invest in stocks. However, if this were the case, then stocks as a share of total assets would have increased over this period, which it did not (it fell from 13 to 7 percent between 2001 and 2007). Moreover, they did not go into other assets. In fact, the rise in housing prices almost fully explains the increase in the net worth of the middle class from 2001 to 2007. Of the $16,400 rise in median wealth, gains in housing prices alone accounted for $14,000 or 86 percent of the growth in wealth. Instead, middle class households, experiencing stagnating incomes, expanded their debt almost exclusively in order to finance consumption expenditures.

The question remains whether the consumption financed by the new debt was simply normal consumption or was there a consumption binge (acceleration) during the 2000s emanating from the expanded debt? That is, did the enhanced debt simply sustain usual consumption or did it lead to an expansion of consumption? To provide an answer, I examine two sources of consumption expenditure data. The first is the personal consumption expenditures data provided in the National Income and Product Accounts (NIPA).[14] This is the most comprehensive and reliable data on consumption in the U.S. However, its drawback from the point of view here is that it covers all households, not just middle class households. The data show that total personal expenditures grew at 3.38 percent per year from 1989 to 2001 but only 2.93 percent per year from 2001 to 2007. Thus, according to these data, there was actually a modest slowdown in the growth of consumer spending during the 2000s in comparison to the 1990s.

The second source is the Bureau of Labor Statistics' Consumer Expenditure Survey (CEX).[15] Its advantage is that it provides data on consumer spending by income class group. On the other hand, this data set is subject to sampling error and reporting error. I use the same three years as before. Since the income classes are designated in dollars rather than percentiles, I choose the income class that lies in the median of the distribution of consumer units in each year. The average expenditure of the median income class was virtually unchanged from 1989 to 2001 and also from 2001 to 2007. Thus, the CEX data, like the NIPA data, show no acceleration in consumer spending during the debt splurge of the 2000s. As a result, it can be concluded that the debt build-up of the 2000s went for normal consumption, not enhanced consumption.

6. THE RACIAL DIVIDE REMAINS LARGELY UNCHANGED OVER TIME

Striking differences are found in the wealth holdings of different racial and ethnic groups. In Tables 10 and 11, households are divided into three groups: (i) non-Hispanic whites, (ii) non-Hispanic African-Americans, and (iii) Hispanics.[16] In 2007, while the ratio of mean incomes between non-Hispanic white and non-Hispanic black households was an already low 0.48 and the ratio of median incomes was 0.60, the ratios of mean and median wealth holdings were even lower, at 0.19 and 0.06, respectively, and those of non-home wealth still lower, at 0.14 and 0.01, respectively.[17] The homeownership rate for black households was 49 percent in 2007, a little less than two thirds the rate among whites, and the percentage of black households with zero or negative net worth stood at 33.4, more than double the corresponding percentage among whites.

Between 1982 and 2006, while the average real income of non-Hispanic white households increased by 42 percent and the median by 10 percent, the former rose by only 28 percent for non-Hispanic black households but the latter by 18 percent. As a result, the ratio of mean income slipped from 0.54 in 1982 to 0.48 in 2006, while the ratio of median income rose from 0.56 to 0.60.

---

[14] The data are available from table 1.1.3 of the national accounts at:http://www.bea.gov/national/nipaweb/TableView.asp?SelectedTable/.
[15] The data are available at: http://www.bls.gov/cex/csxstnd.htm#2007.
[16] The residual group, American Indians and Asians, is excluded here.
[17] It should be stressed that the unit of observation is the household, which includes both families (two or more related individuals living together), as well as single adults. As is widely known, the share of female-headed households among African-Americans is much higher than that among whites. This difference partly accounts for the relatively lower income and wealth among African-American households.

Table 10. Household Income and Wealth by Race, 1983-2007
(In thousands, 2007 dollars)

	Means			Medians		
Year	Non-Hispanic Whites	Non-Hispanic African-Americans	Ratio	Non-Hispanic Whites	Non-Hispanic African-Americans	Ratio
A. Income						
1982	64.8	34.9	0.54	45.6	25.4	0.56
1988	71.0	31.6	0.45	47.3	17.9	0.38
1991	70.6	35.3	0.50	43.5	24.6	0.57
1994	64.8	31.3	0.48	43.5	23.1	0.53
1997	73.6	36.2	0.49	47.1	25.4	0.54
2000	88.9	43.0	0.48	51.5	29.3	0.57
2003	85.4	41.8	0.49	52.7	30.7	0.58
2006	92.3	44.6	0.48	50.0	30.0	0.60
B. Net Worth						
1983	316.0	59.5	0.19	91.0	6.1	0.07
1989	373.9	62.7	0.17	108.1	2.8	0.03
1992	361.8	67.2	0.19	90.7	15.3	0.17
1995	329.7	55.5	0.17	83.0	10.0	0.12
1998	408.2	74.1	0.18	103.9	12.7	0.12
2001	545.3	77.7	0.14	124.6	12.5	0.10
2004	586.1	111.3	0.19	129.8	13.0	0.10
2007	652.1	122.7	0.19	143.6	9.3	0.06
C. Non-home Wealth						
1983	232.8	30.0	0.13	25.3	0.0	0.00
1989	282.6	30.7	0.11	34.2	0.0	0.00
1992	278.5	38.3	0.14	27.9	0.2	0.01
1995	256.4	28.9	0.11	24.6	0.3	0.01
1998	324.1	47.8	0.15	47.8	1.5	0.03
2001	432.8	50.6	0.12	49.3	1.3	0.03
2004	441.8	67.5	0.15	39.6	0.3	0.01
2007	495.3	70.7	0.14	43.6	0.5	0.01
D. Homeownership Rate (in Percent)						
1983	68.1	44.3	0.65			
1989	69.3	41.7	0.60			
1992	69.0	48.5	0.70			
1995	69.4	46.8	0.67			
1998	71.8	46.3	0.64			
2001	74.1	47.4	0.64			
2004	75.8	50.1	0.66			
2007	74.8	48.6	0.65			
E. Percent of Households with zero or negative net worth						
1983	11.3	34.1	3.01			
1989	12.1	40.7	3.38			
1992	13.8	31.5	2.28			
1995	15.0	31.3	2.09			
1998	14.8	27.4	1.85			
2001	13.1	30.9	2.35			
2004	13.0	29.4	2.27			
2007	14.5	33.4	2.30			

Source: own computations from the 1983, 1989 1992, 1995, 1998, 2001, 2004, and 2007 SCF.

Households are divided into four racial/ethnic groups: (I) non-Hispanic whites; (ii) non-Hispanic blacks; (iii) Hispanics; and (iv) American Indians, Asians, and others. For 1995, 1998, and 2001, the classification scheme does not explicitly indicate non-Hispanic whites and non-Hispanic blacks for the first two categories so that some Hispanics may have classified themselves as either whites or blacks.

Table 11. Family Income and Wealth for Non-Hispanic Whites and Hispanics, 1983-2007 (In thousands, 2007 dollars)

	Means			Medians		
Year	Non-Hispanic Whites	Hispanics	Ratio	Non-Hispanic Whites	Hispanics	Ratio
A. Income						
1982	64.8	39.2	0.60	45.6	30.2	0.66
1988	71.0	32.4	0.46	47.3	22.7	0.48
1991	70.6	33.3	0.47	43.5	23.2	0.53
1994	64.8	42.0	0.65	43.5	29.9	0.69
1997	73.6	39.6	0.54	47.1	29.3	0.62
2000	88.9	44.0	0.50	51.5	28.1	0.55
2003	85.4	42.2	0.49	52.7	28.5	0.54
2006	92.3	46.4	0.50	50.0	35.0	0.70
B. Net Worth						
1983	316.0	51.4	0.16	91.0	3.5	0.04
1989	373.9	61.5	0.16	108.1	2.3	0.02
1992	361.8	80.4	0.22	90.7	5.4	0.06
1995	329.7	69.8	0.21	83.0	6.8	0.08
1998	408.2	100.8	0.25	103.9	3.8	0.04
2001	545.3	93.8	0.17	124.6	3.5	0.03
2004	586.1	125.6	0.21	129.8	6.1	0.05
2007	652.1	170.4	0.26	143.6	9.1	0.06
C. Non-home Wealth						
1983	232.8	15.2	0.07	25.3	0.0	0.00
1989	282.6	30.1	0.11	34.2	0.0	0.00
1992	278.5	51.7	0.19	27.9	0.0	0.00
1995	256.4	39.8	0.16	24.6	0.0	0.00
1998	324.1	64.1	0.20	47.8	0.0	0.00
2001	432.8	60.3	0.14	49.3	0.3	0.01
2004	441.8	73.5	0.17	39.6	0.1	0.00
2007	495.3	96.3	0.19	43.6	0.4	0.01
D. Homeownership Rate (in Percent)						
1983	68.1	32.6	0.65			
1989	69.3	39.8	0.60			
1992	69.0	43.1	0.70			
1995	69.4	44.4	0.67			
1998	71.8	44.2	0.67			
2001	74.1	44.3	0.60			
2004	75.8	47.7	0.63			
2007	74.8	49.2	0.66			
E. Percent of Households with zero or negative net worth						
1983	11.3	40.3	3.01			
1989	12.1	39.9	3.38			
1992	13.8	41.2	2.28			
1995	15.0	38.3	2.09			
1998	14.8	36.2	2.09			
2001	13.1	35.3	2.69			
2004	13.0	31.3	2.41			
2007	14.5	33.5	2.30			

Source: own computations from the 1983, 1989 1992, 1995, 1998, 2001, 2004, and 2007 SCF.
See footnote to Table 10 for details on racial/ethnic categories.

Between 1983 and 2001, average net worth (in 2001 dollars) rose by a whopping 73 percent for whites but only by 31 percent for black households, so that the net worth ratio fell from 0.19 to 0.14. Most of the slippage occurred between 1998 and 2001, when white net worth surged by a spectacular 34 percent and black net worth advanced by only a respectable 5 percent. Indeed, mean net worth growth among black households was slightly higher in the 1998-2001 years, at 1.55 percent per year, than in the preceding 15 years, at 1.47 percent per year. The difference in the 1998-2001 period was the huge increase in household wealth among white households. However, between 2001 and 2007, mean net worth among black households gained an astounding 58 percent while white wealth advanced only 29 percent, so that by 2007 the net worth ratio was back to 0.19, the same level as in 1983.

It is not clear how much of the sharp drop in the racial wealth gap between 1998 and 2001 and the turnaround between 2001 and 2007 is due to actual wealth changes in the African-American community and how much is due to sampling variability (since the sample sizes of non-Hispanic African Americans are relatively small in all years). However, one salient difference between the two groups is the much higher share of stocks in the white portfolio and the much higher share of principal residences in the portfolio of black households. In 2001, the gross value of principal residences formed 46.3 percent of the gross assets of black households and only 26.9 percent that of white households, while (total) stocks were 25.4 percent of the total assets of whites and only 14.9 percent that of black households.[18] Moreover, while the debt ratio was higher for black than white households in 2001 (debt to asset ratios of 0.324 and 0.115, respectively), the ratio declined for black households from 0.324 in 2001 to 0.297 in 2004 but then bounced back to 0.356. For whites the debt to asset ratio first rose to 0.140 in 2004 but then fell slightly to 0.134 in 2007.

In the case of median wealth, the black-white ratio first increased from 7 to 12 percent between 1983 and 1998 and then diminished to 10 percent in 2001, where it remained in 2004. In this case, median wealth for white households grew by 25 percent between 1998 and 2004 but by only 2.1 percent among black households. Median wealth among black households actually dipped by 29 percent between 2004 and 2007, reflecting in part the rising share of black households with zero or negative net worth, while it rose by 11 percent among white households, and the ratio of median wealth between blacks and whites fell to 0.06 in 2007, a little less than the ratio in 1983.

Average non-home wealth also increased somewhat more for black than white households between 1983 and 1998, so that the ratio rose from 13 to 15 percent. However, between 1998 and 2001, mean non-home wealth among white households also surged by 34 percent but inched up only 6 percent among black households, so that the ratio dwindled back to 0.12 – even lower than in 1983. Once again there was a notable recovery from 2001 to 2004, where mean non-home wealth climbed by 33 percent among blacks but was virtually unchanged among white households, so that by 2004 the ratio was up to 0.15, the same level as in 2001. The ratio then dipped a bit, to 0.14, in 2007. The reasons are here also the lower share of non-home assets held in the form of stocks by black households and the decrease in their debt ratio over the 2001-2004 period followed by a rise in their debt ratio from 2004 to 2007.

The median non-home wealth of non-Hispanic black households also increased, from virtually zero in 1983 to a positive $1,100 in 2001, and the corresponding ratio also grew, from zero to 3 percent. However, from 2001 to 2004, median non-home wealth among blacks toppled to only $300 and the corresponding ratio fell to only 1 percent. The reason for the decline is the faster growth of debt among black middle class households than among whites. There followed a slight recover in median non-home wealth among blacks to $500 in 2007 but the racial ratio remained at 0.01.

---

[18] Also, see Gittleman and Wolff (2004) for additional evidence from the PSID.

The homeownership rate of black households grew from 44.3 to 47.4 percent between 1983 and 2001 but relative to white households, the homeownership rate first increased from a ratio of 0.65 in 1983 to 0.67 in 1998 and then slipped to 0.64 in 2001. The change over the 1998-2001 period primarily reflected a big jump in the white homeownership rate, of 2.3 percentage points. However, from 2001 to 2004, the black homeownership rate surged to a little over half, while the white homeownership rate moved up to only 75.8 percent. As a result, the homeownership rate ratio recovered a bit to 0.66 by 2004. The homeownership rates dropped a bit for both black and white households between 2004 and 2007, and the ratio of homeownership rates fell slightly, to 0.65.

In contrast, the percentage of black households reporting zero or negative net worth fell from 34.1 percent in 1983 to 27.4 percent in 1998 (and likewise declined relative to white households) but then retreated to 30.9 percent in 2001 (and also rose relative to the corresponding rate for white households).[19] In 2004, the share of black households with non-positive wealth dipped a bit again, to 29.4 percent, and also fell a bit relative to the corresponding share of white households. However, in the ensuing three years the share of black households with zero or negative wealth surged again, reaching 33.4 percent in 2007. The share of white households reporting non-positive wealth was also up in 2007 and the black-white ratio also rose a bit from 2004 to 2007.

The picture is somewhat different for Hispanics (see Table 11). The ratio of mean income between Hispanics and non-Hispanic whites in 2007 was 0.50, almost the same as that between African-American and white households. However, the ratio of median income was 0.70, much higher than the 0.60 ratio between black and white households. The ratio of mean net worth was 0.26 compared to a ratio of 0.19 between blacks and whites and the ratio of mean non-home wealth 0.19, compared to a ratio of 0.14 between blacks and whites. However, the ratios of medians were 0.06 and 0.01, respectively, almost identical to those between blacks and whites. The Hispanic homeownership rate was 49 percent, almost identical to that of non-Hispanic black households, and 34 percent of Hispanic households reported zero or negative wealth, almost the same as African-Americans.

Progress among Hispanic households over the period from 1983 to 2007 was generally a positive story. Mean household income for Hispanics grew by 18 percent and median household income by 16 percent, so that the ratio of mean income slid from 60 to 50 percent while that of median income advanced from 66 to 70 percent. In fact, from 2004 to 2007 median income for Hispanics grew by an astonishing 23 percent while that for non-Hispanic whites declined by 5 percent.[20]

Between 1983 and 1998, mean wealth almost doubled for Hispanic households and mean non-home wealth grew more than four-fold but between 1989 and 2001 both declined in absolute terms. As a result, the ratio of mean net worth climbed from 16 percent in 1983 to 25 percent in 1998 and then tumbled to 17 percent in 2001, and the ratio of mean non-home wealth jumped from 7 to 20 percent between 1983 and 1998 then fell off to 14 percent in

---

[19] There is a large amount of variation in the income and wealth figures for both blacks and Hispanics on a year by year basis. This is probably a reflection of the small sample sizes for these two groups and the associated sampling variability, as well as some changes in the wording of questions on race and ethnicity over the eight surveys.

[20] In contrast, according the CPS data, median household income among Hispanics grew by only 4.4 percent from 2003 to 2006 and that among non-Hispanic whites by 0.1 percent. It is not clear why there is such a large discrepancy between the SCF and CPS data.

2001. However, both recovered in 2004. Mean net worth among Hispanics climbed by 32 percent between 2001 and 2004 and mean non-home wealth by 22 percent, and the corresponding ratios advanced to 21 percent and 17 percent, respectively. Another wealth surge occurred from 2004 to 2007 for Hispanics. Mean net worth among Hispanics gained 36 percent and mean non-home wealth advanced by 31 percent and the corresponding ratios climbed to 26 and 19 percent, respectively, quite a bit higher than those between black and white households.

On the other hand, from 1983 to 2007, median wealth among Hispanics remained largely unchanged, as did median non-home wealth (at virtually zero!), so that the ratio of both median wealth and median non-home wealth between Hispanics and non-Hispanic whites stayed virtually the same. In contrast, the homeownership rate among Hispanic households surged from 33 to 44 percent between 1983 and 1998 and the ratio of homeownership rates between the two groups grew from 0.65 in 1983 to 0.67 in 1998. No progress was made among Hispanics in the homeownership rate between 1998 and 2001, so that the homeownership ratio fell back to 0.60. However, between 2001 and 2007, the Hispanic homeownership rose once again, to 49 percent, about the same as black households, and the homeownership ratio recovered to 0.66.

The percentage of Hispanic households with zero or negative net worth fell rather steadily over time, from 40 percent in 1983 to 31 percent in 2004, and the share relative to white household tumbled from a ratio of 3.01 to 2.41. Here, too, the ratio first spiked upward from 2.1 in 1998 to 2.7 in 2001 before recovering partway to 2.4 in 2004. However, from 2004 to 2007, the share of Hispanics with non-positive wealth rose to 34 percent, almost the same as among black households, though the ratio with white households fell to 2.3.

Despite some progress from 2001 to 2007, the respective wealth gaps between African-Americans and Hispanics on the one hand and non-Hispanic whites on the other were still much greater than the corresponding income gaps in 2007. While mean income ratios were of the order of 50 percent, mean wealth ratios were of the order of 20-25 percent. Median non-home wealth among non-Hispanic black and Hispanic households was still virtually zero in 2007 and the percent with zero or negative net worth was around a third, in contrast to 15 percent among non-Hispanic white households (a difference that appears to mirror the gap in poverty rates). While blacks and Hispanics were left out of the wealth surge of the years 1998 to 2001 because of relatively low stock ownership (see Section 8 below for more details), they actually benefited from this (and the relatively high share of houses in their portfolio) in the 2001-2007 period. However, all three racial/ethnic groups saw an increase in their debt to asset ratio from 2001 to 2007.[21]

---

[21] One important reason for the wealth gap is differences in inheritances. According to my calculations from the SCF data, 24.1 percent of white households in 1998 reported receiving an inheritance over their life time, compared to 11.0 percent of black households, and the average bequest among white inheritors was 115 thousand dollars (present value in 1998) and only 32 thousand dollars among black inheritors. Thus, inheritances appear to play a vital role in explaining the large wealth gap, particularly in light of the fact that black families appear to save more than white families at similar income levels (see, for example, Blau and Graham, 1990; Oliver and Shapiro, 1997; and Gittleman and Wolff, 2004).

7. WEALTH SHIFTS FROM THE YOUNG TO THE OLD

As shown in Table 12, the cross-sectional age-wealth profiles of 1983, 1989, 1992, 1995, 1998, 2001, 2004, and 2007 generally follow the predicted hump-shaped pattern of the life-cycle model (see, for example, Modigliani and Brumberg, 1954). Mean wealth increases with age up through age 65 or so and then falls off. Non-home wealth has an almost identical profile, though the peak is generally somewhat higher than for net worth. Homeownership rates also have a similar profile, though the fall-off after the peak age is much more attenuated than for the wealth numbers (and in 2004 they actually show a steady rise with age). In 2007, the wealth of elderly households (age 65 and over) averaged 75 percent higher than the non-elderly and their homeownership rate was 21 percentage points higher.

Despite the apparent similarity in the profiles, there have been notable shifts in the relative wealth holdings of age groups between 1983 and 2007. The relative wealth of the youngest age group, under 35 years of age, expanded from 21 percent of the overall mean in 1983 to 29 percent in 1989 but then collapsed to only 17 percent in 2007. In 2007, the mean wealth of the youngest age group was $91,200, which was only slightly more than the mean wealth of this age group in 1989 ($88,500). The mean NW of the next youngest age group, 35-44, relative to the overall mean remained fairly steady at around 0.71 from 1983 to 1992 and then dipped to 0.65 in 1995 where it generally remained until 2004 and then tumbled to 0.58 in 2007. The relative wealth of the next youngest age group, 45-54, also declined rather steadily over time, from 1.53 in 1983 to 1.19 in 2007. The relative wealth of age group 55-64 gained rather steadily over time from 1.67 in 1983 to 1.91 in 2004 but then fell to 1.69 in 2007. The relative net worth of age group 65-74 plummeted from 1.93 in 1983 to 1.61 in 1989, regained some of the lost ground, reaching 1.72 in 2001, and then underwent another steep drop, to 1.57 in 2004, but again recovered to 1.86 in 2007. The wealth of the oldest age group, age 75 and over, gained substantially, from only 5 percent above the mean in 1983 to 32 percent in 1995 but then fell back to 16 percent in 2007, though still above its 1983 level.

Results for non-home wealth are very similar. The average non-home wealth of the youngest age group climbed from 17 to 28 percent of the overall mean from 1983 to 1989 and then plummeted to only 15 percent in 2007. The mean non-home wealth of age group 45-54 and 65-74 also fell over the 1983-2004 period, whereas that of age group 55-64 rose. Two patterns were somewhat different. The relative mean non-home wealth of age group 35-44 rose from 0.59 in 1983 to 0.68 in 1989 and then declined to 0.54 in 2007, below its 1983 level, while that of the oldest age group rose from 10 percent above the mean in 1983 to 27 percent above the mean in 1983 and then fell back to 10 percent above the mean in 2007 (the same as its 1983 position).

Changes in homeownership rates tend to mirror these trends. While the overall ownership rate increased by 5.2 percentage points from 63.4 to 68.6 percent between 1983 and 2007, the share of households in the youngest age group owning their own home increased by only 2.1 percentage points. The homeownership rate of households between 35 and 44 of age actually fell by 2.3 percentage points, and that of age group 45 to 54 years of age declined by 0.9 percentage points. Big gains in homeownership were recorded by the older age groups: 3.9

Table 12. Age-Wealth Profiles and Homeownership Rates by Age, 1983-2007

Age	1983	1989	1992	1995	1998	2001	2004	2007
A. Mean Net Worth (Ratio to Overall Mean)								
Overall	1.00	1.00	1.00	1.00	1.00	1.00	1.00	1.00
Under 35	0.21	0.29	0.20	0.16	0.22	0.19	0.14	0.17
35-44	0.71	0.72	0.71	0.65	0.68	0.64	0.65	0.58
45-54	1.53	1.50	1.42	1.39	1.27	1.25	1.21	1.19
55-64	1.67	1.58	1.82	1.81	1.91	1.86	1.91	1.69
65-74	1.93	1.61	1.59	1.71	1.68	1.72	1.57	1.86
75 & over	1.05	1.26	1.20	1.32	1.12	1.20	1.19	1.16
B. Mean Non-home Wealth (Ratio to Overall Mean)								
Overall	1.00	1.00	1.00	1.00	1.00	1.00	1.00	1.00
Under 35	0.17	0.28	0.18	0.14	0.21	0.19	0.12	0.15
35-44	0.59	0.68	0.69	0.62	0.67	0.61	0.64	0.54
45-54	1.53	1.48	1.45	1.43	1.31	1.27	1.24	1.19
55-64	1.72	1.60	1.89	1.86	1.99	1.94	1.97	1.80
65-74	2.12	1.69	1.60	1.75	1.66	1.74	1.61	1.86
75 & over	1.10	1.27	1.14	1.26	1.00	1.11	1.08	1.10
C. Homeownership Rate (in Percent)								
Overall	63.4	62.8	64.1	64.7	66.3	67.7	69.1	68.6
Under 35	38.7	36.3	36.8	37.9	39.2	40.2	41.5	40.8
35-44	68.4	64.1	64.4	64.7	66.7	67.6	68.6	66.1
45-54	78.2	75.1	75.5	75.4	74.5	76.1	77.3	77.3
55-64	77.0	79.2	77.9	82.3	80.6	83.2	79.1	80.9
65-74	78.3	78.1	78.8	79.4	81.7	82.5	81.2	85.5
75 & over	69.4	70.2	78.1	72.5	76.9	76.2	85.1	77.0

Source: own computations from the 1983, 1989 1992, 1995, 1998, 2001, 2004, and 2007 SCF.
Households are classified according to the age of the householder

Table 13. Composition of Household Wealth by Age Class, 2007 (Percent of gross assets)

Asset	All	Under 35	35-44	45-54	55-64	65-74	75 & over
Principal residence	32.8	54.3	43.7	33.8	25.6	28.2	30.2
Liquid assets (bank deposits, money market funds, and cash surrender value of life insurance)	6.6	5.7	5.4	6.4	6.3	6.1	10.5
Pension accounts	12.1	6.0	10.7	13.0	15.8	12.9	5.0
Corporate stock, financial securities, mutual funds, and personal trusts	15.5	4.2	8.6	13.1	16.4	20.5	25.6
Unincorporated business equity other real estate	31.3	28.7	30.1	32.0	34.4	30.2	27.1
Miscellaneous assets	1.7	1.2	1.5	1.7	1.5	2.1	1.6
Total assets	100.0	100.0	100.0	100.0	100.0	100.0	100.0
Memo (selected ratios in percent):							
Debt / equity ratio	18.1	92.7	41.3	20.2	11.9	7.1	2.1
Debt / income ratio	118.7	167.5	156.5	118.2	100.0	79.7	29.9
Net home equity / total assets[a]	21.4	18.8	21.3	20.9	18.1	23.4	28.7
Principal residence debt / house value	34.9	65.4	51.4	38.3	29.2	16.9	4.9
All stocks / total assets[b]	16.8	5.9	11.2	15.1	19.4	21.5	20.0

Source: own computations from the 2007 Surveys of Consumer Finances. Households are classified into age class according to the age of the household head.

a. Ratio of gross value of principal residence less mortgage debt on principal residence to total assets.

b. Includes direct ownership of stock shares and indirect ownership through mutual funds, trusts, and IRAs, Keogh plans, 401(k) plans, and other retirement accounts

c. Financial securities exclude U.S. government savings bonds in this tabulation.

percentage points for age group 55-64, 7.1 percentage points for age group 65-74, and 7.6 percentage points for the oldest age group.[22] By 2007, homeownership rates rose monotonically with age up to age group 65-74 and then dropped for the oldest age group. The statistics point to a relative shifting of home ownership away from younger towards older households between 1983 and 2007.

Changes in the relative wealth position of different age groups depend in large measure on relative asset price movements and differences in asset composition. The latter are highlighted in Table 13 for the year 2007. The gross value of the principal residence comprised over half the value of total assets for age group 35 and under, and its share of total assets fell off with age to about a quarter for age group 55-64 and then rose to 30 percent for age group 75 and over. Liquid assets as a share of total assets remained relatively flat with age group at around 6 percent except for the oldest group for whom it was 11 percent, perhaps reflecting the relative financial conservativeness of older people. Pension accounts as a share of total assets rose from 4 percent for the youngest group to 16 percent for age group 55 to 64 and then fell off to 5 percent for the oldest age group. This pattern likely reflects the build-up of retirement assets until retirement age and then a decline as these retirement assets are liquidated.[23] Corporate stock and financial securities showed a steady rise with age, from a 4 percent share for the youngest group to a 26 percent share for the oldest. A similar pattern was evident for total stocks as a percentage of all assets. Unincorporated business equity and non-home real estate was relatively flat as a share of total assets with age, about 30 percent.

There was a pronounced fall off of debt with age. The debt to equity ratio declined from 93 percent for the youngest group to 2 percent for the oldest, the debt to income ratio from 168 percent to 30 percent, and principal residence debt as a share of house value from 65 to 5 percent. As a result of the latter, net home equity as a proportion of total assets rose from 19 to 29 percent from the youngest to oldest age group.

Younger households were thus more heavily invested in homes and more heavily in debt whereas the portfolio of older households was more heavily skewed to financial assets, particularly corporate stock. As a result, younger households benefit relatively when housing prices rise and inflation is strong while older households benefit relatively from rising stock prices. Changes in the relative net worth position of age groups over the 1983 to 2007 period were thus largely due to these relative asset price movements.

8. STOCK OWNERSHIP FIRST RISES AND THEN FALLS

Tables 14a and 14b report on overall stock ownership trends from 1983 to 2007. The proportion of households who owned corporate stock shares directly declined a bit between 1983 and 1989, from 13.7 to 13.1 percent, while the share that owned any stocks or mutual funds plunged over these years, from 24.4 to 19.9 percent.[24] In contrast, the share of

---

[22] As with racial minorities, the sample size is relatively small for age group 75 and over, so that the huge increase in the homeownership rate between 2001 and 2004 (almost 9 percentage points) may be ascribable to sampling variation.

[23] This pattern may also be partly a cohort effect since 401(k) plans and other defined contribution plans were not widely introduced into the workplace until after 1989.

[24] The 1983 data do no permit an estimation of indirect stock ownership, so that we present the results for 1983 and 1989 separately from the other years.

households owning stocks and mutual funds worth $5,000 or more (in 1995 dollars) was stable over this period; and, indeed, the proportion with holdings of $10,000 or more and with $25,000 or more actually rose over this period. These changes over the 1983-1989 period might reflect the steep drop in the stock market in 1987 and the consequent exit of small fund holders after 1987. Yet, despite a 62 percent real increase in stock prices (as measured by the Standard and Poor 500 index), stocks plus mutual funds as a share of total household asset actually dipped form 9.0 percent in 1983 to 6.9 percent in 1989.

Table 14a. Stock Ownership, 1983 and 1989 (Percent of households holding stocks)

Stock Type	1983	1989
Direct stock holdings only	13.7	13.1
Stocks and mutual funds		
1. Any holdings		
2. Holdings worth $5,000 or more[a]	24.4	19.9
3. Holdings worth $10,000 or more[a]	14.5	14.6
4. Holdings worth $25,000 or more[a]	10.8	12.3
Memo:	6.2	8.4
Stocks plus mutual funds as a percent 9.0 of total assets	9.0	6.9
Percentage change in S&P 500 Index, in constant dollars over period		61.7

Source: own computations from the 1983 and 1989 Survey of Consumer Finances
a. 1995 dollars

Table 14b. Stock Ownership, 1989-2007 (Percent of households holding stocks)

Stock Type	1989	1992	1995	1998	2001	2004	2007	1989-2007
Direct stock holdings only	13.1	14.8	15.2	19.2	21.3	20.7	17.9	
Indirect stock holdings only	23.5	29.3	34.8	43.4	47.7	44.0	44.4	
1. Through mutual funds	5.9	8.4	11.3	15.2	16.7	14.1	10.6	
2. Through pension accounts	19.5	24.8	29.2	37.4	41.4	38.0	40.2	
3. Through trust funds	1.6	1.2	1.9	2.4	5.1	4.7	4.1	
All stock holdings[a]								
1. Any holdings	31.7	37.2	40.4	48.2	51.9	48.6	49.1	
2. Stock worth $5,000 or more[b]	22.6	27.3	29.5	36.3	40.1	34.9	34.6	
3. Stock worth $10,000 or more[b]	18.5	21.8	23.9	31.8	35.1	29.8	29.6	
4. Stock worth $25,000 or more[b]	10.5	13.1	16.6	24.3	27.1	22.5	22.1	
Memo:								
Direct plus indirect stocks as a percent of total assets	10.2	13.7	16.8	22.6	24.5	17.5	16.8	
Percentage change in S&P 500 Index, in constant dollars over period		13.8	20.0	87.3	1.3	-11.2	19.0	173.6

Source: own computations from the 1989, 1992, 1995, 1998, 2001, 2004, and 2007 Survey of Consumer Finances.
a. Includes direct ownership of stock shares and indirect ownership through mutual funds, trusts, and IRAs, Keogh plans, 401(k) plans, and other retirement accounts. b. 1995 dollars

In contrast, the years 1989 to 2001 saw a substantial increase in stock ownership (see Table 14b). The share of households with direct ownership of stock climbed from 13.1 percent in 1989 to 21.3 percent in 2001, while the share with some stock owned either outright or indirectly through mutual funds, trusts, or various pension accounts surged from 31.7 to 51.9 percent. Much of the increase was fueled by the growth in pension accounts like IRAs, Keogh plans, and 401(k) plans. Between 1989 and 2001, the share of households owning stock through a pension account more than doubled, accounting for the bulk of the overall increase in stock ownership. Indirect ownership of stocks through mutual funds also greatly expanded over the 1989-2001 period, from 5.9 to 16.7 percent, as did indirect ownership through trust funds, from 1.6 to 5.1 percent. All told, the share of households with indirect ownership of stocks more than doubled, from 23.5 percent in 1989 to 47.7 percent in 2001.

Table 14c. Distribution of Stock Ownership by Asset Type, 1989-2007(Percent of total stock held in each asset type)

Stock Type	1989	1992	1995	1998	2001	2004	2007	Change 1989-2007
Direct stock holdings	54.0	49.4	36.7	42.6	38.5	37.1	37.1	-16.9
Indirect stock holdings only	46.0	50.6	63.3	57.4	61.5	62.9	62.9	16.9
1. Through mutual funds	8.5	10.9	17.9	16.3	16.0	21.9	21.3	12.8
2. Through pension accounts	24.4	34.1	37.9	32.9	33.5	30.9	31.4	7.0
3. Through trust funds	13.2	5.6	7.6	8.2	12.0	8.1	7.2	-6.0
Memo:								
Stocks held in pension accounts/total value of pension accounts	32.6	44.8	67.5	64.1	66.3	45.6	43.6	11.1

Source: own computations from the 1989, 1992, 1995, 1998, 2001, 2004, and 2007 Survey of Consumer Finances
a. Includes direct ownership of stock shares and indirect ownership through mutual funds, trusts, and IRAs, Keogh plans, 401(k) plans, and other retirement accounts.

The next three years, 2001-2007, saw a retrenchment in stock ownership. This trend probably reflected the sharp drop in the stock market from 2000 to 2001, its rather anemic recovery through 2004, and its subsequent rebound from 2004 to 2007. Direct stock ownership declined only slightly from 21.3 percent in 2001 to 20.7 percent in 2004 but then plummeted in 2007 to 17.9 percent. Indirect stock ownership fell by 3.3 percentage points from 2001 to 2007. this was largely due to a sharp decline in stock ownership through mutual funds (down by 6.1 percentage points). Stock ownership through pension accounts was down by 3.4 percentage points from 2001 to 2004 but then rose by 2.2 percentage points from 2004 to 2007 as the stock market recovered.

By 2004 the share of households who owned stock directly or indirectly dipped below half, down to 48.6 percent, about the same level as in 1998 and down from its peak of 51.9 percent in 2001. However, it did increase slightly to 49.1 percent in 2007. Moreover, many of these families had only a minor stake in the stock market in 2007, with only 35 percent with total stock holdings worth $5,000 (in 1995 dollars) or more, down from 40 percent in 2001; only 30 percent owned $10,000 or more of stock, down from 35 percent in 2001; and only 22 percent owned $25,000 or more of stocks, down from 27 percent six years earlier.

Direct plus indirect ownership of stocks as a percent of total household assets did more than double from 10.2 in 1989 to 24.5 in 2001. This increase may reflect in large measure the 171 percent surge in stock prices over these years. However, between 2001 and 2007, the share plummeted to 16.8 percent. This change is a result not only of the relative stagnation of the stock market over these years but also of the withdrawal of many families from the stock market.

Table 12c shows the distribution of total stocks owned by vehicle of ownership. Here there are very marked time trends. Direct stock holdings as a share of total stock holdings fell almost continuously over time, from 54 percent in 1989 to 37 percent in 2007. The only deviation occurred in 1998, when direct stock ownership took an upward spike. This may reflect the stock market frenzy of the late 1990s. In contrast, stock held in mutual funds as a share of total stock rose almost continuously over time, from 8.5 percent in 1983 to 21 percent in 2007, while that held in trust funds declined by 6 percentage points.

The most interesting pattern is with regard to stock held in pension accounts (including IRAs). Its share of total stocks first increased from 24 percent in 1989 to 38 percent in 1995 but then fell off to 31 percent in 2007. The trend after 1995 seems to reflect a substitution of stock holdings in mutual funds for those in pension plans as investors looked for safer retirement accounts (see below). Likewise the share of the total value of pension plans held as stock more than doubled between 1989 and 1995, from 33 to 68 percent, remained at this level through 2001, and then plummeted to 44 percent in 2007. The sharp tail-off in stock ownership in pension plans between 2001 and 2004 likely reflects the lethargic performance of the stock market over this period (and its precipitous fall from 2000 to 2002) and the search for more secure investments among plan holders.

Stock ownership is also highly skewed by wealth and income class. As shown in Table 15a, 93 percent of the very rich (the top one percent) reported owning stock either directly or indirectly in 2007, compared to 48 percent of the middle quintile and 16 percent of the poorest 20 percent. While 88 percent of the very rich also reported stocks worth $10,000 or more, only 22 percent of the middle quintile and 2 percent of the bottom quintile did so. The top one percent of households owned 38 percent of all stocks, the top five percent 69 percent, the top 10 percent 81 percent, and the top quintile over 90 percent.

Table 15a. Concentration of Stock Ownership by Wealth Class, 2007

Wealth Class	Percent of Households Owning Stock Worth More Than			Percent of Stock Owned	
	Zero	$4,999	$9,999	Shares	Cumulative
Top one percent	92.6	89.1	88.4	38.3	38.3
Next four percent	92.2	90.7	89.5	30.8	69.1
Next five percent	86.8	85.0	81.4	12.1	81.2
Next ten percent	82.1	77.1	71.2	9.9	91.1
Second quintile	65.4	54.3	47.1	6.4	97.5
Third quintile	47.7	28.9	22.1	1.9	99.4
Fourth quintile	30.3	12.3	8.7	0.5	99.9
Bottom quintile	16.3	3.5	2.0	0.1	100.0
All	49.1	36.3	31.6	100.0	

Note: Includes direct ownership of stock shares and indirect ownership through mutual funds, trusts, and IRAS,

Keogh plans, 401(k) plans, and other retirement accounts. All figures are in 2007 dollars.

Table 15b. Concentration of Stock Ownership by Income Class, 2007

Income Level	Share of Households	Percent of Households Owning Stock Worth More Than Zero	$4,999	$9,999	Percent of Stock Owned Shares	Cumulative	Cumulative-2001
$250,000 or more	3.6	95.4	93.4	91.3	53.7	53.7	40.6
$100,000-$249,999	15.5	84.5	71.0	63.7	21.5	75.2	68.6
$75,000-$99,999	10.4	71.1	55.6	49.6	9.0	84.3	77.4
$50,000-$74,999	17.5	58.1	40.7	34.9	7.7	92.0	89.3
$25,000-$49,999	27.1	39.3	23.6	19.0	5.7	97.7	97.6
$15,000-$24,999	12.7	23.1	15.7	11.9	1.1	98.8	98.9
Under $15,000	13.3	11.2	5.0	4.3	1.2	100.0	100.0
All	100.0	49.1	36.3	31.8	100.0		

Note: Includes direct ownership of stock shares and indirect ownership through mutual funds, trusts, and IRAs, Keogh plans, 401(k) plans, and other retirement accounts. All figures are in 2007 dollars.

Stock ownership also tails off by income class (see Table 15b). Whereas 94 percent of households in the top 3.6 percent of income recipients (those who earned $250,000 or more) owned stock in 2007, 39 percent of the middle class (incomes between 25 and 50 thousand), 23 percent of the lower middle class (incomes between 15 and 25 thousand), and only 11 percent of poor households (income under $15,000) reported stock ownership. The comparable ownership figures for stock holdings of $10,000 or more are 91 percent for the top income class, 19 percent for the middle class, 12 percent for the lower middle class, and 4 percent for the poor. Moreover, 84 percent of all stocks were owned by households earning $75,000 or more (the top 30 percent) and 92 percent by those earning $50,000 or more in terms of income.

Another notable development in the 2000s was an increase in the concentration of stock ownership, as shown in the last column of Tables 15a and 15b. The share of total stock owned by the richest one percent in terms of wealth increased from 33.5 percent in 2001 to 38.3 percent in 2007 and that of the richest 5 percent from 62.3 to 69.1 percent. In terms of income , the share of total stock owned by the top income class jumped from 40.6 to 53.7 percent (though, it should be noted their share of total households also rose, from 2.7 to 3.6 percent) and that of the top two income classes from 68.6 to 75.2 percent. One result of the stock market bust of the early 2000s was a withdrawal of middle class families from the stock market.

Thus, in terms of wealth or income, substantial stock holdings have still not penetrated much beyond the reach of the rich and the upper middle class. The big winners from the stock market boom of the late 1990s (as well as the big losers in the early 2000s) were these groups, while the middle class and the poor did not see sizable benefits from the bull market (or losses when the stock market tanked in 2000-2002). It is also apparent which groups benefit the most from the preferential tax treatment of capital gains.

9. AN UPDATE TO 2009

A complete update of the wealth figures to 2009 is beyond the scope of the present study. However, it is possible to provide a partial update of the wealth figures to July 1, 2009 based on two notable developments. The first is that house prices fell by 23.5 percent in real terms,[25] and the second is that the S&P 500 index was down by 40.9 percent in real terms.[26] A somewhat rough update, based on the change in housing and stock prices shows a marked deterioration in middle class wealth. According to my estimates, while mean wealth (in 2007 dollars) fell by 17.3 percent between 2007 and 2009 to $443,600, median wealth plunged by an astounding 36.1 percent to $65,400 (about the same level as in 1992!).

Trends in inequality are also interesting. According to previous research (Wolff, 2002a), wealth inequality is very sensitive and positively related to the ratio of stock prices to housing prices, since the former is heavily concentrated among the rich and the latter is the chief asset of the middle class.[27] The fact that stock prices fell more than housing prices, at least from 2007 to mid-2009 should lead to a decline in wealth inequality over these two years. However, instead, the results show a fairly steep rise in wealth inequality, with the Gini coefficient climbing from 0.834 to 0.865. The share of the top one percent advanced from 34.6 to 37.1 percent, that of the top 5 percent from 61.8 to 65.0 percent, and that of the top quintile from 85.0 to 87.7 percent, while that of the second quintile fell from 10.9 to 10.0 percent, that of the middle quintile from 4.0 to 3.1 percent, and that of the bottom two quintiles from 0.2 to -0.8 percent. There was also a large expansion in the share of households with zero or negative net worth, from 18.6 to 24.1 percent.

On the surface, these results appear somewhat surprisingly in light of the earlier regression results. However, while stock prices fell more than house prices, houses were a much larger share of the gross assets of the middle class than stocks were of the rich. As shown in Table 6, the gross value of principal residence comprised 65.1 percent of the gross assets of the three middle wealth quintiles in 2007, whereas stocks made up 21.4 percent of the gross assets of the top one percent and 18.6 percent of the next 19 percent. As a result, the middle class took a bigger relative hit from the decline in home prices on their net worth than the top 20 percent did from the stock market decline. This is also reflected in the fact that median wealth dropped much more in percentage terms than mean wealth.

We can see how the rising debt of the middle class made them vulnerable to income shocks and set the stage for the mortgage crises of 2008 and 2009 and the resulting financial meltdown. The rapid decline in house prices over these two years (on the order of 24 percent) left many middle class families (I estimate 16.6 percent of homeowners) "underwater"

---

[25] This figure is based on the National Association of Realtors Median Sales Price of Existing Single-Family Homes for Metropolitan Areas.

[26] I assume that there are no additional savings (or dissavings) and no portfolio adjustments (except those caused by price changes of homes and stock).

[27] The regression was run of a wealth inequality index, measured by the share of marketable wealth held by the top one percent of households (WLTH) on income inequality, measured by the share of income received by the top five percent of families (INC), and the ratio of stock prices (the Standard and Poor index) to housing prices (RATIO), with 21 data points between 1922 and 1998. It yields:
WLTH = 5.10 + 1.27 INC + 0.26 RATIO, $R2 = 0.64$, $N = 21$
   (0.9)   (4.2)   (2.5)
with t-ratios shown in parentheses. Both variables are statistically significant (INC at the 1 percent level and RATIO at the 5 percent level) and with the expected (positive) sign. Also, the fit is quite good, even for this simple model.

(greater mortgage debt than the value of their homes) and, coupled with a sharp spike in unemployment, unable (or unwilling) to repay their mortgage loans.[28]

10. SUMMARY AND CONCLUDING COMMENTS

The years 2001 to 2004 witnessed an explosion of household debt and gave evidence of the middle class squeeze. Median wealth declined by 0.7 percent after a period of robust growth from 1998 to 2001. The only other times in the recent past that median wealth has declined were during recessionary periods. While 2001 was a recession year, 2002-2004 was a period of expansion, so the decline in median wealth was almost unprecedented. Moreover, median non-home wealth (total wealth less home equity) fell by a staggering 27 percent from 2001 to 2004. While the share of households with non-positive net worth declined slightly, the percent of households with zero or negative non-home wealth rose substantially, by 2.5 percentage points, from 2001 to 2004 Median income also fell by 1.6 percent from 2001 to 2004.

The mid-2000s, from 2004 to 2007, was a period of recovery. Median household income rose by 3.2 percent. From 2004 to 2007 median wealth grew sharply, by 19.9 percent. Over the 2001-2007 period it increased by 19.1 percent, even faster than during the 1990s (and 1980s). Median non-home wealth also showed a sizeable increase from 2004 to 2007, by 17.6 percent, though it was down by 13.5 percent overall the whole 2001 to 2007 period. However, the share of households with zero or negative net worth increased by 1.6 percentage point to reach its highest level over the years 1983 to 2007, though the percent with non-positive non-home wealth fell slightly.

Wealth inequality was up slightly from 2001 to 2004 and again from 2004 to 2007,while the inequality of non-home wealth was up sharply from 2001 to 2004, with the share of top one percent increasing by 2.5 percentage points, after a marked decline from 1998 to 2001, and it was up again a bit from 2004 to 2007. Income inequality actually fell from 2000 to 2003 but then rose sharply from 2003 to 2006, for a net increase over the six years (an increase of 0.12 Gini points). The number of households worth $1,000,000 or more, $5,000,000 or more, and especially $10,000,000 or more surged during the 1990s and once again from 2001 to 2007.

The mean wealth of the top one percent jumped to 18.5 million dollars in 2007. The percentage increase in net worth (also that of non-home wealth and income) from 1983 to 2007 was much greater for the top wealth (and income) groups than for those lower in the distribution. Moreover, the average wealth of the poorest 40 percent declined by 63 percent between 1983 and 2007, and by 2007 had fallen to only $2,200. All in all, the greatest gains

---

[28] Two papers which appeared subsequent to the first draft of my paper have also called attention to the growing debt during the 200s and have reached similar conclusions to mine. The first, Mian and Sufi (2009), using data from a national consumer credit bureau over the years 1997 to 2008, reported that the debt-to-income ratio for U.S. households roughly doubled between 2002 and 2007. They also found that money extracted from increased home equity loans is not used to purchase new real estate or pay down credit card balances but rather the borrowed funds are used for real expenditures (though they do not estimate whether the new debt expanded existing consumption or enhanced it). The second, Khandani, Lo, and Merton (2009), simulated the effect of the housing price decline from June 2006 to December 2008 and estimated a total loss of $1.5 trillion in the U.S. housing market. They also found that a significant percentage of home owners wound up with negative home equity.

in wealth and income were enjoyed by the upper 20 percent, particularly the top one percent, of the respective distributions. Between 1983 and 2007, the top one percent received 35 percent of the total growth in net worth, 43 percent of the total growth in non-home wealth, and 44 percent of the total increase in income. The figures for the top 20 percent are 89 percent, 94 percent, and 87 percent, respectively.

The biggest story for the early and mid 2000s is the sharply rising debt to income ratio, reaching its highest level in almost 25 years, at 119% in 2007. Also the debt-equity ratio (ratio of debt to net worth) was way up, from 14.3 percent in 2001 to 18.1 percent in 2007. Most of the rising debt was from increased mortgages on homes. In contrast during the late 1990s, indebtedness fell substantially and by 2001 the overall debt-equity ratio was lower than in 1983. The proportion of households reporting zero or negative net worth, after increasing from 15.5 percent in 1983 to 18.0 percent in 1998, fell to 17.6 percent in 2001, but then increased to 18.6 percent in 2007.

Another notable trend is the big increase in the value of homes as a share of total assets from 2001 to 2007 and corresponding fall in the value of stocks held to total assets. As shown above, these two changes largely mirror relative price movements over the period, particularly from 2001 to 2004. Pension accounts as a share of total assets also fell off a bit from 2001 to 2007. Net equity in owner-occupied housing as a share of total assets fell sharply from 23.8 percent in 1983 to 18.2 percent in 1998 and then rebounded to 21.4 percent in 2007, reflecting rising mortgage debt on homeowner's property between 1983 and 1998, which grew from 21 to 37 percent, before retreating somewhat to 35 percent in 2007.

Evidence of the middle class squeeze is that for the middle three wealth quintiles there was a huge increase in the debt-income ratio from 100 to 157 percent from 2001 to 2007 and an almost doubling of the debt-equity ratio from 31.7 to 61.1 percent. Moreover, total stocks as a share of total assets fell off from 12.6 to 7.0 percent for the middle class. The debt-equity ratio was also much higher among the middle 60 percent of households in 2007, at 0.61, than among the top one percent (0.028) or the next 19 percent (0.121). The evidence, moreover, suggests that middle class households, experiencing stagnating incomes, expanded their debt almost exclusively in order to finance normal consumption expenditures.

The percent of all households with a defined contribution pension plan also fell from 52.2 to 49.7 from 2001 to 2004 but then recovered to 52.2 percent in 2007. For the middle class, there was a slight increase from 2001 to 2007. The overall stock ownership rate (either directly or indirectly through mutual funds, trust funds, or pension plans) also fell, from 51.9 percent in 2001 to 49.1 percent in 2007. For the middle class, the fall was from 51.1 to 47.8 percent. There was also a pronounced decline in the share of middle class households (and of all households) with $5,000 or more of stocks and with $10,000 or more of stocks.

The concentration of investment type assets generally remained as high in 2007 as during the previous two decades. About 90 percent of the total value of stock shares, bonds, trusts, and business equity, and about 80 percent of non-home real estate were held by the top 10 percent of households. Stock ownership is also highly skewed by wealth and income class. The top one percent of households classified by wealth owned 38 percent of all stocks in 2007, the top 10 percent 81 percent, and the top quintile 91 percent. Moreover, 84 percent of all stocks were owned by households earning $75,000 or more and 92 percent by households with incomes of $50,000 or more.

The racial disparity in wealth holdings, after stabilizing during most of the 1990s, widened in the years between 1998 and 2001, as the ratio of average net worth holdings dropped sharply from 0.18 to 0.14 and the ratio of median net worth from 0.12 to 0.10. From 2001 to 2007 the mean wealth gap narrowed again, with the ratio of mean wealth rising to 0.19 but that of median wealth fell to 0.06. The relative gains made by black households in the 2000s are ascribable to the fact that blacks have a higher share of homes and a lower share of stocks in their portfolio than do whites and to the fact that house prices rose relative to stock prices over the period.

Between 1998 and 2001, mean non-home wealth among white households also surged by 34 percent but went up by only 6 percent among black households, so that the ratio dwindled from 0.15 to 0.12 – even lower than in 1983. However, by 2007 the ratio had climbed back to 0.14. The black homeownership rate grew from 44.3 to 50.1 percent between 1983 and 2004 but then slipped to 48.6 percent in 2007, and the homeownership rate relative to white households, after increasing from a ratio of 0.65 in 1983 to 0.67 in 1998, slipped back to 0.64 in 2001 but then recovered slightly to 0.65 in 2004.

Hispanic households also lost ground both in absolute terms and relative to non-Hispanic white households in terms of both net worth and non-home wealth between 1998 and 2001 but then regained the ground in the 2000s. The homeownership rate among Hispanic households, after advancing from 33 percent in 1983 to 44 percent in 1995, leveled off in the ensuing six years but then surged to 49 percent in 2007, and the ratio of homeownership rates advanced from 48 percent in 1983 to 64 percent in 1995, dropped to 60 percent in 2001, but then climbed to 66 percent in 2007.

At least since 1989, wealth shifted in relative terms away from young households under age 55 and particularly those under age 35 and toward households in age group 55 to 74. A similar pattern is found for non-home wealth. The average net worth and non-home wealth of households in age group 75 and over also fell relative to the overall mean between 1989 and 2007.

I also updated the wealth figures to July 1, 2009, on the basis of changes in house and stock prices. My estimates indicate that while mean wealth (in 2007 dollars) fell by 17.3 percent between 2007 and 2009, median wealth plunged by 36.1 percent. The results show a fairly steep rise in wealth inequality, with the Gini coefficient swelling from 0.834 to 0.865 the share of the top one percent advancing from 34.6 to 37.1 percent. I also estimate that 16.6 percent of homeowners were "underwater" with greater mortgage debt than the value of their homes.

REFERENCES

Avery, Robert B., Gregory E. Elliehausen, and Arthur B. Kennickell. 1988. "Measuring Wealth with Survey Data: An Evaluation of the 1983 Survey of Consumer Finances." *Review of Income and Wealth* series 34 (5, December): 339-369.

Blau, Francine D., and John W. Graham. 1990. "Black-White Differences in Wealth and Asset Composition." *Quarterly Journal of Economics,* Vol. 105, No. 1 (May): 321-339.

Board of Governors of the Federal Reserve System. 1998. *"Flow of Funds Accounts of the United States: Flows and Outstanding Second Quarter 1998."* (September 11).

Conley, Dalton. 1999. *Being Black, Living in the Red: Race, Wealth and Social Policy in America.* Berkeley and Los Angeles: University of California Press.

Gittleman, Maury, and Edward N. Wolff. 2004. "Racial Differences in Patterns of Wealth Accumulation." *Journal of Human Resources*, Vol. 39 (1, Winter): 193-227.

Kennickell, Arthur B. 2001. "Modeling Wealth with Multiple Observations of Income: Redesign of the Sample for the 2001 Survey of Consumer Finances," October, *http://www.federalreserve.gov/pubs/oss/oss2/method.html*.

Kennickell, Arthur B., Douglas A. McManus, and R. Louise Woodburn. 1996. "Weighting Design for the 1992 Survey of Consumer Finances." Federal Reserve Board of Washington (March). Unpublished paper.

Kennickell, Arthur B., and R. Louise Woodburn. 1992. "Estimation of Household Net Worth Using Model-Based and Design-Based Weights: Evidence from the 1989 Survey of Consumer Finances. Federal Reserve Board of Washington (April). Unpublished paper.

Kennickell, Arthur B., and R. Louise Woodburn. 1999. "Consistent Weight Design for the 1989, 1992, and 1995 SCFs, and the Distribution of Wealth." *Review of Income and Wealth* series 45 (2, June): 193-216.

Khandani, Amir E., Andrew W. Lo, and Robert C. Merton. 2009. "Systemic Risk and the Refinancing Ratchet Effect," NBER Working Paper No. 15362, September.

Mian, Artif, and Amir Sufi. 2009. "House Prices, Home Equity-Based Borrowing, and the U.S. Household Leverage Crisis," NBER Working Paper No. 15283, August.

Modigliani, Franco, and Richard Brumberg. 1954. "Utility Analysis and the Consumption Function: An Interpretation of Cross-Section Data." In *Post-Keynesian Economics*, edited by K. Kurihara. New Brunswick, N.J.: Rutgers University Press.

Oliver, Melvin L., and Thomas M. Shapiro. 1997. *Black Wealth, White Wealth*. New York: Routledge.

Spilerman, Seymour. 2000. "Wealth and Stratification Processes," *American Review of Sociology*, Vol. 26, No. a, pp. 497-524.

U.S. Council of Economic Advisers. 2004. *Economic Report of the President, 1994*. Washington, DC: United States Government Printing Office.

Wolff, Edward N. 1987. "Estimates of Household Wealth Inequality in the United States, 1962-83." *Review of Income and Wealth* series 33 (3, September): 231-256.

____. 1994. "Trends in Household Wealth in the United States, 1962-1983 and 1983-1989." *Review of Income and Wealth* series 40 (2, June): 143-174.

____. 1996. *TOP HEAVY: A Study of Increasing Inequality of Wealth in America*. New York: New Press.

____. 1998. "Recent Trends in the Size Distribution of Household Wealth." *Journal of Economic Perspectives,* Vol. 12 (3, Summer): 131-150.

____. 2001. "Recent Trends in Wealth Ownership, from 1983 to 1998", in Thomas M. Shapiro and Edward N. Wolff eds., *Assets for the Poor: The Benefits of Spreading Asset Ownership*, New York: Russell Sage Press, pp. 34-73.

____. 2002a. *TOP HEAVY: A Study of Increasing Inequality of Wealth in America*. Newly updated and expanded edition, New York: the New Press.

____. 2002b. *Retirement Insecurity: The Income Shortfalls Awaiting the Soon-to-Retire*, Washington, DC: Economic Policy Institute.

____. 2007. *"Recent Trends in Household Wealth in the United States: Rising Debt and the Middle-Class Squeeze."* Levy Institute Working Paper No. 502, June.

APPENDIX: DATA SOURCES AND METHODS

I applied several adjustments to the underlying SCF data as follows. First, in some years, the SCF also supplied alternative sets of weights. For the 1983 SCF, I use the so-called "Full Sample 1983 Composite Weights" because this set of weights provides the closest correspondence between the national balance sheet totals derived from the sample and those in the Federal Reserve Board Flow of Funds. For the same reason, results for the 1989 SCF are based on the average of SRC-Design-S1 series (X40131 in the database itself) and the SRC Designed Based weights (X40125); and results for the 1992, 1995, 1998, 2001, 2004, and 2007 SCF rely on the Designed-Base Weights (X42000) -- a partially design-based weight constructed on the basis of original selection probabilities and frame information and adjusted for non-response. The 1998, 2001, 2004, and 2007 weights are actually partially Designed-Based weights (X42001), which account for the systematic deviation from the CPS estimates of homeownership rates by racial and ethnic groups.

Second, in the case of the 1992 SCF, this set of weights produced major anomalies in the size distribution of income for 1991. As a result, I modified the weights somewhat to conform to the size distribution of income as reported in the Internal Revenue Service's Statistics of Income. It should be noted at the outset that there appeared to be a substantial change in the sampling frame used in the 1992 Survey in comparison to the 1989 Survey. For consistency with the earlier results, I adjusted the weights used in the 1992 Survey of Consumer Finances.

The problem can be seen most easily in the following table.

Comparison of SOI and SCF Size Distributions				
Adjusted Gross Income or Household Income [Current $]	SCF Distribution: Percentage of All Households[a] 1989	1992	SOI Distribution: Percentage of All Tax Returns[b] 1989	1992
Under $100,000	95.7	94.9	97.4	96.7
100,000-199,999	3.107	3.948	1.864	2.474
200,000-499,999	0.895	0.892	0.546	0.657
500,000-999,999	0.187	0.182	0.103	0.124
1,000,000 or more	0.073	0.040	0.051	0.059
Of Which:				
1,000,000-3,999,999	0.0550	0.0293		
4,000,000-6,999,999	0.0128	0.0021		
7,000,000 or more	0.0049	0.0002		
Total	100.0	100.0	100.0	100.0

a. Source: own computations from the 1989 and 1992 SCF.
b. Sources: "Selected Historical and Other Data," Statistics of Income Bulletin, Winter 1993-94, Vol. 13, No. 4, pp. 179-80; "Selected Historical and Other Data," Statistics of Income Bulletin, Winter 1994-95, Vol. 15, No. 3, pp. 180-81.

A comparison of weights used in the 1989 and 1992 SCF shows a very sharp attenuation in the weights at the top of the income distribution. According to these figures, the percentage of households with incomes between $1,000,000 and $4,000,000 declined from 0.055 to 0.029, or by almost half; the percentage in the income range $4,000,000 to $7,000,000 fell from 0.013 to 0.002, or by over 80 percent; and the percentage with incomes of $7,000,000 or more decreased from 0.0049 to 0.0002, or by over 95 percent. These changes are highly implausible -- particularly in light of results from the Current Population Survey or CPS (available on the Internet), which show a slightly rising degree of income inequality over this period (the Gini coefficient increased from 0.427 to 0.428).

The table also compares the size distribution of income computed from the Internal Revenue Service Statistics of Income (SOI) in 1989 and 1992 with that from the two SCF files. The SOI figures are based on actual tax returns filed in the two years. There are three major differences between the two data sources. First, the SOI data use the tax return as the unit of observation, whereas the SCF figures are based on the household unit. Second, individuals who do not file tax returns are excluded from the SOI tabulations. Third, the size distribution for the SOI data is based on adjusted gross income (AGI), whereas the SCF distributions are based on total household income.

Despite the differences in concept and measurement, trends in the size distribution of AGI can give a rough approximation to actual changes in the size distribution of household (Census) income. What is most striking is that the SOI figures show a slight increase in the percent of units in income class $1,000,000 and more, from 0.051 in 1989 to 0.059 percent in 1992, whereas the SCF figures show a sharp decline, from 0.073 to 0.040 percent.

Results from the SOI data fail to provide any independent corroboration for the sharp decline in the number of households with incomes of $1,000,000 or more between 1989 and 1992. Accordingly, I adjusted the 1992 weights to conform to the 1989 weighting scheme. The adjustment factors for the 1992 weights are given by the inverse of the normalized ratio of weights between 1992 and 1989, shown in the last column of the preceding table:

Income in 1989 Dollars	Adjustment Factors for 1992 Weights
Under 200,000	0.992
200,000-999,999	1.459
1,000,000-3,999,999	1.877
4,000,000-6,999,999	4.844
7,000,000 or more	12.258

The resulting size distribution of income for 1989 and 1992 is as follows:

	1989 SCF	1992 SCF
Income Shares (in Percent)	Using Original Weights	Using Adjusted Weights
Share of the Top 1%	16.4	15.7
Share of the Top 5%	29.7	30.5
Share of the Top 10%	40.1	41.1
Share of the Top 20%	55.3	56.4
Gini Coefficient:	0.521	0.528

The calculations show a slight increase in overall income inequality, as measured by the Gini coefficient, a result that is consistent with both the SOI and the CPS data.

Third, the Federal Reserve Board imputes information for missing items in the SCF. However, despite this procedure, there still remain discrepancies for several assets between the total balance sheet value computed from the survey sample and the Flow of Funds data. As a result, the results presented below are based on my adjustments to the original asset and liability values in the surveys. This takes the form of the alignment of asset and liability totals from the survey data to the corresponding national balance sheet totals. In most cases, this entails a proportional adjustment of reported values of balance sheet items in the survey data (see Wolff, 1987, 1994, 1996, and 1998 for details).

The adjustment factors by asset type and year are as follows:

	1983 SCF	1989 SCF	1992 SCF	1995 SCF
Checking Accounts	1.68			
Savings and Time Deposits	1.50			
All Deposits		1.37	1.32	
Financial Securities	1.20			
Stocks and Mutual Funds	1.06			
Trusts		1.66	1.41	1.45
Stocks and bonds				1.23
Non-Mortgage Debt	1.16			

No adjustments were made to other asset and debt components, or to the 1998, 2001, 2004, or 2007 SCF.

It should be noted that the alignment has very little effect on the measurement of wealth inequality -- both the Gini coefficient and the quantile shares. However, it is important to make these adjustments when comparing changes in mean wealth both overall and by asset type.

In: Economics of Wealth in the 21st Century
Editor: Jason M. Gonzalez

ISBN: 978-1-61122-805-2
©2011 Nova Science Publishers, Inc.

Chapter 2

WHEN THE MARKET DOES NOT DELIVER: AN INCLUSIVE GROWTH EXPERIMENT FALLS VICTIM TO WEALTH CONSTRAINTS

Roswitha M. King[*]

Oestfold University CollegeHalden, Norway

ABSTRACT

This paper explains one aspect of the challenges faced by regional development policy. At issue is a policy for the development and expansion of small and medium sized enterprises (SMEs). The causes and dynamics of difficulties with SME development policies are analyzed in a game theory framework, in which "policy failure" arises as an equilibrium phenomenon. The model results deliver a cautionary note: that indiscriminate application of market criteria may be counterproductive in an environment characterized by severe constraints on material wealth accumulation.

INTRODUCTION

Against the backdrop of the ongoing global economic crisis some countries have experienced extreme swings in economic growth over the past 5 years. Much descriptive narrative reflects these breaks and extreme amplitudes of economic performance. However, for people residing at the subsistence level far removed from the halls of economic power – a very large group of people indeed – the high growth phase came and left without noticeable benefits. These large disadvantaged regions of the world have now gone from a bad situation to a worse situation. Public policy is seen as an appropriate avenue for intervention, however, its effectiveness has often been disappointing.

---

[*] Roswitha M. King, Associate Professor of Economics, Oestfold University College, Department of Economics, Remmen,1757 Halden,Norway, e-mail: roswitha.king@hiof.no, Tel. +(47) 69 21 52 64 Fax. + (47) 69 21 52 02

The purpose of this paper is to document, analyze, and hopefully deliver a lesson learned from a policy failure in regional development that is based on a misconception of what the market can and cannot deliver.

The analysis is carried out in a game theory framework, in which "policy failure" arises as an equilibrium phenomenon.

The key findings point to a 'double-failure' in the following sense: If the belief of what the market can deliver is wrong then the public policy will fail. If, on the other hand, the belief is correct, public policy will again be a failure in that it is unnecessary – as the market can take care of matters by itself.

In this paper we focus on a policy, widely applied, for example, in Eastern Europe, to promote the formation of small and medium sized enterprises (SME).

Small and medium size enterprises are an important pillar of market economies. They typically provide a large share of employment. They contribute substantially to GDP, and often are the main engines for innovation. SMEs have been essential for the transition from planned economy to market economy in the countries of Central and Eastern Europe. Their importance, however, has generally been under-appreciated. SME issues have often been overshadowed by public pre-occupation with privatization of large state-owned enterprises.

Recognizing this relative neglect of SMEs the European Commission provided financing and consultation services targeted on potential entrepreneurs, as part of its pre-EU-accession program in Central and Eastern Europe. For example, the European Commission dedicated significant amounts of funds under its Phare program to SME support structures.

The Phare program is one of the three pre-accession instruments[1] financed by the European Union and targeted toward the countries of Central and Eastern Europe. Its principal purpose is/was to assist the EU applicant countries in preparing for EU membership.

The program's name comes from its original (1989) orientation toward Poland and Hungary - "Poland and Hungary: Assistance for Restructuring their Economies" (Phare). But the program soon expanded to cover also the other East European EU acceding countries during their periods of massive economic restructuring and political change. Until 2000 also the countries of the Western Balkans (Albania, Macedonia, and Bosnia-Herzegovina) received financing from Phare.

Initially Phare focused on delivering know-how and technical assistance. Subsequently it provided investment assistance in the areas of environmental protection and infrastructure. As it became clear that East European countries would become members of the EU (after the publication of Agenda 2000) Phare's objective became: (i) To strengthen public institutions so that they can function effectively within the European Union; (ii) To assist candidate countries to attain compliance with the extensive body of EU legislation; (iii) to promote economic and social cohesion.

Phare's financial assistance is given in the form of grants rather than loans – either independently or with recipient- or third party co-financing requirement. A significant part of co-financing has been provided by institutions, such as the World Bank, the European Bank for Reconstruction and Development, and the European Investment Bank.

---

[1] The other two instruments are the Special Accession Program for Agriculture and Rural Development (SAPARD) and the Instrument for Structural Policies for Pre-Accession (ISPA), with the latter concentrating on infrastructure projects, particularly in environmental and transport fields.

Despite considerable Phare investments into SME development projects there remains the nagging impression that results have been disappointing. For example, the European Union's Phare Final Synthesis Report, *"An evaluation of Phare-financed programmes in support of SMEs"*, of February 2000 comes to the following sobering assessment: "Overall, it is disagreeable to have to conclude that Phares' contribution to the establishment of institutional support structures in Central and Eastern Europe has been extremely disappointing."[2]

A network of Phare-financed business support centers was super-imposed upon a region that already had a scattering of private business support centers[3]. Analysis had revealed that the private business support centers had concentrated on dealing with larger, already well established companies, and had neglected the smaller companies and start-up companies, who, in fact, had a greater need for support. The Phare-financed business support centers were targeted exactly on this "neglected" group, and were directed toward the economically less prosperous regions, further away from the major cities.

This paper uses a game theoretic framework to examine the reasons behind this widespread institutional/policy failure. The particular model of this paper is framed by strongly simplifying assumptions, and is to be understood as a benchmark model. It incorporates just enough elements to "produce" institutional/policy failure as an equilibrium outcome.

In a wider context this approach also provides an analytical platform on which alternative policy experiments can be investigated before real-life formulation and implementation. This may filter out some costly policy failures due to unrecognized design flaws – an issue of particular relevance to post-communist economies, as real-life experience with market supporting institutions and policies is limited to date.

The agents (players) in this strategic situation are a publicly sponsored consulting agency, a private consulting firm, and a candidate SME, which is a potential client of the agency/firm.

There are three possible outcomes that are relevant for this analysis: (i) formation of a SME with the assistance of a public consulting agency, (ii) formation of a SME with the assistance of a private consulting firm, and (iii) <u>no</u> SME formation.

THE MODEL

Economic Agents

We consider 3 economic agents, or formally, the set of agents is denoted $N = \{1, 2, 3\}$.

Agent 1: a private consulting firm; Agent 2: a public consulting agency; Agent 3: a potential entrepreneur of a start-up SME, hereafter referred to as candidate SME.

---

[2] Phare Final Synthesis Report, "An Evaluation of Phare-Financed programmes in support of SMEs, Publisher: The European Commission. February 2000, page 136.
[3] For empirical studies on the business environment for SMEs in Turkey see Acma (2003), and Akca et al. (2003)., for Hungary see: Szabo (1997); for larger regional groupings , e.g. Visigrad Countries, OSCE, see Szabo (2002), (2003), as well as UNECE Biennium Review 2000-2001, with regard to Romania see Nistor (2003), Pop et al (2003); with regard to the impact of EU accession see Wach et al (2003) and Kraftova et al (2003); with regard to market-orientation of policies see Hallberg (2001).

Set Of (Physical) Outcomes

We let Z denote the set of outcomes, with typical element z^i. Outcomes are situations arising from the actions of the agents. In our case we let Z consists of three elements, i.e.

$Z = \{z^1, z^2, z^3\}$, where[4] the superscript enumerates the elements of Z.

z^1 denotes the situation, where the candidate SME (agent 3) accepts the price quote of the public consulting agency (agent 2); this directly implies the start-up of a new SME.

z^2 denotes the situation, where the candidate SME accepts the price quote of the private consulting firm (agent 1); this also directly implies the start-up of a new SME.

z^3 denotes the situation, where the candidate SME does not accept any of the price quotes. This directly implies that no new SME is formed. This outcome represents policy failure.

Utility Functions

Agents' preferences are assumed to be represented by utility functions, and utilities are defined over outcomes.

Each agent's preferences are represented by a utility function U_i, $i \in N$, which maps from the set of (physical) outcomes, Z, to the set of real numbers, $\Re$; i.e. $U_i : Z \to \Re$.

Letting P_1 denote the price quote per unit of consulting services of the private consulting firm, P_2 the price quote per unit of consulting services of the public consulting agency, $c > 0$ the cost of supplying a unit of consulting services, and $R_3 > 0$, the reservation price per unit of consulting service of the candidate SME[5], we define agents' utility functions as follows. Note that subscript indexes agents and superscript enumerates the elements of Z.

$U_1(z^1) = 0$ utility of private consulting firm arising from outcome z^1
$U_2(z^1) = P_2 - c$ utility of public consulting agency arising from outcome z^1
$U_3(z^1) = -P_2 + R_3$ utility of candidate SME arising from outcome z^1
$U_1(z^2) = P_1 - c$ utility of private consulting firm arising from outcome z^2
$U_2(z^2) = 0$ utility of public consulting agency arising from outcome z^2
$U_3(z^2) = -P_1 + R_3$ utility of candidate SME arising from outcome z^2
$U_1(z^3) = 0$ utility of private consulting firm arising from outcome z^3
$U_2(z^3) = 0$ utility of public consulting agency arising from outcome z^3
$U_3(z^3) = 0$ utility of candidate SME arising from outcome z^3

We assume that $P_1, P_2, c, R_3 \in \Re^{++}$, where $\Re^{++}$ denotes the set of positive real numbers.

It should be noted that cost, c, is not indexed, which implies that government consulting agency and private consulting firm are assumed to have identical operating costs. We assume $R_3 < c$, capturing the idea that the financial resources of the candidate SME are very modest.

---

[4] Here an element zi, i= 1,2,3 of Z is a "joint" outcome, and not agent i's (individualized) sub-outcome.
[5] Under reservation price we mean the highest price that a candidate SME would be willing to pay.

We rule out the case where the entrepreneur becomes a client of both the private and the public consulting firm.

Special Restrictions

Special restrictions, ξ_2, apply to the public consulting agency (agent 2): it must be *self-financing*[6]. If the agency is unable to cover its expenses by the fees it earns from consulting services, it must close down. The same requirement is, of course, valid for the private consulting firm (agent 2). This implies the requirement $P_i - c \geq 0$ for $i = 1, 2$.

THE IMPLIED GAME IN STRATIC FORM

The above narrative suggests a game in strategic form along the following lines:

Strategies

For player 1 and player 2 a strategy is a price quote per unit of consulting service, P_1 and P_2 respectively. For player 3 a strategy is to "accept" or "reject" a price offer. We restrict attention to pure strategies.

Formally: Let S_i denote a *set of pure strategies* of player i, $i \in N$, with typical element s_i. For i=1,2 we define $S_i = \Re^{++}$ with typical element $s_i = P_i$, interpreted as a price quote per unit of consulting services. For player 3 there are three types of pure strategies: "accept player 1's price offer", "accept player 2's price offer", "reject both price offers".

We define $S = S_1 \times S_2 \times S_3$, with typical element $s = (s_1, s_2, s_3)$ to be the joint strategy space.

Payoff Functions

We define player i's payoff function, $\pi_i : S \to \Re$, for $i \in N$, and we write $\pi = (\pi_1, \pi_2, \pi_3)$.

We define the game to be $\Gamma(S, \pi)$.

In an operational sense, we assume that player i's payoff function equals his/her utility function as defined above.

To solve the game $\Gamma(S, \pi)$ we apply the solution concept of Nash Equilibrium

Nash Equilibria Of $\Gamma(S, \pi)$

The set *of pure strategy Nash equilibria* of the game Γ is defined by

NE $(\Gamma) = \{ s^* = (s_i^*, s_{-i}^*) \in S: \pi_i(s^*) \geq \pi_i(s_i, s_{-i}^*), \forall s_i \in S_i, i \in N \}$,

---

[6] To be more precise, the public consulting agency receives public funds for its start-up cost, but, after that, must cover its operating costs from the fee income it generates.

where (s_i, s_{-i}^*) denotes the strategy tuple derived from $s^* = (s_i^*, s_{-i}^*)$, by replacing its ith component s_i^* by an alternative strategy, s_i, and where s_{-i}^* represents the components of the strategy tuple s^*, associated with the players other than i.

In the following we display the implied game in strategic form:

		Public Consulting agency $P_2 < R_3$	(column player) $P_2 = R_3$	Player 2 $P_2 > R_3$
Private Consulting firm (row player) Player 1	$P_1 < R_3$	If 1's offer is chosen: (-), (0) If 2's offer is chosen: (0), (-)	(-), (0)	(-), (0)
	$P_1 = R_3$	(0), (-)	If 1's offer is chosen (-), (0) If 2's offer is chosen (0), (-) If both are rejected (0), (0)	If 1's offer chosen (-), (0) If both are rejected (0),(0) C
	$P_1 > R_3$	(0), (-)	If 2's offer is chosen (0), (-) If both are rejected (0), (0)	(0), (0) A

Figure 1.

EXPLANATION OF THE STRATEGIC FORM GAME Γ

Figure 1, below, illustrates the game in strategic (normal)form representing our strategic situation. The entries inside the shaded cells represent the payoff to player 1 and 2, i.e. the private consulting firm and the public consulting agency respectively, with the first element of each pair representing player 1's payoff, and the second element player 2's payoff. Note that several of the shaded cells contain multiple pairs of payoffs, depending on whether player 3 accepts the offer of player 1, or of player 2, or rejects both offers. A payoff "(−)" means that the respective player has negative payoff, while a payoff "(0)" has a payoff of zero.

The entries at the margins of the matrix show the strategies of player 1 and 2 respectively.

Strategy "$P_i < R_3$", i= 1,2, means that player *i* makes a price offer that lies below player 3's reservation value R_3. Strategy "$P_i = R_3$", i= 1,2, means that player *i* makes a price offer that is equal to player 3's reservation value R_3. Strategy "$P_i > R_3$", i= 1,2, means that player i makes a price offer that lies above player 3's reservation value R_3.

RESULTS

Policy Failure as Equilibrium Outcome

The game has a four Nash equilibria. All four equilibria are outcome equivalent: the candidate SME rejects both price offers and no SME is formed. This is interpreted as policy failure. The reason why the policy lacks effectiveness is explained by the following dilemma. If the publicly subsidized agency offers a price that is low enough to be affordable by the candidate SME, the consulting agency makes a loss and is not economically viable. If, on the other hand, the publicly sponsored agency offers a price, at which it is economically viable, then it prices itself out of the local market. The policy design flaw lies in the requirement that the consulting agency has to be self-financing, and consequently has to charge market prices, while targeting a clientele with insufficient financial resources to pay market prices for consulting services. On the other hand, suppose that the candidate SME could afford market prices. But then it could just avail itself of the services of the private consulting firm. The government sponsored consulting agencies would not be needed at all, and again the policy would be flawed, in that it would be unnecessary

The self-financing rule ξ_2, to which the public consulting agency is subjected, and which is associated with the design flaw, is reflected in the model in several ways. It is implicit in the public agency's utility function, $U_2 = P_2 - c$, for the case that the client accepts price and services. It is of the same form as the utility function of the private consulting firm,

$U_1 = P_1 - c$, which is subject to normal market conditions. The utility function is, in effect, a profit function, consisting of the difference between revenue and costs. It shows that, as far as operating costs are concerned, the government agency does not receive any subsidies or other transfer payments from the government.[7] The self-financing rule requires that, in equilibrium, we have $U_2 \geq 0$. This implies that the equilibrium outcomes incorporate the self-financing requirement. As we will see below, the Nash equilibrium satisfies the condition $U_2 \geq 0$.

Nash Equilibria

I now turn to an explanation of the equilibria. (Formal proofs are given in the appendix)
The strategy sets S_1 and S_2 of player 1 and 2, in principle, contain infinitely many elements, corresponding to the infinite number of potential prices that the respective agent could quote. However, we group an agent's price offers into three types: "greater than R_3", "smaller than R_3" and "equal to R_3", where $R_3 \in \Re^{++}$ is the candidate SME's reservation price, as mentioned above.

---

[7] The reason we call it "publicly sponsored agency" or "subsidized agency", is the assumption that the agency received a subsidy to finance the startup cost, but not the cost of operating. There are concrete example, for example in Latvia, where this form of partial public financing occurred.

In the Nash equilibrium A (bottom right cell) both the private firm and the publicly sponsored agency offer a price, P_1 and P_2 respectively, which is higher then the candidate SME's reservation price, R_3. The candidate SME rejects both offers. This leads to the "policy failure" payoff pair (0),(0). No SME is formed. This equilibrium is a clear case where the government consulting firm (and also the private firm) prices itself out of the local market.

In equilibrium B (bottom center cell) the private firm, player 1, offers a price, P_1, which exceeds the candidate SME's reservation price. The government consulting firm, player 2, offers a price, P_2, which equals the reservation price R_3. The candidate SME (player 3) rejects both offers, although player 2's offer is affordable. It should be noted that player 3 rejects player 1's price offer, P_1, because $R_3 < P_1$. But player 3 is indifferent between accepting or rejecting player 2's price offer P_2, because $R_3 = P_2$. However the acceptance, by player 3, of player 2's price offer is not part of a Nash equilibrium, because in that case player 2's price offer P_2 (=R_3) is not a best response to player 3's acceptance of such offer. It would give negative payoff to Player 2. Player 2 would be better off to change to the strategy of offering a price that exceeds player 3's reservation price ($P_2 > R_3$) – having the offer rejected, and thereby obtaining utility of zero. This case illustrates the difficulty of making business agreements under conditions of severe constraints on financial resources of the target clientele. While the price offered by the government consulting firm is affordable by the target clientele, it still does not come to a contract. The dual constraints of self-financing requirement of the government agency, together with the very low reservation price of the potential SME leave no room for mutually beneficial agreement.

Equilibrium C (centre right cell) is analogous to equilibrium B; only this time it is the private firm, which offers a price equal to the candidate SME's reservation price R_3, while the public agency offers a price, P_2, which exceeds R_3. The candidate SME rejects both offers. Commentary analogous to that of equilibrium B applies.

In equilibrium D (centre cell) the private consulting firm and the public agency offer identical prices, which equal the reservation price R_3, which is affordable by the prospective SME. The candidate SME rejects all offers. Analogous commentary as for equilibrium B applies, except that here both the private and the public agency find it disadvantageous to offer a contract, given that the candidate SME accepts it. This leaves the rejection of affordable price offers as the only equilibrium behavior. (We recall that player 3 is indifferent between accepting and rejecting the price offers.) Again, we have a case, where the dual constraints of self-financing for the consulting firm, coupled with the extremely low ability to pay of the candidate SME, prevent the policy from being effective.

Several observations are in order: Although the four equilibria differ in their strategies, and in their reasons why a consultancy contract fails to materialize, all lead to the same outcome of "policy failure". Furthermore, as can be verified by the definition of the players' utility functions that each of the four equilibria satisfies the self-financing condition ξ_2. Under the assumptions of the model the self-financing requirement is satisfied if $U_2 \geq 0$, where U_2 denotes the utility function of the public consulting agency (agent 2).

INTERPRETATION

One of the fundamental difficulties behind the real world institutional/policy failure, which inspired this research, lies in an "identity problem" on the part of business support centers and agencies, created for the purpose of helping prospective entrepreneurs get started with the formation and management of small businesses. The experience of Phare-financed small business support centers illustrates the problem quite well. Given that Phare support for SMEs was known to be available only for a limited number of years, this immediately raised the issue of sustainability of the business support centers beyond the exit date of Phare financing. Rather than focusing on establishing close relations with local government units in order to secure future public funding, conventional wisdom steered policy in the direction of making the business centers "self-supporting", i.e. profitable, and thereby independent of public financing. This stemmed from the desire to avoid dependence on subsidies in a region, where subsidies had been all-too-familiar during the time of central planning. This meant that, beyond Phare financing for the initial start-up costs, this genre of business support centers had to cover operating costs by fee income. The requirement to be self-financing forced the consulting agencies to charge market rates for their services. However, the target clientele, consisting of low budget candidate start-up companies, were not in a position to afford market rates - one of the reasons that the Phare program focused on this clientele in the first place.

This exposed the following internal inconsistency: the business support centers could not fulfill their principal mandate, while at the same time satisfying the subsidiary goal of being self-financing. The sub-goal of financial independence was revealed to be inconsistent with the principal goal of reaching the low budget clientele. The Phare-funded business support centers became increasingly similar to private sector business consulting firms, in that they favored larger clients with more substantive business history, while tending to avoid their original mandate of seeking out the very entrepreneurs who could not afford private consulting firms.

To make matters worse, private sector non-Phare funded business consulting firms were put at a distinct disadvantage relative to the Phare-subsidized[8] competitors. This, in fact, has led to an apparent violation of one of the prime directives of the Phare project: not to substitute for private initiatives or national development initiatives, but to seek out projects that would otherwise not receive attention and support by either private interests or national public interests, some of which might have a public good feature.

Instead of focusing on long-run SME development processes, which typically receive scarce attention from private firms or capital-constrained national governments, Phare-financed business consulting centers were forced to concentrate on their own short-term survival as businesses.

CONCLUSION

We present a model, which explains how and why well-intentioned market-oriented economic development policies may fail in environments characterized by severe constraints

---

[8] The subsidy is restricted to the start-up costs, and does not apply to operating costs.

on financial resources. Combining elements of mechanism design theory and game theory, the model exposes a policy design flaw. This design flaw leads to the publicly subsidized consulting centers failing in their mission to seek out and support exactly those prospective entrepreneurs, who need assistance most urgently, and for whose benefit the initiative was created. The model produces "policy failure" as an equilibrium outcome.

The real world policy flaw is two-fold. First the severe constraints on financial resources among the target clients are not given due consideration. Second, if the target clientele were able to pay market prices, there would be no need for public agencies in the first place, since private consulting firms could offer their services at market prices, and furthermore, would not be exposed to "unfair" competition from start-up-cost-subsidized agencies. The model results deliver a cautionary note: market behavior and market standards that are desirable in well endowed economies may be misplaced in environments below a certain threshold of wealth accumulation.

Or, in the words of the Phare report, "As institutions which support bottom-up SME development and the wider economic development processes which underpin successful SME development, it is not possible to reconcile this specific function with the need to generate sufficient funds from fee income in order to survive. There are virtually no examples of BSCs (business support centers)[9] in the western economies which survive without public funding of some sort."[10]

APPENDIX

The appendix contains:

- A list of the Nash equilibria of the game Γ
- Proof that $s^*(1)$, $s^*(2)$, $s^*(3)$, and $s^*(4)$ are Nash Equilibria
- Proof that there are no other Nash equilibria.

- List of Nash Equilibria for the game $\Gamma(S, \pi)$

The following is a list of the Nash equilibria, $s^*(1)$, $s^*(2)$, $s^*(3)$, $s^*(4)$, associated with the game $\Gamma(S, \pi)$. We recall that R_3 denotes the reservation price of the candidate SME, player 3.

(A) $s^*(1) = (s_1^*(1), s_2^*(1), s_3^*(1))$, where

$s_1^*(1)$ is described by $P_1 > R_3$, with P_1 being the strategic variable of player 1;
$s_2^*(1)$ is described by $P_2 > R_3$ for all decision nodes of player 2 with player 2' strategic variable P_2.
$s_3^*(1)$ is described as follows for i,j = 1,2, i≠j: (i) If $P_i \geq R_3$ and $P_j \geq R_3$ then reject all offers. (ii) If

---

[9] Expression in parenthesis added.
[10] Phare Final Synthesis Report, "An evaluation of Phare-financed programmes in support of SMEs, February 2000, page 140.

$P_i < R_3$ and $P_j \geq R_3$ then accept player i's offer. (iii) If $P_i < R_3$ and $P_j < R_3$ and $P_i \neq P_j$ then accept
min$\{P_i, P_j\}$. (iv) If $P_i = P_j < R_3$ then accept the government agency's offer.

(B) $s^*(2) = (s_1^*(2), s_2^*(2), s_3^*(2))$, where

$s_1^*(2)$ is described by $P_1 > R_3$, with P_1 being the strategic variable of player 1;
$s_2^*(2)$ is described by $P_2 = R_3$ for all decision nodes of player 2, with player 2's strategic variable P_2;
$s_3^*(2)$ is described as follows for i,j = 1,2, i≠j: (i) If $P_i \geq R_3$ and $P_j \geq R_3$ then reject all offers. (ii) If
$P_i < R_3$ and $P_j \geq R_3$ then accept player i's offer. (iii) If $P_i < R_3$ and $P_j < R_3$ and $P_i \neq P_j$ then accept
min$\{P_i, P_j\}$. (iv) If $P_i = P_j < R_3$ then accept the government agency's offer.

(C) $s^*(3) = (s_1^*(3), s_2^*(3), s_3^*(3))$, where

$s_1^*(3)$ is described by $P_1 = R_3$, with P_1 being the strategic variable of player 1;
$s_2^*(3)$ is described by $P_2 > R_3$ for all decision nodes of player 2, with player 2's strategic variable P_2;
$s_3^*(3)$ is described as follows for i,j = 1,2, i≠j: (i) If $P_i \geq R_3$ and $P_j \geq R_3$ then reject all offers. (ii) If
$P_i < R_3$ and $P_j \geq R_3$ then accept player i's offer. (iii) If $P_i < R_3$ and $P_j < R_3$ and $P_i \neq P_j$ then accept
min$\{P_i, P_j\}$. (iv) If $P_i = P_j < R_3$ then accept the government agency's offer.

(D) $s^*(4) = (s_1^*(4), s_2^*(4), s_3^*(4))$, where

$s_1^*(4)$ is described by $P_1 = R_3$, with P_1 being the strategic variable of player 1;
$s_2^*(4)$ is described by $P_2 = R_3$ for all decision nodes of player 2, with player 2's strategic variable P_2;
$s_3^*(4)$ is described as follows for i,j = 1,2, i≠j: (i) If $P_i \geq R_3$ and $P_j \geq R_3$ then reject all offers. (ii) If
$P_i < R_3$ and $P_j \geq R_3$ then accept player i's offer. (iii) If $P_i < R_3$ and $P_j < R_3$ and $P_i \neq P_j$ then accept
min$\{P_i, P_j\}$. (iv) If $P_i = P_j < R_3$ then accept the government agency's offer.

Remark: An analogous set of 4 Nash equilibria exist, where part (iv) of s_3^* reads "If $P_i = P_j < R_3$ then accept the private consultancy firm's offer. This set of equilibria is outcome equivalent to the above set of 4 equilibria. Detail is not provided here.

- Proof that $s^*(1)$, $s^*(2)$, $s^*(3)$, and $s^*(4)$ are Nash Equilibria

The proof is by contradiction. We say "suppose that $s^*(j)$, j = 1,2,3,4, is *not* a Nash equilibrium. By the definition of Nash equilibrium this implies that for some player i, i =

1,2,3 there exists an alternative strategy s_i', which gives higher payoff to that player i, given that the other players remain at their "*" strategies. Then we show that there does not exist such a payoff improving strategy for player i.

A: To show that strategy triple $s^*(1) = (s_1^*(1), s_2^*(1), s_3^*(1))$ is a Nash equilibrium:

Suppose $s^*(1) = (s_1^*(1), s_2^*(1), s_3^*(1))$ is not a Nash equilibrium. Then there exist some alternative strategy s_i' for some player i, i= 1,2,3, such that $\pi_i(s_i', s_{-i}^*(1)) > \pi_i(s^*(1))$. Here π_i denotes player i's payoff function, $(s_i', s_{-i}^*(1))$ denotes a strategy triple such that player i plays the alternative strategy s_i', while the players other than i play their designated "*" equilibrium strategies.

First we examine whether there exist such payoff improving strategy for Player 3, given that the other players' strategies remain at $s_1^*(1)$, and $s_2^*(1)$. Given $s_1^*(1), s_2^*(1)$, as defined above, only part (i) of player 3's strategy is relevant in the sense of being potentially payoff-altering for player 3. There are two alternatives for player 3 to choose: accept player 1's offer, or alternatively, accept player 2's offer. But since $P_1 > R_3$ and $P_2 > R_3$ either one of these alternative strategies would lead to

$\pi_3(s_3', s_{-3}^*(1)) < 0 = \pi_3(s^*(1))$, and thus would result in a lower payoff for player 3.

We now examine the possibility for player 1 to have a payoff improving alternative strategy s_1', given that the other players' strategies remain at $s_2^*(1)$ and $s_3^*(1)$. The two possible alternative strategies are to announce a price P_1, such that $P_1 < R_3$ or to announce a price P_1, such that $P_1 = R_3$. In both cases, however we would have $\pi_1(s_1', s_{-1}^*(1)) \leq 0 = \pi_1(s^*(1))$, given player 1's utility function, and given the assumption
$R_3 < c$. This can be seen as follows: There are two cases: Either player 1's offer gets accepted, or it does not get accepted. If it gets accepted, then $\pi_1(s_1', s_{-1}^*(1)) < 0$, since $P_1 \leq R_3 < c$. If it does not get accepted, then $\pi_1(i_1', s_{-1}^*(1)) = 0$. Thus we have $\pi_1(s_1', s_{-1}^*(1)) \leq 0 = \pi_1(s^*(1))$, and this would not be a profitable alternative strategy for player 1.

It remains to examine the possibility for player 2 to have a payoff improving alternative strategy, s_2', given that the other players strategies remain at $s_1^*(1)$ and $s_3^*(1)$. The possible alternative strategies are to offer a price P_2, such that $P_2 < R_3$, or to offer a price P_2, such that $P_2 = R_3$. Following a line of reasoning analogous to that of player 1 above, we conclude that $\pi_2(s_2', s_{-2}^*(1)) \leq 0 = \pi_2(s^*(1))$, and this is not a profitable alternative strategy for player 2.

We conclude that $s^*(1) = (s_1^*(1), s_2^*(1), s_3^*(1))$ is a Nash equilibrium.

B: To show that strategy triple $s^*(2) = (s_1^*(2), s_2^*(2), s_3^*(2))$ is a Nash equilibrium:

Suppose $s^*(2) = (s_1^*(2), s_2^*(2), s_3^*(2))$ is not a Nash equilibrium. Then there exist some alternative strategy s_i' for some player i, i= 1,2,3, such that $\pi_i(s_i', s_{-i}^*(2)) > \pi_i(s^*(2))$. Here π_i denotes player i's payoff function, $(s_i', s_{-i}^*(2))$ denotes a strategy triple such that player i plays the alternative strategy s_i', while the players other than i play their designated "*" equilibrium strategies.

Examining player 3: Given $s_1^*(2), s_2^*(2)$, as defined above, only part (i) of player 3's strategy is relevant in the sense of being potentially payoff-altering for player 3. There are two alternatives for player 3 to choose: accept player 1's offer, or alternatively, accept player 2's offer. But since $P_1>R_3$, accepting player 1's offer would lead to $\pi_3(s_3', s_{-3}*(2)) < 0 = \pi_3(s*(2))$, and would only make player three worse off. Since $P_2 = R_3$ accepting player 2's offer would lead to $\pi_3(s_3', s_{-3}*(2)) = 0 = \pi_3(s*(2))$, which also does not make player 3 better off.

We now examine the possibility for player 1 to have a payoff improving alternative strategy s_1', given that the other players' strategies remain at $s_2*(3)$ and $s_3*(2)$. The two possible alternative strategies are to announce a price P_1, such that $P_1<R_3$ or to announce a price P_1, such that $P_1 = R_3$. In both cases, however we would have $\pi_1(s_1', s_{-1}*(2)) \leq 0 = \pi_1(s*(2))$, given player 1's utility function, and given the assumption

$R_3 < c$. This would not be a profitable alternative strategy for player 1.

It remains to examine the possibility for player 2 to have a payoff improving alternative strategy, s_2', given that the other players strategies remain at $s_1*(2)$ and $s_3*(2)$. The possible alternative candidate strategies

are to offer a price P_2, such that $P_2 < R_3$, or to offer a price P_2, such that $P_2 > R_3$. Following a line of reasoning analogous to that of player 1 above, we conclude that $\pi_2(s_2', s_{-2}*(2)) \leq 0 = \pi_2(s*(2))$, and this is not a profitable alternative strategy for player 2.

We conclude that $s*(2) = (s_1*(2), s_2*(2), s_3*(2))$ is a Nash equilibrium.

C: To show that strategy triple $s*(3) = (s_1*(3), s_2*(3), s_3*(3))$ is a Nash equilibrium:

Suppose $s*(3) = (s_1*(3), s_2*(3), s_3*(3))$ is not a Nash equilibrium. Then there exist some alternative strategy s_i' for some player i, $i= 1,2,3$, such that $\pi_i(s_i', s_{-i}*(3)) > \pi_i(s*(3))$

Examining player 3: Given $s_1*(3)$, $s_2*(3)$, as defined above, only part (i) of player 3's strategy is relevant in the sense of being potentially payoff-altering for player 3. There are two alternatives for player 3 to choose: accept player 1's offer, or alternatively, accept player 2's offer. But since $P_1=R_3$, accepting player 1's offer would lead to $\pi_3(s_3', s_{-3}*(3)) = 0 = \pi_3(s*(3))$, and this would not make player 3 better off. Since $P_2 > R_3$, accepting player 2's offer would lead to $\pi_3(s_3', s_{-3}*(3)) < 0 = \pi_3(s*(2))$, which would make player 3 worse off.

We now examine the possibility for player 1 to have a payoff improving alternative strategy s_1', given that the other players' strategies remain at $s_2*(3)$ and $s_3*(3)$. The two possible alternative strategies are to announce a price P_1, such that $P_1<R_3$ or to announce a price P_1, such that $P_1 > R_3$. In both cases, however we would have $\pi_1(s_1', s_{-1}*(3)) \leq 0 = \pi_1(s*(3))$, given player 1's utility function, and given the assumption

$R_3 < c$. This can be seen as follows: Suppose $P_1<R_3$. Either player 1's offer gets accepted, or it does not get accepted. If it gets accepted, then $\pi_1(s_1', s_{-1}*(3)) < 0$, since $P_1 \leq R_3 < c$. If it gets rejected then

$\pi_1(s_1', s_{-1}*(3)) = 0$. Suppose $P_1 > R_3$ then $\pi_1(s_1', s_{-1}*(3)) = 0$, since, according to $s_3*(3)$, player 1's offer gets rejected. So player 1 does not get an improvement from using alternative strategies.

It remains to examine the possibility for player 2 to have a payoff improving alternative strategy, s_2', given that the other players strategies remain at $s_1*(3)$ and $s_3*(3)$. The possible alternative strategies are to offer a price P_2, such that $P_2 < R_3$, or to offer a price P_2, such that $P_2 = R_3$. Following a line of reasoning analogous to that of player 1 above, we conclude that $\pi_2(s_2', s_{-2}*(3)) \leq 0 = \pi_2(s*(3))$, and this is not a profitable alternative strategy for player 2.

We conclude that $s^*(3) = (s_1^*(3), s_2^*(3), s_3^*(3))$ is a Nash equilibrium.

D: To show that strategy triple $s^*(4) = (s_1^*(4), s_2^*(4), s_3^*(4))$ is a Nash equilibrium:

Examining player 3: : Given $s_1^*(4)$, $s_2^*(4)$, as defined above, only part (i) of player 3's strategy is relevant in the sense of being potentially payoff-altering for player 3. There are two alternatives for player 3 to choose: accept player 1's offer, or alternatively, accept player 2's offer. But since $P_1=P_2=R_3$, accepting player 1's or player 2's offer would lead to $\pi_3(s_3', s_{-3}^*(4)) = 0 = \pi_3(s^*(4))$, and this would not make player 3 better off.

We now examine the possibility for player 1 to have a payoff improving alternative strategy s_1', given that the other players' strategies remain at $s_2^*(4)$ and $s_3^*(4)$. The two possible alternative strategies are to announce a price P_1, such that $P_1 < R_3$ or to announce a price P_1, such that $P_1 > R_3$. In both cases, however we would have $\pi_1(s_1', s_{-1}^*(4)) \leq 0 = \pi_1(s^*(4))$, given player 1's utility function, and given the assumption $R_3 < c$. The line of reasoning is analogous to the one given in B.3 for player 1.

Examining player 2: The possible alternative strategies are to offer a price P_2, such that $P_2 < R_3$, or to offer a price P_2, such that $P_2 > R_3$. Following a line of reasoning analogous to that of player 1 in B.3, we conclude that $\pi_2(s_2', s_{-2}^*(4)) \leq 0 = \pi_2(s^*(4))$, and this is not a profitable alternative strategy for player 2.

We conclude that $s^*(4) = (s_1^*(4), s_2^*(4), s_3^*(4))$ is a Nash equilibrium.

- Proof that there are no others

I now show that there are no other Nash equilibria besides the ones described above, $s^*(1), s^*(2), s^*(3), s^*(4)$.

First To show that player 1's strategy of offering a price P_1 less than R_3 cannot be part of a Nash equilibrium.

Suppose player 1 offers a price P_1, such that $P_1 < R_3$. There are a number of cases to consider.

Case 1: Player 1's offer is P_1, such that $P_1 < R_3$, player 1's offer gets accepted by player 3, and player 2 plays an arbitrary strategy. We refer to this as *case 1 scenario*. By the definition of player 1's utility function this would give negative utility to player 1, since we assume that $R_3 < c$. Here player 1 could obtain higher utility, given that the other players do not change their case 1 scenario strategies, by changing to strategy $P_1 > R_3$. So, a strategy triple, as suggested, is not a Nash equilibrium.

Case 2: Player 1's offer is P_1, such that $P_1 < R_3$, and player 3 rejects all offers. Player 2 plays an arbitrary strategy. *(Case 2 scenario)*. Here player 3 receives zero utility. Player 3 could improve by changing to a strategy of accepting player 1's offer, and thereby receiving positive utility $U_3 = R_3 - P_1 > 0$, given that the other players remain at their case 2 scenario strategies. So, a strategy triple, as suggested, is not a Nash Equilibrium.

Case 3: Player 1's offer is P_1, such that $P_1 < R_3$, player 3 rejects player 1's offer, but accepts player 2's offer P_2, and $P_2 \leq R_3$. Here player 2 receives negative utility, owing to the assumption $R_3 < c$. Player 2 could improve by changing to a strategy $P_2 > R_3$, given that the other players remain at their case 3 scenario strategies. So, a strategy triple, as suggested, is not a Nash equilibrium.

*Case 4:*Player 1's offer is P_1, such that $P_1 < R_3$, player 3 rejects player 1's offer, but accepts player 2's offer P_2, and $P_2 > R_3$. Here player 3 receives negative utility. Player 3 could improve by rejecting all offers, thereby receiving zero utility, given that the other players remain at the case 4 scenario strategies. So, a strategy triple, as suggested, is not a Nash equilibrium.

As the above scenarios exhaust the relevant strategic possibilities, associated with player 1's strategy of offering a price P_1, such that $P_1 < R_3$, the preceding analysis implies that there are no Nash equilibria that include playera 1's strategy of offering a price P_1 such that $P_1 < R_3$

Second

Case 5: Player 1's offer is P_1, such that $P_1 = R_3$, and player 1's offer gets rejected by player 3. Here we have several sub-cases, accounting for different strategic situations with regard to player 2.

Subcase 5.1 Suppose player 2's offer P_2 also is rejected, and satisfies $P_2 < R_3$. Then player 3, who under this scenario receives utility of zero, could improve by changing to a strategy of accepting player 2's offer, thereby receiving positive utility.

Subcase 5.2 Suppose player 2's offer P_2 also is rejected, and satisfies $P_2 = R_3$. This is equilibrium

s*(4).

Subcase 5.3 Suppose player 2's offer P_2 also is rejected, and satisfies $P_2 > R_3$. This is equilibrium

s*(3).

Subcase 5.4 Suppose player 2's offer P_2 gets accepted and satisfies $P_2 < R_3$. Then player 2 gets negative utility, which could be improved upon by changing to an alternative strategy of $P_2 > c$,

($c > R_3$ by assumption) which would give positive utility to player 2.

Subcase 5.5 Suppose player 2's offer P_2 gets accepted and satisfies $P_2 = R_3$. Then player 2 gets negative utility, owing to the assumption of $R_3 < c$. Player 2 could obtain positive utility by changing to an alternative strategy of $P_1 > c$. So the suggested strategy triple cannot be a Nash equilibrium.

Subcase 5.6 Suppose player 2's offer P_2 gets accepted and satisfies $P_2 > R_3$. This would give negative utility to player 3. Changing to an alternative strategy of rejecting all offers, while the other players remain at their original strategies, player 3 could obtain zero utility, which would be an improvement. So, also this strategy triple cannot be a Nash equilibrium.

Case 6: Player 1's offer is P_1, such that $P_1 = R_3$, and player 1's offer gets accepted by player 3. Player 2 uses an arbitrary strategy. Then player 1 receives negative utility, due to the assumption that $R_3 < c$. By changing to an alternative strategy, $P_1 > R_3$, player 1 could obtain positive utility, given the usual assumption, that the other players remain at their initial strategies.

As the above scenarios exhaust the relevant strategic possibilities, associated with player 1's strategy of offering a price P_1, such that $P_1 = R_3$, the preceding analysis implies that there are no additional Nash equilibria, that include such a strategy by player 1.

Third

*Case 7:*Player 1's offer is P_1, such that $P_1 > R_3$, and player 3 accepts player 1's offer. Player 2 plays an arbitrary strategy. This leads to negative utility for player 3. Player 3 could improve upon this by changing to a strategy of rejecting player 1's offer, thereby securing utility zero, given that the other players remain at their postulated strategies. So there can be no Nash equilibrium such that $P_1 > R_3$, and player 3 accepts player 1's offer.

Case 8: Player 1's offer is P_1, such that $P_1 > R_3$, and player 3 rejects player 1's offer. We consider several sub-cases, accounting for different strategic situations with regard to player 2.

Subcase 8.1 Suppose player 2's offer is accepted and satisfies $P_2 > R_3$. This gives negative utility to player 3. Player 3 could improve upon this by changing to a strategy of rejecting player 2's offer, thereby obtaining utility value of zero.

Subcase 8.2 Suppose player 2s offer is accepted and satisfies $P_2 \leq R_3$. This gives negative utility to player 2, owing to the assumption $R_3 < c$. Player 2 could improve upon this by changing to a strategy of offering P_2, such that $P_2 > c$, which would give player 2 positive utility.

Subcase 8.3 Suppose player 3 rejects both offers, and $P_2 < R_3$. Here player 3 receives utility of zero, which could be improved upon by player 3 switching to a strategy of accepting player 2's offer and thereby receiving positive utility.

Subcase 8.4 Suppose player 3 rejects both offers, and $P_2 = R_3$. This is equilibrium s*(2).

Subcase 8.5 Suppose player 3 rejects both offers, and $P_2 > R_3$. This is equilibrium s*(1).

In the above sub-cases, when I say that player i, i = 1,2,3, can be made better off by changing to an alternative strategy, it should be understood that this is true, *given that the other players remain at their designated subcase x strategies*, as required by the definition of Nash equilibrium.

As the above scenarios exhaust the relevant strategic possibilities, associated with player 1's strategy of offering a price P_1, such that $P_1 > R_3$, the preceding analysis implies that there are no additional Nash equilibria, besides the ones listed above.

ABOUT THE AUTHOR

Brief Bio: Roswitha M. King studied economics at the University of Minnesota in Minneapolis, USA and received her PhD from this institution in 1998 with dissertation advisor Prof. Leonid Hurwicz. Thereafter she moved to Riga, Latvia, to study economics of transition from centrally planned to market economies. In Riga she was employed at the EuroFaculty, a European Academic Development Project for Eastern Europe and taught at the University of Latvia. Since 2006 Roswitha M. King is associate professor at Oestfold University College in Halden, Norway, while maintaining her connection with Riga as senior research fellow at the Centre for European and Transition Studies at the University of Latvia. Dr. King's research interests are international economics and economic policy analysis

REFERENCES

Acma, Bulent (2003), "Innovations and Entrepreneurship : Case Study of Southeastern Anatolia Region and the Southeastern Anatolia Project (GAP) in Turkey, Papers and Proceedings of the International Conference *Small and Medium Enterprises in European Economies,* Babes-Bolyai University Cluj- Napoca, October 17-18, 2003.

Akca, Hazan, Murat Sayili and Kemal Esengun (2003), "The Concept of Entrepreneurship in Small and Medium-Sized Agricultural Enterprises in Turkey", Papers and Proceedings of the International Conference *Small and Medium Enterprises in European Economies,* Babes-Bolyai University Cluj- Napoca, October 17-18, 2003.

"An evaluation of Phare-financed programmes in support of SMEs"; Phare Final Synthesis Report, February 2000. Report produced for the Evaluation Unit of the Common Service for External Relations (SCR) of the European Commission.

Ayyagari, Meghana, Thorsten Beck, and Asli Demirgüc-Kunt (2003), "Small and Medium Enterprises across the Globe: A New Database, *World Bank Policy Research Working Paper 3127,* August 2003.

Elster, John, Claus Offe, and Ulrich K. Preuss (1998), *Institutional Design in Post-communist Societies,* Cambridge University Press.

EUR-LEX: 96/280/EC: Commission Recommendation of 3 April 1996 concerning the definition of small and medium-sized enterprises, *Official Journal L* 107, 30/04/1996 P. 0004 - 0009

Hallberg, Kristin(2001): A Market-Oriented Strategy For Small and Medium-Scale Enterprises. *IFC Discussion Paper # 48.*

Hurwicz, Leonid (1972), "On Informationally Decentralized Systems", Chapter 14 in C. B. McGuire and Roy Radner, eds. *Decision and Organization,* North Holland.

___ (1973), "The Design of Mechanisms for Resource Allocation", *The American Economic Review,* Vol. 63.

___ (1986), "Incentive Aspects of Decentralization", in: *Handbook of Mathematical Economics*, Chapter 28.

Kraftova, Ivana and Jiri Kraft (2003) "Position of Small and Medium Enterprises in the Czech Republic Before its Entrance into the EU, Papers and Proceedings of the International Conference *Small and Medium Enterprises in European Economies,* Babes-Bolyai University Cluj-Napoca, October 17-18, 2003.

Nistor, Ioann Alin (2003), "Enterprise Size and Profitability – Problems related to the Nature of the SME in Romania", Papers and Proceedings of the International Conference *Small and Medium Enterprises in European Economies,* Babes-Bolyai University Cluj-Napoca, October 17-18, 2003.

Petrakis, P.E. (2002), *"Social and Economic Factors Affecting Entrepreneurship Perspectives", Working Paper.*

Pop, Cornelia, Dana Bako, and Ioanna Circo (2002), "Financing Programs Available for Romanian SMEs", Papers and Proceedings of the International Conference *Small and Medium Enterprises in European Economies,* Babes-Bolyai University Cluj-Napoca, October 17-18, 2003.

Romania, Ministry for SMEs and Co-Operatives, "Small and Medium-Sized Enterprises in Romania
http://www.unece.org/indust/sme/Romanian%20SME%20sector%20presentation.pdf
(date accessed: November 6, 2005)

"Small and Medium-sized Enterprises in Countries in Transition" *Biennium Review 2000-2001,* UNECE, OPA/AC.32/1, 2003.

Szabo, Antal, Regional Adviser on Entrepreneurship and SMEs, UN Economic Commission for Europe, "Development of the SME sector in the Visegrad Countries"; UN-ECE

Operational Activities *http://www.unece.org/indust/sme/visegrad.htm (date accessed: July 3, 2006)*

_____ (2003) *"The Development of the SME Sector in the Various Regions of the OSCE"*, paper prepared for the 3rd OSCE Parliamentary Assembly Conference on Sub-Regional Co-operation: Small and Medium-Sized Businesses, held on 14-15 May 2003 in the Swiss Parliament in Bern.

_____ (1997) "Development of Entrepreneurship and Small and Medium-Sized Enterprises in Hungary. Working paper prepared for the workshop on The Role of SMEs in Economy and Practical Lessons Learned by Transition Countries in Promotion of Entrepreneurship, held 26.-28 February 1997 in Minsk, UN- ECE; *www.unece.org/indust/sme/hu-study.htm (date accessed: Aug. 12, 2006)*

"The State in a Changing World", World Development Report 1997. World Bank 1997.

"Latvia, Human Development Report" (1998) UNDP

Wach, Krzysz and Rafael Morawczynski (2003), "Impact of the European Union Accession on Polish Small and Medium-Sized Enterprises, Papers and Proceedings of the International Conference *Small and Medium Enterprises in European Economies,* Babes-Bolyai University Cluj-Napoca, October 17-18, 2003.

In: Economics of Wealth in the 21st Century
Editor: Jason M. Gonzalez

ISBN: 978-1-61122-805-2
©2011 Nova Science Publishers, Inc.

Chapter 3

CAN WE EXPLAIN AWAY THE BLACK-WHITE WEALTH GAP?

Zhu Xiao Di and Yi Xu

Joint Center for Housing Studies, Harvard University, Cambridge, MA, USA

ABSTRACT

The racial gap in wealth in the U.S. is a large and persistent social issue, an important concern for both sociologists and public policy makers. Study after study has found this to be true: no one has found any set of factors that can explain it away. However, none of these studies used the data that best capture the total aggregate household wealth in the U.S. and therefore the real wealth gap between white and black households: the Federal Reserve's SCF data set. To reinvestigate this gap, therefore, we used the latest SCF data, collected in 2007. Our findings confirm that the black/white wealth gap cannot be explained away even using the best available data capturing household wealth.

Keywords: household wealth, racial wealth gap.

INTRODUCTION

In the 15 years since Oliver and Shapiro (1995) published their groundbreaking *Black Wealth, White Wealth*, the gap in household wealth between blacks and whites has become well known and drawn much public attention. Many studies have been published, including Dalton Conley's well-known *Being Black, Living in the Red* (1999). A paper by Scholz and Levine (2003) summarized these previous studies very carefully; some of the studies they included, now nearly 20 years old, drew little attention at the time, such as those by Blau and Graham (1990) and Long and Caudill (1992). Clearly, researchers have been trying to explain the racial wealth gap by looking at other factors.

Researchers have suggested a few factors that have proven significant, both theoretically and empirically. First, differences in household income and some demographic differences between blacks and whites, such as age, marriage status and family size, can explain some of the wealth gap. Second, inheritances and the intergenerational transfer of wealth when parents are still alive also play an important role in people accumulating wealth. Third, strategies and opportunities in financial management and investment may lead to differences in wealth. Altonji and Doraszelski (2005) further explored the impact of permanent incomes instead of current ones.

But so far no researchers have paid attention to the warning by Scholz and Levine (2003) about data source and sampling methods. Because a relatively small proportion of households hold a large amount of wealth, conventional sampling methods can fail to include a large quantity of household wealth. These methods include random and representative samples and those taken from administrative records on those receiving government assistance and thus limited to relatively poorer households. Therefore, analyses based on these datasets, such as the Panel Survey of Income Dynamics (PSID), actually miss the wealth in the high end of the distribution, and thus they may not accurately present the sharp difference in the household wealth between blacks and whites. Scholz and Levine argued that the Federal Reserve's dataset, the Survey of Consumer Finances (SCF), is really the only one in the United States that over-samples wealthy households and therefore fully presents the racial wealth gap.

In this paper we use the most recent SCF data, collected in 2007 and released in 2009, to explore the same issue: can the black/white wealth gap be explained away by factors that previous researchers have explored using other datasets? We set the level of household wealth as the dependent variable, and controlled for current household income and education (often seen as a proxy for permanent income), and demographic variables such as age, size of household and marriage status, the amount of inheritance and gifts received, and investment habits (owning homes, stocks, etc.).

To our surprise, the black/white dummy in our OLS model did not prove to be statistically significant. This finding seems to suggest that the black/white gap in household wealth can be explained away entirely by the factors we controlled for. Is that right? Can we say that we now have a satisfying answer to this important sociological and perhaps moral question? Not quite yet. Further analysis has convinced us that we should not be fooled by the insignificance of the parameter estimate in the above model. We will tell the full story of our discovery but first we describe our data and methodology in comparison with those used in previous studies and comments made on them by other researchers.

Data and Methodology

The data source we used in this paper is the SCF micro data of 2007. The survey is conducted every three years by the Federal Reserve, and it takes the bank approximately 18 months to release the micro dataset for public use. Because the survey over-samples wealthy households, it captures the aggregate amount of household wealth more accurately than any other dataset on wealth in the United States.

The major limitation of the dataset is its small sample size, since each survey interviews fewer than 5,000 households. The publicly released data actually contains over 20,000 observations, and the SCF website explains why:

Missing data in the survey have been imputed five times using a multiple imputation technique. The information is stored in five separate and internally coherent imputation replicates (implicates). Thus, for the 4,422 families interviewed for the survey, there are 22,110 records in the data set. Four observations were deleted for the public version of the dataset for purposes of disclosure avoidance; thus, there are 22,090 records in the public dataset for 4,418 families.[1]

The SCF also created a new deflated weight to be used for all five sets of implicates so that the weighted estimates still represent the total number of households in the United States, not five times as many.

The greatest strength of the SCF is that it over-samples wealthy households in order to capture, as closely as possible, the full magnitude of household wealth in this country. Roughly a third of the sample is drawn from a listing of households known as wealthy. Because of the way the SCF deals with missing data, researchers have to make adjustments in calculating standard errors in the regression models, unless they choose to use only one of the five sets of implicates. Many regression packages will treat each of the five implicates as an independent observation, which inflates the reported significance of the results. The SCF website suggests that users can simply "multiply the standard errors of the regression (on all observations) by the square root of five"[2] as a safe and adequate way to make the adjustment. To avoid this cumbersome readjustment procedure, we decided to use only the first set of implicates with the original weights that adjust the sample size to the actual number of households in the United States.

In terms of methodology, all the previous studies on this issue have taken one of two approaches: the decomposing method or the indicator method. Both have limitations. The decomposing method, also known as the Blinder-Oaxaca (B-O) method, uses a sample that is either white alone or black alone to run a regression and then applies the results to the other side of the sample (i.e. black or white, respectively) to predict wealth. In doing this it assumes the other sample has similar characteristics in independent variables, and tries to see if that might explain the racial wealth gap.

Previous researchers (e.g. Altonji and Doraszelski, 2001; Barsky, Bound, Charles, and Lupton, 2002) have discovered a major and annoying problem with this method: if they develop a model using the white sample, they can "explain" away much more of the racial wealth gap than if they use the corresponding black sample. Even though these researchers took great pains to improve the B-O method and came up with some sophisticated remedies, it is not intuitively easy to understand or explain why such a discrepancy occurs in the first place when one chooses the white or black sample to run the model.

Scholz and Levine (2003) are not satisfied with this method because they think "there is no *a priori* reason to prefer one approach to the other." We believe that if the B-O method has to be used, the white sample should be used to run the regression and not the black. For most independent variables such as income and age, the white sample has a wider range than the black sample; for example, the black population includes few high-income households. Therefore it makes sense to apply estimates from the white sample to the black sample rather than vice versa. A regression run from the black sample is only accurate for a narrower range

---

[1] http://www.federalreserve.gov/pubs/oss/oss2/2007/scf2007data.html
[2] http://www.federalreserve.gov/pubs/oss/oss2/faq.html

of the white sample. Therefore, it is not appropriate to apply the black regression estimates to the white sample for those white households with very high incomes.

The second method involves using an indicator. Oliver and Shapiro (1995), Smith (1995), Hurst, Luoh, and Stafford (1998), and Conley (1999, 2001) all added a dummy indicator variable of black and white to the side of the independent variables in the regression equation. In the words of Scholz and Levine (2003),[3] conditioning on other covariates, the coefficient on the indicator variable should reflect wealth differences across racial and ethnic groups that are unexplained by other factors. An insignificant indicator variable suggests wealth differentials can be completely explained by factors such as income, education, and household composition rather than by race or ethnicity.

Meanwhile, however, they also contend that such an approach is restrictive, because a "linear regression with an indicator implies that the slope of the wealth function with respect to all other covariates is the same for both races, and only the intercept of the function is shifted up or down" If that is their major concern, however, it should be possible to detect these differences using a set of interaction variables that connect the black/white dummy variable and the other independent variables. Therefore, we feel more comfortable taking this approach than the B-O approach and believe it is totally legitimate to use this method. Moreover, the criticism by Scholz and Levine (2003) does not make much sense or even appear to be fair, as long as the interaction variables are included as we suggest above.

In our investigation, we built three models. In Model A, the dependent variable is simply the level of household net wealth expressed in dollars. This model has a weakness, however. A linear regression model requires or assumes that depending on the independent variables, the distribution of the dependent variable would be roughly normal; in other words, it assumes a normal distribution in errors. However, actual wealth distribution is known to be far from normal, with a long tail on the right side.

Because the SCF survey over-samples wealthy households, it shows a much longer right tail than the datasets used in some previous studies, such as the PSID data. Even researchers using the PSID data, such as Altonji and Doraszelski (2005), trim off the outliers in their sample so that their model will fit better. They acknowledge that excluding the outliers did somewhat reduce the size of the wealth gap between whites and blacks, but they state that their main findings are not sensitive to that trimming process. Because of the SCF's over-sampling, our data set includes many more wealthy households than the PSID dataset. Even if we were to trim off the top 5 percent of the sample, we might not meet the same level of normality assumption as in the PSID data. Potential violation of linearity is another concern: because of the heavy right tail nature of this sampling method, our predictions are likely to be seriously in error, especially when we extrapolate beyond the range of the sample data. Fortunately, a log transformation could cure both problems.

However, many households have negative net wealth because they hold large debts; therefore, a direct log transformation would eliminate all these households from the data. Therefore, we shifted the dependent variable upward by $391,001 to make sure that all the observations were strictly positive before we proceeded with the log transformation. Then, we just need to deduct that $391,001 when we convert the dependent variable from its logged form back to the dollar amount.

---

[3] http://www.econ.wisc.edu/~scholz/Research/Wealth_survey_v5.pdf

Our Model B took a different approach. Since the slope of the wealth function with respect to all other covariates may not be the same for black and white households, as Scholz and Levine (2003) argue, for Model B we created interaction variables between the black/white dummy and each of the other independent variables. This helps us to predict the various black/white wealth differences according to the different levels of all covariates such as education and the age of the household head. There is still a potential problem, namely multicollinearity, because we included both education and household income in the model while education is strongly related to income. Therefore, we built Model C, which excludes education as an independent variable.

Table 1 provides some descriptive statistics on the SCF data we used.

FINDINGS FROM OLS REGRESSION MODELS

Our three models tell our whole story one step at a time. As we mentioned in the introduction, once we controlled for socioeconomic and demographic factors, as well as for differences in wealth transfer and investments, the black/white dummy variable did seem to indicate that the racial wealth gap may have been entirely "explained" away by these independent variables when the level of household wealth in dollars is used as the dependent variable, as shown in Model A in Table 2.

We also did step-by-step modeling to test the relative impact of each set of these factors. It turns out that household income is the most important indicator of household wealth and that none of the other factors can begin to compete with its influence. Using household income alone, the model can explain 40 percent of the variation in household wealth.

The amount of inheritance or gifts received turns out to be the next most important influence, with an R-square of 0.03 when used alone as the independent variable. Education variables that can be viewed as a proxy for permanent income achieve an R-square of 0.02 when used as the sole independent variable. None of the other independent variables can explain more than 1 percent of the variations in the dependent variable of household wealth.

As we explained above, there is one problem with Model A: that the distribution of wealth is so far away from a normal distribution. In Model B we used log wealth instead, and the coefficient for the black/white dummy variable became statistically significant; this indicates that the racial wealth gap may NOT be explained away by the independent variables, once we have addressed the normality assumption by using a log transformation.

In Model B we also included a few interaction variables, but that is not the reason why the black/white dummy variable became significant, because it was still insignificant when we tried including the interaction variables in Model A. In Model B we found that the black/white dummy variable interacts significantly with three other factors: educational level of college or more, the age of the household head, and whether the household is directly or indirectly holding some stock wealth. These suggest several points that should raise sociological concerns. First, while a college education often leads to more household wealth, its value is different for the two races in our sample: it is less valuable for a black person than for a white. One possible reason here is that measuring education by level alone could be a rough measurement and if black college graduates in general are less likely to have graduated from top-rate institutions it could lead to the result as we see in our model. Second, compared

Table 1: Descriptive Statistics of the Sample Using the 2007 SCF Data

Variable	All (N=3928) Mean	Maximum	Minimum	Median	White (N=3518) Mean	Maximum	Minimum	Median	Black (N=410) Mean	Maximum	Minimum	Median
Household Net wealth	594,890.08	1,146,457,000	-391,000	133,900	673,468.39	1,146,457,000	-391,000	162,400	133,286.19	40,855,000	-85,500	17,100
log(networth+$391001)	13.38	20.86	12.01	13.17	13.43	20.86	12.01	13.22	13.08	17.54	12.63	12.92
Household Income	88,126.40	186,819,144	0	48,335	95,323.95	186,819,144	0	51,420	45,844.80	19,745,280	0	30,852
Age of Household Head	51.22	95	18	50	52.16	95	19	51	45.72	91	18	44
Inheritance/gift Received	34379.01	50,352,000	0	0	39,283.89	50,352,000	0	0	5,565.59	300,000	0	0
High School	32.1%				31.8%				33.4%			
Some College	24.0%				23.1%				29.6%			
College or Higher	31.0%				32.9%				20.2%			
Male-headed Households	21.2%				20.8%				23.1%			
Female-headed Households	28.7%				25.8%				45.7%			
Number of Persons in Household	2.47				2.45				2.60			
Homeownership	71.0%				74.8%				48.5%			
Having stock wealth	53.3%				57.4%				28.9%			

Table 2. Regression Model Estimation

Parameter	Model A	Model B	Model C (without education variables)
Dependent variable	Household Net Wealth	Log (net wealth + $391,001)	Log (net wealth + $391,001)
Intercept	-722665**	12.55**	12.79**
Black or white (1=black, 0=white)	-29159	0.29**	0.03
Household Income	5.82**	0.00**	0.00**
High School	12632	0.06*	
Some College	56917	0.11**	
College or Higher	274167	0.41**	
Age of Household Head	12468**	-0.01	0.00
Male-headed Households	-20564	0.01**	0.00**
Female-headed Households	-81303	-0.06*	-0.08**
Inheritance/gift Received	1.54**	-0.14**	-0.16**
Homeownership	31438	0.00**	0.00**
Having Stock Wealth	114963	0.28**	0.38**
Number of Persons in Household	-16623	0.00	-0.01
Interaction between black/white and College+		-0.25**	
Interaction between black/white and Age		0.00**	
Interaction between black/white and Having Stock Wealth		-0.17**	-0.24**
Interaction between Homeownership and Age		0.01**	0.01**
R-Square	42.27%	41.68%	37.6%

** Significant at 1% level
* Significant at 5% level

to white households, black households are likely to have smaller amounts invested in stock equity. Therefore, for black households our model assigns less value to the dummy variable of having stock equity. Third, the only variable that seems to favor blacks over whites is the age of the household head. The model suggests that, as black households grow older, they catch up with the wealth of white ones to a certain degree.

A few detailed numbers may convey some of the differences in household wealth between white and black households suggested by our Model B. Suppose we are comparing two households that both consists of only a married couple, headed by a 51-year-old person with a college education; the couple owns its home and some stocks, either directly or indirectly. Its household income is at the sample mean level, i.e. $88,126 and it has received some inheritance/gifts, also at the sample mean level of $34,379. If this is a black household, our model predicts its household wealth to be $282,125, but if it is a white one, its predicted wealth would be $593,312.

Using Model B we can also see how education and age play different roles in accumulating wealth. For example, take as the example a white married couple household with no one else present, whose head is aged 35 and has only high school education; it owns the home and some stocks, has received $5,000 as inheritance or gift, and has a household income of $30,000. Its predicted household wealth would be $168,230. By the time the household head reaches age 55, the accumulated household wealth would become $307,917. If the household head manages to graduate from college before age 55, the household wealth would be $598,776. In contrast, for a black household with all the same variables, its predicted wealth at age 35 would be $140,971, reaching $214,163 by age of 55, and even with an educational level improved to a college degree, it would have just $273,247 in household wealth.

On the other hand, take a black married couple with only a high school education at age 25; they do not own their home or any stocks, have received $5,000 of inheritance or gift, and have a household income of $30,000. Their predicted household wealth would be merely $2,925 and increase to $41,385 with a college education. Their white counterparts, with a college education, would have $80,693 in wealth, but if they had just a high school education their predicted wealth would be negative $57,921. This negative figure seems surprising but may reflect one of two possibilities: either a young white household is more likely to be willing to take on debt or lenders are more likely to be willing to lend it money, for example, in the form of education loans.

We have noted that black and white households have very different levels of household income and receive different amount of inheritances/gifts. Remembering this, what happens if we apply these two variables at the sample means of black and white separately instead of the sample means of the entire sample? That is, we use the white income of $95,324 with inheritance/gifts at $39,284 and the black income of $45,845 and inheritance/gifts at $5,566. Then the predicted wealth gap would be $431,889 for whites vs. $244,812 for blacks.

Many earlier studies have included education as an independent variable even though household income is already in the model, but we noticed a potential problem with this practice. We found a high correlation between education and income; in fact the education variable can even be used as a proxy for permanent income, while the income variable reflects only the current income level, which changes from year to year. To put both of them in as independent variables may only create confusion. Therefore, to predict the wealth gap between whites and blacks, we also built a regression model without education variables, as shown in Model C.

We should point out that the interaction between the age of household head and the black/white dummy variable also became insignificant and therefore we excluded it from our Model C. This difference or change from Model B seems to suggest a need to rethink our earlier observation that to some extent black households catch up with the wealth of white households as they grow older. They do not catch up because of an improved education, because Model B already controls for education. Instead, we suggest, it is simply due to behavior changes, perhaps a higher savings rate at a later age.

Finally, not surprisingly, our models B and C indicate some interaction between home ownership and age. That means that the positive correlation between homeownership and household wealth grows even stronger as people age. This reflects the fact that most households become homeowners by taking out home mortgage loans and gradually pay back these loans while they age, so their home equity grows. Thus our models predict a larger value of wealth for older rather than younger homeowners.

CONCLUSION

In this paper, to reinvestigate the black/white wealth gap, we used the Federal Reserve's SCF data, the best data for capturing the total aggregate wealth and therefore the wealth gap among different households, especially the racial wealth gap between white and black households. On first blush, it seemed we could explain away the entire wealth gap by pointing to the covariates in our model: household income, age and education level of household head, size and marriage status of household, amount of inheritance or gifts received by the household, and whether the household owns its home or any stocks, directly or indirectly.

Further investigation, however, reveals this is not so. An improved model uses log transformation to attain a more normal distribution of wealth—its dependent variable. In this model, the OLS regression still reveals significant differences in wealth holdings between black and white households after controlling for the variables listed just above.

These new findings use a better dataset that records a stronger and true racial dividing line in household wealth holdings; they provide more definitive evidence that the black/white wealth gap cannot be explained away by all the covariates in the model. Household income remains by far the most influential factor in household wealth accumulation. Other factors do play some role in distinguishing the amount of wealth held by black and white households; these factors include intergenerational wealth transfer through inheritance and gift-giving, homeownership and equity stock holdings, and other social-economic factors such as age, household size and marital status, as well as education. Still, all of them together, and combined with household income, cannot fully explain the large racial wealth gap in this country.

REFERENCES

Altonji, Joseph G. and Ulrich Doraszelski. 2001. "The Role of Permanent Income and Demographics in Black/White Differences in Wealth." *National Bureau of Economic Research Working Paper 8473*. Cambridge, MA: NBER.

Altonji, Joseph G. and Ulrich Doraszelski. 2005. "The Role of Permanent Income and Demographics in Black/White Differences in Wealth." *The Journal of Human Resources*, Vol. 40, No. 1 (Winter, 2005), pp. 1-30.

Barsky, Robert B., John Bound, Charles Kerwin, and J.P. Lupton. 2002. "Accounting for the black-white wealth gap: A nonparametric approach." *Journal of the American Statistical Association*, 97(459): 663-673.

Blau, Francine D. and John W. Graham. 1990. "Black-White Differences in Wealth and Asset Composition." *Quarterly Journal of Economics*, 105(2): 321-339.

Conley, Dalton, 1999. *Being Black, Living in the Red: Race, Wealth and Social Policy in America*. Berkeley: University of California Press.

Conley, Dalton, 2001. "Decomposing the Black-White Wealth Gap: The Role of Parental Resources, Inheritance, and Investment Dynamics," *Sociological Inquiry*, Vol. 71, No. 1 (Winter 2001), pp. 39-66.

Hurst, Erik, Ming Ching Luoh, and Frank P. Stafford. 1998. "The Wealth Dynamics of American Families, 1984-94." *Brookings Papers on Economic Activity* 1: 267-337.

Long, James E. and Steven B. Caudill. 1992. "Racial Differences in Homeownership and Housing Wealth." *Economic Inquiry* 30(1): 83-100.

Oliver, Melvin and Thomas Sharpiro. 1995. *Black Wealth, White Wealth*. New York and London: Routledge.

Scholz, John Karl and Kara Levine. 2003. "U.S. Black-White Wealth Inequality: A Survey," in *Social Inequality*, Kathryn Neckerman (ed.), Russell Sage Foundation, 2003.

Smith, James P. 1995. "Racial and Ethnic Differences in Wealth in the Health and Retirement Study." *Journal of Human Resources* 30(0), Suppl: S158-83.

In: Economics of Wealth in the 21st Century
Editor: Jason M. Gonzalez

ISBN 978-1-61122-805-2
© 2011 Nova Science Publishers, Inc.

Chapter 4

CONSILIENT APPROACHES TO MODELING WEALTH

Bernard C. Beaudreau[*]
Department of Economics, Université Laval
Québec, Canada

Abstract

With the productivity slowdown in the mid-1970's came a renewed interest in all questions pertaining to the wealth of nations (levels, growth, role of technology). Neglected for most of the 20th century, economic growth soon dominated and continues to dominate both the academic and public agendas. In time, new models and approaches were forthcoming. Examples include the Ak approach developed by Paul Romer (1987, 1990). While convincing, these models suffered from a number of shortcomings, not the least of which were weak fundamentals. Specifically, while most attributed variations in growth to technological change, little was known about technology *per se*. Some responded by modeling technological change (Aghion and Howitt 1998) while others called for a fundamental reexamination of the very way in which material processes were modeled in economics (Kummel *et al.* 1998, Beaudreau 1995, 1998, 1999). The upshot of the latter class of models is the belief that models of material processes in economics, like in all other physical sciences, should be consistent with the laws of physics, specifically classical mechanics and thermodynamics. This paper examines these models, historically, theoretically and empirically. They are shown to have a history that extends back in time to the 1920s and 1930s when physicists, engineers and economists alike proposed new approaches to understanding wealth, approaches that were consistent with basic physics.

Keywords: Consilience, Growth, Unified science, Growth slowdown.

1. Introduction

Since Adam Smith's *magnum opus*, An Inquiry into the Nature and Causes of the Wealth of Nations, published in 1776, scholars have examined the workings of material processes with

---
[*] E-mail address: bernard.beaudreau@ecn.ulaval.ca

the hope of better understanding wealth, specifically, its underlying "nature" and "causes." Those in the natural sciences focused on the physics of the new technology that was the steam engine, while those in the moral sciences focused on the fallout from the resulting massive increase in material wealth. The cornerstone, in both cases, was a model of wealth *per se*. Its causes, its equations of motion.

With the benefit of hindsight, the steam engine was an enigma to both. Natural philosophers were at a loss to explain its workings as were moral philosophers. Physicists struggled with the concept of steam as a force. Moral philosophers, accustomed to labor-based material processes also struggled with the steam engine. Was it a form of labor? Or was it capital? How exactly did it affect productivity?

Both would devote the next century writings the equations of motion of steam engine-based material processes. In the case of the natural philosophy, the result was the field of thermodynamics and its three laws. In the case of moral philosophy, the result was classical—including Marxian—and neoclassical economics, with their emphasis on capital and labor. Interestingly and surprisingly, the two parted ways. Thermodynamics dominated 19th century physics, while moral philosophy gave way to economics and business administration. For roughly two centuries, the two led what were largely independent existences, with few attempts at integration.

The productivity slowdown of the 1970s (Maddison 1987) thrusted the problem of wealth into the forefront, a place it had rarely found itself over the course of history. Why did growth suddenly plummet? Why was its impact global? And why have Western industrialized nations, despite what have been and continue to be Herculean measures at fostering growth, failed to renew with the growth rates of lore? This has prompted a lot of soul searching on the part of the economics profession. It has led to innovations on many fronts, from Paul Romer's *Ak* model, to Philippe Aghion and Peter Howitt's modeling of Joseph Schumpeter's notion of creative destruction. Another is a class of models that draws from thermodynamics and process engineering. The upshot of this literature is simple, namely that energy matters. More specifically, energy, the cornerstone of all known material processes in the universe, matters a lot. And, furthermore, the productivity slowdown and ensuing lower growth rates owe, in large measure, to a marked decrease in energy availability that began with the two OPEC-induced energy crises in the 1970s. Unlike mainstream models that violate, for the most part, the laws of physics and thermodynamics, these models are consilient with them.[1]

This paper examines these models in detail, historically, methodologically and empirically. The emphasis will be on drawing parallels between the physics and economics literature on the subject of material processes. That is, identifying common themes across both fields. The discussion will be organized around three themes namely history, methodology and evidence. To this end, we begin by presenting a consilient model of material processes in the form of Beaudreau (1998)'s *Energy-Organization* model which is consistent with the

---

[1] In his 1840 synthesis The Philosophy of the Inductive Sciences, William Whewell coined the word "consilience" to describe the "jumping together" of regularity across scientific disciplines. As Edward O. Wilson points out in his 1998 book *Consilience, The Unity of Knowledge*, the unity of knowledge is as old as science itself, extending back in time to the ancient Greeks. Consilience, argues Wilson, has since been the mother's milk of the natural sciences. More importantly, the central idea is that all tangible phenomena, from the birth of stars to the workings of social institutions, are based on material processes that are ultimately reducible, however long and tortuous the sequences, to the laws of physics" [Wilson (1998),291].

laws of physics as well as with the basic principles of material processes as seen by the economics profession. This will be followed by a brief history of the literature on material processes beginning with Adam Smith's work on the steam engine. The history of steam and its influence on economics is told from the point of view of moral and natural philosophy, both of which were at a lost to understand the new technology. Next, we examine three consilient approaches to material processes, including The *Addendum Approach*, the *Ecological Approach* and the *Fundamentals Approach*. Which is followed by a brief discussion of the politics of consilience. Here we examine the underlying politics of production theory asking the question why have consilient models been eschewed in large measure by the economics profession?

2. The Energy-Organization Framework

To introduce the notion of consilience in the context of growth models and to provide a jargon for the task at hand (examine a particular class of models), we begin by introducing the *Energy-Organization* framework (Beaudreau 1998). Drawing from material process sciences (engineering, biology), the Energy-Organization framework models wealth in terms of two universal factor inputs, namely broadly-defined energy and broadly-defined organization. Both are necessary conditions in all material processes whether it be in biology, chemistry, engineering or economics. The model is formalized in terms of Equation 1 where $W(t)$, $E(t)$, $T(t)$, and $S(t)$ refer to wealth, energy, tools and supervision at time t. η refers to second-law efficiency, which, as shown, is a function of $T(t)$ and $S(t)$.

$$W(t) = \eta[T(t), S(t)]E(t) \qquad (1)$$

$\eta[T(t), S(t)]$ corresponds to the broadly-defined organization input, while $E(t)$ corresponds to the broadly-defined energy input. While $E(t)$ is sometimes referred to as energy consumption *per se*, technically it refers to available work or negentropy. As energy cannot be created nor destroyed, it follows that energy is not consumed *per se*, but rather entropy is increased. Second-law efficiency (i.e. η) is assumed to be increasing in tools and supervision. For the sake of discussion, it will be assumed that the latter are qualitative and not quantitative variables. That is, second-law efficiency is increasing in the quality of tools and the quality of supervision.

This model is consilient in the sense that it describes virtually all known material processes, be they in process engineering, biology or economics. As such, all material processes are powered by energy. Energy and energy alone is productive in the physical sense. Tools and supervision are necessary factor inputs, but not productive in the physical sense.[2] They affect output via their effect on second-law efficiency which is, by definition, bounded from above.[3] Lastly, this equation is consistent with the laws of classical mechanics and thermodynamics, making for a truly consilient model of material processes.

---

[2]According to Betts (1989): Machinery is used to change the magnitude, direction and point of application of required forces in order to make tasks easier. The output of useful work from any machine, however, can never exceed the total input of work and energy. (Betts 1989, 172)

[3]Historically, second-law efficiency is highly stable. Few innovations have and can make a significant difference.

It can be used to study human thermodynamics, industrial processes, celestial motion and economic growth. For example, it predicts that growth will be increasing in energy use, with causality running from the latter to the former (Beaudreau 2010). As a corollary, it predicts that energy-poor countries will, in the absence of imports, be on average poorer than energy-rich countries. A good example is Cuba where the energy constraint tightened with the end of Soviet imports of fossil fuels. The number one issue facing Cuba today is energy, specifically, an acute shortage of energy.

3. Early Literature

Equation 1 is the product of centuries of scientific advances, beginning with Sir Issac Newton's work in the 17th century (classical mechanics). In this section, we examine the historical record in search of consilient approaches to modeling wealth. To begin with, it is important to note that the very practice of modeling (or formalizing) wealth *per se* is relatively recent, having its origins in the 18th century. Which raises the question why? Why was wealth *per se* ignored prior to the 18th century? Why was it not studied in imperial Rome, by far the richest of all empires and civilizations? The reason, we believe, is simple, namely that there was no reason to. Scholars and scribes, poets and priests understood that wealth was an increasing function of labor/work which explains in part the use of slaves as a measure of wealth. Formally, slaves were the principal source of energy/force and hence the basis of wealth.

But is this true. Are slaves a source of energy? Is human labor the source of all wealth? The first to cast doubt on the received wisdom were the French Physiocrats who attributed all wealth invariably to agriculture. According to them, agriculture was the only source of a surplus and hence the only source of wealth. How are we to understand this puzzling result? While dismissed by most, their argument does stand up to further scrutiny. The key to understanding and appreciating it lies in the very source of human energy/force, namely broadly-defined food. As most know only too well, food (carbohydrates and proteins) is what powers human life in general and human force in particular. Put differently, the human body is not a source of energy, but rather an energy transmission device, transforming glucose into motion. As such, having slaves but not having the wherewithal to feed them is a burden, not an asset.

With this as a backdrop, we are better able to appreciate the consilient nature of the Physiocrats argument, namely that agriculture in general and agricultural surpluses in particular, being the source of human energy, are the basis of wealth in general. Recurrent agricultural surpluses, by providing the wherewithal to fuel more physical work, are a necessary condition for greater wealth.[4] This was reflected in the pro-agricultural policies of Louis IV. Not only were the Physiocrats consilient in their approach to modeling wealth, they were the first to invoke scientific principles in the study of wealth. To Francois Quesnay, Nicolas Baudeau, Anne-Robert Jacques Turgot and others, the economy was to be likened to the human body which accounts for the root *physio* in word Physiocrat.

---

[4] the Physiocrats viewed the production of goods and services as consumption of the agricultural surplus.

3.1. The Mystery of Steam

At roughly the same time, developments in Great Britain were laying the basis for the greatest industrial revolution of all times. In 1769, James Watt, a chemist, put the finishing touches on a new atmospheric steam engine equipped with an external condenser. The up-shot was a marked increase in second-law efficiency, making the steam engine a viable technology and a universal source of work. This simple innovation would shape the course of history, catapulting Great Britain, Europe and the rest of the world into the industrial revolution, the defining characteristic of which was a massive increase in wealth.

It represents one of the few episodes in the history of technology where science had to play catch-up. That is, a new technology that could not be understood in terms of the knowledge of the day. At the end of the 18th century, the physics (natural philosophy) of steam were as much a mystery as the economics (moral philosophy) of steam. What was it? How did it behave? Was it a source of power? If so, which? Such were the questions confronting physicists (i.e. natural philosophers) at the end of the 18th century.

Economists were in a similar position. In fact, their predicament was compounded by the total absence of a science of wealth *per se*. Such was the case for Adam Smith: faced with the task of making sense of the new technology and the immense wealth that the steam engine offered without the benefit of a theory of wealth let alone a theory of steam. Unfazed by the immensity of the task before him, he published *An Inquiry into the Nature and Causes of the Wealth of Nations* (Smith 1776). In Chapter 1, he laid out his theory of wealth, based in large measure on labor. Wealth was an increasing function of the labor input. Labor productivity, he maintained, was influenced by three factors, namely specialization, specialization-related time savings, and mechanization (Smith 1776,7). By the latter, it should be understood the steam engine.

Just how did Smith see the steam engine? As a source of power, as a source of work? What was the relationship between the steam engine and conventional labor? It could be argued that the steam engine was as much a mystery to him as it was to most of his contemporaries. Judging from the many references found in the *Wealth of Nations*, it could be argued that he understood/appreciated (*i*) elementary classical mechanics, according to which all work is the result of the application of force, and (*ii*) that the machine itself was not a source of work, but rather steam was. Interestingly, he referred to the new technology as "fire power" in keeping with classical mechanics. In his eyes, the ultimate source of force was the fire that transformed water into steam.

While Smith sought in earnest to understand the causes of the wealth of nations, science was not his main preoccupation. Acutely aware of the immense potential that steam offered, he devoted most of his time and effort to the question of realizing it. How best could Great Britain make the transition to this new "industrial society?" Which led him to the question of institutions, notably free markets. The steam engine *per se* fell into oblivion, lost in the mnemonic mechanization. Mechanization increased productivity by decree. The underlying science was of little concern.

For the remainder of the 18th century and the beginning of the 19th century, steam and fire power was nested in mechanization, although not always explicitly. Wealth was increasing in mechanization or so it was believed. Interest in energy *per se*, however, was rekindled in the 1820s, the result of a series of crises. As it turned out, the new "industrial economy" was prone to cyclical behavior. Despite its infinite potential, it oftentimes found itself in crisis. Which resulted in the emergence of a new field in economics, namely macroeconomics. One of the first to examine the problem of the business cycle was industrialist Robert Owen according to whom low wages and income relative to potential output were the leading cause of stagnation. In his view, technological change in the form of the steam engine had increased potential output; however income lagged behind. Like Adam Smith before him, he did not content himself with simple references to the steam engine, but attempted to delve further into the matter. The following excerpt bears witness to a desire on his part to understand the underlying principles that were responsible for the massive increase in output that resulted from the steam engine.

> It is well known that, during the last half century in particular, Great Britain, beyond any other nation, has progressively increased its powers of production, by a rapid advancement in scientific improvements and arrangements, introduced, more or less, into all the departments of productive industry throughout the empire. The amount of this new productive power cannot, for want of proper data, be very accurately estimated; but your Reporter has ascertained from facts which none will dispute, that its increase has been enormous;—that, compared with the manual labour of the whole population of Great Britain and Ireland, it is, at least, as forty to one, and may be easily made as 100 to one; and that this increase may be extended to other countries; that it is already sufficient to saturate the world with wealth and that the power of creating wealth may be made to advance perpetually in an accelerating ratio. [Owen (1820),246]

As we shall show, the macroeconomic problem as described by Owen would play an important role in the development of consilient models of economic growth. Owen, realizing full well that human labor no longer powered 19th-century material processes, nonetheless advocated a form of the labor theory of value. Output, he argued, should be returned to labor in the form of labor certificates. Which raises the question: is this not a contradiction? Yes and no. It is important to remember his purpose: increasing overall income, not elaborating a theory of production. Steam had increased output (value of) by more than its costs, making for substantial rents (energy rents, surplus). According to Owen, these rents should be captured by labor.

This energy-energy rent-wage triad was to form the basis of an intellectual movement that would shake the foundations of capitalism in the 19th century namely Marxian economics. Borrowing extensively from Owen, Karl Marx set out to revolutionize energy rent sharing. Like Owen before him, he believed that recurrent crises were the result of low wages. Also like Owen, he advocated raising wages, but went further advocating eliminating profits altogether (since capital was not physically productive).

The corresponding theoretical basis was the classical labor theory of value according to which labor and labor alone was/is physically productive. Are we to understand that both Owen and Marx actually believed this? We argue that the labor theory of value had little-to-nothing to do with their views on wealth creation and everything to do with their macroeconomic policy prescriptions. Specifically, both advocated higher wages to increase income and expenditure and chose the labor theory of value as the corresponding rationalization.

Surprisingly, Karl Marx was one of the first 19th century economists to not only understand classical mechanics but to invoke it as a basis for wealth creation. For example, in Chapters 14 and 15 of *Das Capital*, published in 1867, he presented what is by far the most scientifically accurate "scientific" description of production processes both before and after the industrial revolution. Consider, for example, the following passage which describes the role of tools and power in "heterogeneous" and "serial" manufactures, the former referring to the domestic system, and the latter, to the factory system.

> Mathematicians and mechanicians, and in this they are followed by a few English economists, call a tool a simple machine, and a machine a complex tool. They see no essential difference between them, and even give the name of machine to the simple mechanical powers, the lever, the inclined plane, the screw, the wedge, etc. As a matter of fact, every machine is a combination of those simple powers, no matter how they may be disguised. From the economic standpoint, this explanation is worth nothing, because the historical element is wanting. Another explanation of the difference between tool and machine is that, in the case of the tool, man is the motive power, while the motive power of a machine is something different from man, is, for instance, an animal, water, wind. and so on. According to this, a plough drawn by oxen, which is a contrivance common to the most different epochs, would be a machine, while Claussen's circular loom, which, worked by a single labourer, weaves 96,000 picks per minute, would be a mere tool. Nay, this very loom. though a tool when worked by hand, would, if worked by steam, be a machine. And, since the application of animal power is one of man's earliest inventions, production by machinery would have preceded production by handicrafts. When in 1735, John Wyalt brought out his spinning machine and began the industrial revolution of the eighteenth century, not a word did he say about an ass driving it instead of a man. and yet this part fell to the ass. He described it as a machine "to spin without fingers." All fully developed machinery consists of three essentially different parts, the motor mechanism, the transmitting mechanism, and finally the tool of working machine. The motor mechanism is that which puts the whole in motion. It either generates its own motive power, like the steam engine, the caloric engine, the electro-magnetic machine, etc., or it receives its impulse from some already existing natural force, like the water-wheel from a head of water, the windmill from wind, etc. The transmitting mechanism, composed of flywheels, shafting, cogwheels, pulleys, straps, ropes, bands, pinions, and gearing of the most varied kinds, regulates the motion, changes its form where necessary, as, for instance, from linear to circular, and divides and distributes it among the working machines. These two parts of the whole mechanism are there solely for putting the working machines in motion, by means of which motion the subject of labour is seized upon and modified as desired. The tool or working machine is that part of machinery with which the industrial revolution of the eighteenth century started. And, to

> this day it constantly serves as such a starting point whenever a handicraft, or a manufacture, is turned into industry carried on by machinery. (Marx 1991, 181)

Set against the first seven chapters of *Das Kapital* based in large measure on the labor theory of value, one cannot help but question Marx's integrity as a scholar. There, he extols the merits of the classical labor theory of value according to which labor and labor alone is physically productive. And then, in Chapter 17, he outlines a theory of production based on classical mechanics, one that is orthogonal to the former. Clearly, both can't be true.

This leads us to the next point, namely that by the mid-19th century, the debate over the nature and causes of the wealth of nations had degenerated into a debate over the question of distribution with Marx invoking the Classical labor theory of value to justify higher wages and the classical economists defending the *status quo*, specifically capital's right to profits and rents.

Meanwhile, in physics (natural philosophy), a theory of the steam engine in the form of thermodynamics was taking shape, complete with a set of laws (i.e. the laws of thermodynamics). Most cite Sadi Carnots 1824 paper *Reflections on the Motive Power of Fire* as the starting point for thermodynamics as a modern science. Carnot defined "motive power" to be the expression of the useful effect that a motor is capable of producing. In 1843, James Joule experimentally found the mechanical equivalent of heat. In 1845, he reported his best-known experiment, involving the use of a falling weight to spin a paddle-wheel in an barrel of water, which allowed him to estimate a mechanical equivalent of heat of 819 ftlbf/Btu (4.41 J/cal). This led to the theory of conservation of energy and explained why heat can do a work.

The name "thermodynamics," however, did not arrive until some twenty-five years later when, in 1849, the British mathematician and physicist William Thomson (Lord Kelvin) coined the term thermodynamics in a paper on the efficiency of steam engines. In 1850, the famed mathematical physicist Rudolf Clausius originated and defined the term enthalpy H to be the total heat content of the system and defined the term entropy S to be the heat lost or turned into waste. In association with Clausius, in 1871, a Scottish mathematician and physicist James Clerk Maxwell formulated a new branch of thermodynamics called Statistical Thermodynamics, which functions to analyze large numbers of particles at equilibrium, i.e., systems where no changes are occurring, such that only their average properties as temperature T, pressure P, and volume V become important. Soon thereafter, in 1875, the Austrian physicist Ludwig Boltzmann formulated a precise connection between entropy S and molecular motion.

Clearly, the two fields (economics and physics) had embarked on diametrically opposed paths, paths that were never to cross. As physicists probed further the relationship between heat and work, economists were involved in a internecine debate over the respective roles of capital and labor in the creation and distribution of wealth, a debate that was to last a century (i.e. neoclassical versus Marxian distribution theory). The irony is that, according to classical mechanics and thermodynamics, neither labor (in the 19th century) nor capital is physically productive—energy and energy alone is physically productive.

There were exceptions. Economists in general were not impervious to both the role of coal in material processes and the rise of thermodynamics. For example, William Stanley

Jevons, one of the founders of neoclassical economics, published in 1865 a work entitled *The Coal Question*, in which he questioned the sustainability of Great Britain's fossil fuel-based wealth. It is important to remember that Jevons was one of the architects of the neoclassical revolution according to which wealth was an increasing function of labor and capital. In the *Introduction* (The Coal Question) he remarks:

> Day by Day it becomes more evident that the Coal we happily possess in excellent quality and abundance is the mainspring of modern material civilization. As the source of fire, it is the source at once of mechanical motion and of chemical change. Accordingly it is the chief agent in almost every improvement or discovery in the arts which the present age brings forth.... And as the source especially of steam and iron, coal is all powerful. This age has been called the Iron Age, and it is true that iron is the material of most great novelties. By its strength, endurance, and wide range of qualities, this metal is fitted to the the fulcrum and lever of great works, while steam is the motive power. But coal alone can command in sufficient abundance either the iron or the steam; and coal, therefore, commands this age—the Age of Coal. Coal in truth stands not beside, but entirely above all other commodities, It is the material source of the energy of the country?the universal aid?the factor in everything we do. With coal almost any feat is possible or easy; without it we are thrown back into the laborious poverty of early times. With such facts familiarly before us, it can be no matter of surprise that year by year we make larger draughts upon a material of such myriad qualities of such miraculous powers. But it is at the same time impossible that men of foresight should not turn to compare with some anxiety the masses yearly drawn with the quantities known or supposed to lies within these islands. (Jevons 1865, 2)

Jevons personifies economic thought as it pertains to the role of energy in wealth creation, in the 19th century. At a visceral level, most are acutely aware of the importance of coal to Great Britain's wealth. However, intellectually coal is absent from all formalizations of wealth.

3.2. The 20th Century

Despite major advances in the physics of steam (i.e. thermodynamics), the economics of steam remained woefully underdeveloped. Let us now turn to the early 20th century which witnessed another paradigm energy-related technological shock in the form of electromagnetic power (hereafter electric power). Recognized by most as the single most important cause of the second industrial revolution, electric power fueled the meteoric growth of the U.S. economy in the early 20th century. Not only did it raise throughput levels to dizzying heights, it spawned a whole new set of industries collectively known as modernity (electric lights, appliances, automobiles etc). Never before in the history of civilization did man consume as much energy. It powered his industrial processes, heated his house, drove his appliances (automobiles included) (Nye 1990).

As we pointed out, the 19th century closed with little in the way of a consilient approach to understanding material processes. Wealth continued to be seen as an increasing function of labor and capital. Would a technology shock the likes of which had been seen only once before in history be sufficient to push economics along the path of consilience? As we shall argue, the answer is no. Economics remained firmly entrenched in its archaic models of wealth creation. That is not to say, however, that there were no attempts at consilience. We shall focus on two, namely Nobel-laureate Frederick Soddy's *Cartesian Economics* and the *Technocracy* movement in the U.S. Both were attempts by non-economists to break the stranglehold of neoclassical economics and move the profession onto the path of consilience.

Post-WWI Great Britain was but a figment of its former, 19th century self. Inflation was high, unemployment was high, its exports had collapsed and the future seemed grim, especially in light of the mercurial rise of the U.S. as the dominant player. Inevitably, questions arose as to why? How and why did Great Britain fall from grace? The dominant view at the time (Beaudreau 1995) placed the blame squarely on the war, specifically on the demise of the Gold Standard. One of the casualties of the war had been the suspension of convertibility and pre-war parities, itself the result of price inflation. The Bank of England and the Treasury called for a return to pre-WWI parities.

It was against this background that Frederick Soddy begged to differ. In his view, Great Britain's demise owed not to the value of its currency (i.e. the exchange rate) but rather to its failure to electrify—that is, adopt the new process technologies developed in the U.S. The problem, however, was convincing the powers that be. As pointed out earlier, neoclassical economics was devoid of energy. To argue that economic stagnation and decline owed to the failure to adopt a new energy transmission technology (electro-magnetic power) bordered on folly. Which is why he devoted two lectures to the task of rewriting economics, specifically production theory, in "Cartesian" terms. Cartesian economics was one of the first attempts at a consilient theory of production, one that eliminated the seams between economics and physics. According to Soddy:

> Let us now leave generalities and concentrate upon the question as to what precisely humdrum mechanical science can contribute to economics. It insists primarily on the fact that life derives the whole of its physical energy or power, not from anything self-contained in living matter, and still less from an external deity, but solely from the inanimate world. It is dependent for all the necessities of its physical continuance primarily upon the principles of the steam-engine. The principles and ethics of human law and convention must not run counter to those of thermodynamics. For men, no different from any other form of heat engine, the physical problems of life are energy problems. You have to consider the source, the sunshine. It supplies a continuous revenue of energy which is consumed by the living engine in its life. Consumption here does not mean destruction, for destruction, like creation in the world of which we speak is an impossibility, but merely the rendering unfit for further use. All the radiant energy received from the sun sooner or later finds its way into the great energy sink, the ocean of heat energy of temperature uniform with the surroundings, and is incapable of any further transformation. This is the form we know most about. It is the energy of the perpetual thermal agitation of the molecules of which Poincar spoke, and of which we know nothing (of any

individual molecule's motion) and yet know everything (of the statistics of the motion as a whole). And, it is useless [Soddy (1924),10].

Undoubtedly, Cartesian economics ranks as one of the earliest and most comprehensive attempts at consilience in the history of economics. Its breadth is truly remarkable (e.g., agriculture, industry, transportation). Where it comes up short, however, is in the actual formalization of these ideas. For example, the role of the conventional factor inputs, capital and labor, is not well developed. Just what exactly workers do is not clear. Ibid for capital. As shall be argued later, this is a recurrent problem with physics-based attempts at consilience. That is, physicists that wade into economics often ignore the "economics" agenda, focusing for the most part on the laws of basic physics.

Roughly a decade later, we find a second attempt at consilience, but this time in North America. Ironically but not surprisingly, the theater of the second industrial revolution witnessed an economic contraction the likes of which had never been seen before. On October 21, 1929, the Stock Market crashed, unleashing forces that transformed a decade of robust economic growth into the greatest of all economic downturns, the Great Depression. The economics profession was caught off-guard, offering little in the way of diagnoses and even less by way of policy prescriptions. What had gone wrong and how to fix it? Such was the scientific and policy agenda in the early 1930's.

While economists continued to grapple with the fallout, a group of engineers and physicists called for a major overhaul of the science of wealth. To their way of thinking, economics had failed in its quest to understand the equations of motion of wealth creation. Foremost among the shortcomings was the absence of energy. According to Howard Scott and Walter Rautenstrauch, the fathers of technocracy, energy was the basis of all wealth, the source of all value (Akin 1977). With missionary zeal, the Technocrats set out to reform economics and reframe the debate over the causes of the Great Depression. Like Robert Owen in the 19th century, they argued that the downturn was the result of an energy-related technology shock which had opened up a gap between potential output and actual income. Income and expenditure had not increased commensurately with potential output. And the chief cause of the latter was the electrification of U.S. industry.

Technocracy and Cartesian economics were surprisingly similar. Both held that wealth was, is and always will be an increasing function of energy consumption. Both argued that capital and labor were "organizational inputs" in the E-O sense. And both were met with the same derision from the economics profession. To the latter, Technocracy offered little in the way of novelty (Director 1933). While it enjoyed popular support, it made little inroads into mainstream economics with the result that at the end of the 1930's, energy was no more a part of production theory than it had been at the beginning.

Hampering convergence across the fields of thermodynamics and economics in this era was the question of form, *per se*. For example, the Technocrats and their neoclassical counterparts spoke a different language. Like Frederick Soddy, Howard Scott and Walter Rautenstrauch recast material processes in terms of simple physics, ignoring the "economics agenda" (Scott 1933). Capital and labor were ignored, the emphasis being placed on energy. Not surprisingly, the end result was less than satisfactory. Combined with the rise of *Keynesian* economics, this spelt the end of Technocracy as an alternative to mainstream neoclassical production theory.

4. The Oil Crises: The Dawning of a New Era

As has been shown, interest in new, alternative approaches to modeling wealth have come on the heels of crises. As it turns, history was to repeat itself in the 1970's with two, genuine energy-related crises, namely the Oil Crises of 1973 and 1979. Both were the result of decisions on the part of OPEC to restrict petroleum exports, resulting in shortages, lineups and considerably higher energy prices. While previous crises (i.e. the downturns in 19th century Great Britain and 20th century America) were only indirectly linked to energy (steam and electric power), these crises were truly energy related and energy based. And the fallout was swift. In the wake of higher energy prices, stagnation, lower average growth and budgetary chaos (deficits and debt) came numerous attempts at revisiting production theory. Some were more radical than others. Running through them all, however, was a desire to somehow incorporate energy into production theory. For the purposes of exposition, we shall distinguish between three distinct approaches, namely *Addendum*, *Ecological* and *Fundamentals*. The Addendum Approach incorporates energy into mainstream production theory, essentially as an addendum. There is no underlying theory other than the assumption that it, like all other factor inputs, is physically productive. The Ecological Approach dispenses with traditional production theory in favor of thermodynamics, especially the notion of entropy. The third and final approach, the Fundamentals Approach is analogous to the first two; however, whereas they do not impose any structure on the relationships, it goes further and invokes the laws of physics (classical mechanics and thermodynamics)—hence, the fundamentals approach.

4.1. The Addendum Approach

Perhaps the best way to understand this approach as well as the two others is in terms of its starting point. The starting point for the Addendum approach is the neoclassical, two factor model with all its assumptions and implications. That is, both capital and labor are physically productive, diminishing marginal productivity and factor substitution. Against this background, energy is simply added as either a third or nth+1 factor. As the neoclassical approach is open ended (i.e. does not impose any formal structure), no additional assumptions are needed. The upshot of this approach is that each and every factor input is physically productive. Actual (i.e. measured) physical productivity however is (will be) revealed by the data. Typically, output elasticities are estimated. Historically, these have been used to either infer or justify a given functional distribution of income. That is, if labor's output elasticity is 0.70, then labor receives (or is entitled to) 70 percent of income. The most widely cited study is Berndt and Woods (1975) where the standard two-factor neoclassical production function is expanded to include energy, materials and services (KLEMS). The idea here is that capital, labor, energy, materials and services are all factor inputs and all physically productive. While there is *a priori* structure, the structure emerges from the data. Using data from U.S. manufacturing, they find an energy output elasticity of 0.04 which leads them to conclude that energy is, at best, a negligible factor input.[5]

In the 1980s, a group of physicists led by Reiner Kummel of the University of Wurzburg adopted a similar approach, that is, augment the standard neoclassical production function

---

[5] Another example of the *Addendum* approach is Jorgenson (1981, 1983).

Table 1. Kummel, Henn and Lindenberger's Output Elasticities: U.S., Germany and Japanese Manufacturing

Input	U.S. 1960–1993	Germany 1960–1989	Japan 1965–1992
E	0.45	0.50	0.45
L	0.21	0.05	0.21
K	0.36	0.45	0.34

Source: Kummel, Henn, and Lindenberger (2002), 423.

by including energy. Using an estimation technique known as *Linex*, they provided a radically different set of output elasticities (see Table 1).[6]

The problem with this approach, in our view, are the underlying fundamentals. Despite being physicists, the authors view capital and labor as being physically productive, providing estimates of each's output elasticity. Which is surprising as such measures violate the laws of classical mechanics and thermodynamics. Capital (tools and equipment) are not physically productive, nor is latter-day labor which is a supervisory input. An increase in capital, *ceteris paribus*, cannot increase output no more than an increase in labor can increase output. Which raises the question why? Why did physicists ignore the basic laws of physics. While we have no definitive answers, we believe that part of the reason has to do with the conciliatory nature of the exercise. Wanting to be relevant to economists, they conceded the starting point and simply appended energy—the missing factor. Or, it could be argued that because the notion of productivity (total, average and marginal) is so foreign to physicists, they were taken off-guard.

4.2. The Ecological Approach

As argued, the *Addendum* Approach is fundamentally neoclassical in nature, being based on the neoclassical tradition of substitutable factor inputs with all that this implies (substitutability, etc). The 1980's and 1990's witnessed the emergence of another approach to understanding wealth, namely ecological economics with its emphasis on the relationship between the ecosystem and material processes. Finding neoclassical production theory to be woefully inadequate in its treatment of resources, it set out to broaden the purview and include resources, defined generally to include minerals, forests and energy. In time, a new taxonomy emerged. Resources were redefined as "natural capital" as opposed to human or man-made capital. No "new" production function was advanced. The upshot of this literature was clear, namely that there are limits to growth, limits imposed by natural capital.

There are five types of capital: financial, natural, produced, human, and social. All are stocks that have the capacity to produce flows of economically desirable outputs. The maintenance of all five kinds of capital is essential for the sustainability of economic devel-

---

[6] The Linex model has recently been replaced by the KLEC model (capital, labor, energy and creativity. See Kummel, Scmid and Lindenberger (2008). Specifically, they found that the energy output elasticities ranging from 0.45 to 0.60, which were radically different from the KLEMS approach, confirming their *a priori* view (i.e. based on physics) that energy was in fact an important factor input.

opment. Financial capital facilitates economic production, though it is not itself productive, referring rather to a system of ownership or control of physical capital. Natural capital is made up of the resources and ecosystem services of the natural world. Produced capital consists of physical assets generated by applying human productive activities to natural capital and capable of providing a flow of goods or services. Human capital refers to the productive capacities of an individual, both inherited and acquired through education and training. Social capital, the most controversial and the hardest to measure, consists of a stock of trust, mutual understanding, shared values and socially held knowledge.

Natural capital is the extension of the economic notion of capital (manufactured means of production) to goods and services relating to the natural environment. Natural capital is thus the stock of natural ecosystems that yields a flow of valuable ecosystem goods or services into the future. For example, a stock of trees or fish provides a flow of new trees or fish, a flow which can be indefinitely sustainable. Natural capital may also provide services like recycling wastes or water catchment and erosion control. Since the flow of services from ecosystems requires that they function as whole systems, the structure and diversity of the system are important components of natural capital.

It is implicitly assumed that all forms of capital yield flows of services and that the latter combine to produce material wealth. In many regards, the approach is akin to Berndt and Wood's KLEMS production function. No particular structure is imposed on the implied "production function" *per se*. Each form of capital is seen as productive. Unfortunately, ecological economics has not, at least not yet, provided a new set of output elasticities. Instead, as Costanza, Cleveland and Perring (1999) point out, "Ecological economics is not a single new discipline based in shared assumptions and theory. It rather represents a commitment among natural and social scientists and practitioners to develop a new understanding of the way in which different living systems interact with one another and to draw lessons from this for both analysis and policy." [15,47]

4.3. The Fundamentals Approach

Both of these two approaches suffer from weak fundamentals. In the case of the Addendum approach, energy is simply added/included in a standard neoclassical production function while in the orthogonal approach, factors are redefined in terms of a new nomenclature built around the concept of capital. Neither attempts what I refer to as a deep integration, one that goes beyond the *definitional* or *integrative* stages and delves into the underlying structure of material processes (work processes) as it relates to the laws of classical mechanics and thermodynamics. For example, Berndt and Wood simply added energy, materials and services to the standard neoclassical production function without any forethought or afterthought. Using factor shares as a proxy for productivity, they came to the conclusion that energy, the only physically productive factor input according to classical mechanics and thermodynamics, was a minor factor input, with an output elasticity in the 0.04-0.06 range.

Finding this approach to be flawed both theoretically and empirically, Beaudreau (1998,1999) presented an alternative framework, one that is consilient with the basic laws of classical mechanics and thermodynamics. As presented above, the *Energy-Organization* (E-O) framework models material processes in terms of two universal factor inputs, namely broadly-defined energy and broadly-defined organization. In keeping with basic physics, the former is assumed to be physically productive while the latter is not. Including in organization are physical capital (machinery and equipment), labor or more appropriately named supervision, management and information. In keeping with classical mechanics, physical capital is not physically productive, but rather is organizationally productive, affecting second-law efficiency. As is conventionally-defined labor. With the advent of the steam engine and the dynamo, labor metamorphisized into a supervisory input which again is not productive physically. All of these are organizational inputs, defined and overseeing the relevant energy-based material processes. According to the E-O framework, they affect output via their effect on second-law efficiency or the "productivity of energy."

We refer to the E-O approach as "the fundamentals approach" in the sense that it is consistent with fundamentals or, more specifically, the fundamental laws of physics. And it bears reminding that it stands alone in this regard. No other attempt at consilience has explored the deeper implications of the laws of physics for material processes in economics, especially for non-energy inputs. No other attempt at consilience has formalized these laws into a tractable and testable model of material processes in economics. The implications for empirical estimates of production functions are significant. For example, it sees all output elasticities other than the energy output elasticity as misspecified. As energy and energy alone is productive, all non-energy output elasticities are irrelevant and, at best, input elasticities. That is, a relationship between output and the required factor input.

5. Insights from the Three Approaches

It is important to point out that despite their shortcomings, these three approaches taken together represent a form of intellectual convergence across physics and economics. As pointed out, historically the steam engine propelled the physics and economics onto two different (and divergent) paths. The former resulted in thermodynamics, while the latter resulted in neoclassical production theory. For two centuries, the two diverged. That is, until the advent of these three approaches. One of the basic tenets of consilience is the universality of the laws of physics (or the laws of the universe). Which implies that only when models of wealth are consistent with the laws of physics will true consilience be attained.

Of course, in addition to being a desirable property, consilience should also be productive in the scientific sense. That is, consilient models should outperform their rivals. In this section, we examine five areas/fields in which this is the case (i.e. consilient models outperform their rivals). They are (i) the limits to growth (ii) the productivity slowdown (iii) information and communication technology and growth and (iv) R&D and growth. We describe each briefly.

5.1. Limits to Growth

The classic article in the *Limits to Growth* literature is by Robert Solow who in 1974 argued that resources per se did not constitute a limit to growth as society could always substitute other factor inputs in their place (Solow 1974). The underlying idea was simple, namely that no one factor input is irreplaceable. Club of Rome arguments for more judicious use of resources were rendered invalid, or so it seemed. The problem with Solow's argument has to do with its underlying fundamentals. More specifically, with the neoclassical approach to wealth where all factor inputs are physically productive and as such interchangeable (Berndt and Wood 1975, Kummel 1982). What happens if this is not the case? Take for example the E-O model described above. As energy is the only physically productive input, it stands to reason that it and it alone is the only true constraint in so far as growth is concerned. And more so, if society runs out of energy (low entropy), then no amount of labor or capital nor materials can make up for it. A result which is consistent with current energy policy the world over. Energy was, is and always will be the *Brahman* of factor inputs as the following quote from Balaji Reddy of *India Daily* attests to.

> This new dangerous third world war is all on trade and energy resources. No country in the world can survive without viable and reliable source of energy without going back to cave ages. The farmers need energy, the factories need energy and in the developed world (who is really under developed these days?) you need energy to travel even a few blocks. At the same time nations also need to generate money to pay for the energy. Energy demand is rising rapidly as people in India and China wake up to the call of American dreams of good life and modern amenities. The Energy supply is stagnant if not declining because of various geopolitical situations and terrorism possibilities.

5.2. The Productivity Slowdown

Thirty-five years after the fact, the productivity slowdown continues to haunt us. What caused this abrupt fall in the rate of growth of output? Why has productivity growth never recovered? Despite an avalanche of research, the jury is still out. In other words, the productivity slowdown remains an enigma. Consilient models, however, provide a glimmer of hope. Reiner Kummel and Bernard Beaudreau provided an alternative explanation, one couched in consilience. According to both, the productivity slowdown resulted from a fall in the rate of growth of energy consumption, itself the result of the oil crises. The key to their argument lies in the energy output elasticity which they estimate to be between 0.54 and 0.60, a result that is consistent with theoretical physics. By calculating the relevant Divisia growth indices, Beaudreau (1998) is able to fully account for the timing and magnitude of the productivity slowdown. In other words, the oil crises, by increasing the price of energy (anticipated future price) contributed to lower energy consumption growth, thus putting an end to productivity growth. The fact that all material processes throughout the world are powered by energy (basic mechanics) explains its universality.

5.3. ICT and Growth

Related to the productivity slowdown is the question of information and communication technology, the proverbial white knight of productivity growth. Throughout the 1980's, 1990's and 2000's, many have harbored and continue to harbor the hope that ICT would restore growth levels in the West and throughout the world to pre-productivity slowdown levels. But in the late 1990's doubt began to creep in. In a 1998 paper, Robert Solow raised what is now known as Information Paradox, namely that we see computers everywhere but in the productivity data. That is, the West has invested massively in ICT without reaping the expected return. This has fueled a debate between the ICT sceptics (Gordon, Beaudreau 2010) and the ICT zealots (David 1990, Jorgenson and Stiroh 2000). It all comes down to a simple question, will ICT—or more appropriately, can ICT—raise growth rates? Surprisingly, no one has either asked or attempted to answer this question. It is generally assumed that ICT is productive (GPT literature). The only exception is Beaudreau (2010) who examines ICT from the point of view of the underlying physics. He argues, quite simply, that because information is not physically productive, it cannot increase growth, except in the exceptional case that its increases second-law efficiency. In addition to being exceptional, the latter cannot be sustained over an extended period of time. In other words, because second-law efficiency is bounded from above, potential gains from ICT are bounded from above. In short, the Information Paradox is not a paradox at all, but rather a reflection of the basic laws of physics.

5.4. R&D and Growth

More generally, the productivity slowdown prompted governments the world over to turn their attention to technology, more specifically to research and development. The growth literature had made one thing clear: most post-WWII growth was the result of R&D (Edward Denison, Moses Abramovitz, Robert Solow). Hence was born the R&D imperative. Since, governments have invested trillions in R&D in the hope of rekindling growth. R&D became the mantra. Absent from the debate was an underlying theory. Just how did R&D contribute to growth? Was all R&D equal, or was it only certain types of R&D?

Conventional models (neoclassical) were of little use in this matter as technology is modeled as a scaler (i.e. parametrically). For example, according to the Solow-Swan model, technology enters the A variable. Hence, anything and everything that increases its value was/is deemed to be good. The consilient models referred to above, however, shed more light on the question. For example, product R&D is distinguished from process R&D, the former being irrelevant to overall economic growth. Second, according to the E-O model, R&D affects growth through second-law efficiency, *ceteris paribus*. And since second-law efficiency is very stable over time, it is unlikely that R&D will, *ceteris paribus*, raise growth rates to their post-WWII levels. Unless of course, it serves to increase energy availability. Hence the chasm. According to conventional models, growth is increased in R&D; however, according to consilient models, it is not, exceptional circumstances notwithstanding.

Clearly, consilient models have much to offer. Indeed, they throw new light on a whole set of issues whose importance and relevance cannot be increase over time. Which raises the question: Why have consilient models of material processes been largely ignored in economics? Why does the basic standard model of production in economics stand in violation of the laws of physics, the very laws that resulted from the steam engine or the dynamo? In short, why have these models been ignored? We examine these questions in the next section.

6. The Politics of Consilience

While the first out of the proverbial gate, moral philosophers have lagged behind natural philosophers throughout the 19th and early part of the 20th century in so far as uncovering the equations of motion of the new energy technology that was the steam (and electricity). Specifically, Adam Smith's *magnum opus*, "The Wealth of Nations" was the first out of the gate. However, in little time, natural philosophers made up lost ground and have since enjoyed a commanding lead in so far as the role of energy in material processes is concerned. As we have shown here, the latter part of the 20th century witnessed a number of attempts on the part of latter moral philosophers to make up lost ground. These have come from engineers-turned-economists as well as economists *per se*. But despite the proliferation of approaches, energy remains the forgotten input in economics, more specifically in wealth material processes as modeled by economists. Which raises the question, why? Why has consilience failed in economics? Why does the dominant model in so far as material processes in economics continue to violate most of the most elementary laws of physics?

In this section, we examine the politics of consilience. Specifically, we look at the factors that have and continue to impede any and all attempts at consilience. Among these are *Inertia*, *Capital Determinism*, and *Fear of the Alternative*.

6.1. Inertia

By inertia, it should be understood the inertia regarding the received wisdom regarding material processes. Most economists today were weaned on the Cobb-Douglas production function, or its functional equivalent. That is, output is increasing in capital and labor. In fact, it's what cognitive psychologists refer to as an automatic thought—output is increasing in capital and labor. When informed that neither capital nor labor is physically productive, their gut reaction is to protest, contest and ultimately deny and/or reject. After all, this amounts to heresy! Lack of training in the physical sciences could explain, in part, this shortcoming.

6.2. Capital Determinism

By this, it should be understood the firmly entrenched view according to which capital and its owners are the leitmotiv of modern-day capitalism. From Adam Smith to David Ricardo to John Hicks to Frederich van Hayek to Martin Feldstein, another automatic thought is that physical capital holds the key to successful economic development and a healthy economy. A good example is former President Ronald Reagan's "trickle-down theory" according to which lower taxes on the rich would benefit the poor via increased savings, investment, and capital-deepening. When growth rates plummeted in the 1970's and 1980's, many including Reagan and Margaret Thatcher blamed the capital-unfriendly polices of a generation of governments. To restore growth would require, according to this view, more capital-friendly policies which were in fact enacted by right-of-center governments in virtually every Western industrialized democracy. It is interesting to note that in spite of this, growth rates remained low throughout this period.

It is our view that of the traditional factors, capital (i.e. its owners) will be the most reluctant to adopt/embrace consilient models of material processes. The reason is simple and lies with the fact that capital is not physically productive, a fact that turns the clock back to the mid-19th century when it had to justify its share of national income in the face of repeated attacks by Marxists and other radicals. The question, of course, is how to remunerate the owners of capital? Clearly, physical productivity is not an option.

6.3. Fear of the Alternative

Perhaps the greatest obstacle is what we call the fear of the unknown. A system of economic beliefs built around basic physics is a frightening thing despite the extensive use of the method of physics (i.e. optimization theory). A good example is the *Continental Committee on Technocracy* referred to above. In a nutshell, all our priors, all our beliefs virtually go out the window. As energy is the only physically productive factor input, it stands to reason that from a legal point of view the owners of energy would be the ultimate proprietors of all wealth. The Technocrats recognized this and proposed a system of distribution based on energy certificates (which would replace money). Income distribution would as such be political in nature. Thus to conclude, the alternatives to the *status quo* implied by a consilient approach to wealth creation are as frightening as they are disquieting. We have just scratched the surface here. Suffice it to say, however, that production theory was, is and will always be a highly-charged issue. With good reason as wealth and property are at stake. It is our view that only if the profession is able to transcend this issues will a consilient class of models of wealth emerge as alternatives to the current models.

7. Implications for Public Policy

For over three decades, public policy regarding growth—or restoring growth to pre-Productivity Slowdown levels—has focused on research and development. Trillions of dollars have been invested in the hope that growth would follow. Theoretically, policy has been based on neoclassical models where technology is parameterized (i.e. the A scaler). Pioneering work by Edward Denison, Moses Abramovitz and Robert Solow showed that most growth could not be explained by traditional factors, but rather by technology (Griliches 1995).

Consilient approaches to growth reject these findings pointing instead to energy deepening as the principal source of growth, the other being improvements in second-law efficiency. Process-based R&D cannot, other than via its effect on second-law efficiency, increase wealth (see Equation 1). To argue—or believe—otherwise is to violate the basic laws of physics. Clearly, while physical capital and supervision are necessary conditions for wealth; however, they are not what drives growth, physically speaking. Rising per capita and per unit-of-capital growth in the 19th and 20th centuries were fueled largely by energy deepening. It therefore stands to reason that a return to high growth rates requires further energy deepening.

The politics of consilience are manifold and multidimensional; however, one thing stands out, as was the case in the 19th century, production theory is a highly-charged, potentially-explosive issue. As we argued earlier, the attribution of property rights (i.e. who gets what) has not only dominated, but also clouded the thinking regarding wealth. It is our view that it will continue to dominate the agenda, especially in light of increasing automation. Clearly, what is needed is a theory of distribution based on a consilient theory of production. That is, one that recognizes energy for what it is, namely the only physically productive factor input.

8. Summary and Conclusions

The steam engine was the proverbial fly in the wealth ointment, throwing both natural and moral philosophy for a loop. As we have shown, in less than a half century, natural philosophy managed to land on its feet, far better for the wear with a new sub-field in the form of thermodynamics. Moral philosophy, however, did not. Two centuries later, economics has not completely digested the steam engine. For the most part, models of wealth continue to be devoid of the only physically productive factor input in the universe, namely energy. Organizational inputs, especially capital and labor, continue to be front and center. There have been exceptions. For two centuries, non-mainstream writers have bemoaned the absence of the most elemental of forces from production theory with little effect. In this paper, we have examined this literature, historically and analytically.

While it is our hope that the profession will move increasingly in the direction of consilient models of wealth, the odds are not in our favor. Cataclysmic events, the likes of the Great Depression and the Productivity Slowdown, failed to make even a dent in neoclassical production theory, which raises the question, what will it take to make a change? What will it take to update production theory along the lines suggested by thermodynamics and classical mechanics? We can only speculate. Perhaps falling energy availability and rising energy costs will have an effect. Or perhaps the end of work (fewer traditional jobs) will force the issue of labor productivity *per se*. Or, the failure of the information and communications technology revolution to restore growth rates in the West to pre-productivity slowdown levels may also force the issue of the role of information in production and productivity.

What remains clear however is the pressing need, theoretically and practically, to update the models of wealth in contemporary moral philosophy and, at the very least, raise the scientific content to the level that natural philosophy had achieved at the end of the 19th century.

References

[1] P. Aghion, P. and P. Howitt, *Endogenous Growth Theory* Cambridge, MA: MIT Press, 1998.

[2] W. E. Akin, *Technocracy and the American Dream, The Technocratic Movement, 1900–1941* Berkeley, CA: University of California Press, 1977.

[3] B.C. Beaudreau, *The Impact of Electric Power on Productivity: The Case of U.S. Manufacturing 1958–1984*, Energy Economics, 17(3) (1995) 231–236.

[4] B.C. Beaudreau, *Energy and Organization: Growth and Distribution Reexamined*, Westport, CT: Greenwood Press, 1998.

[5] B.C. Beaudreau, *Energy and the Rise and Fall of Political Economy*, Westport,CT: Greenwood Press, 1999.

[6] B.C. Beaudreau, The Dynamo and the Computer: An Engineering Perspective on the Modern Productivity Paradox, *International Journal of Productivity and Performance Management,* **59**(1) (2010) 7–17.

[7] E. Berndt and D. O. Wood, Technology, Prices and the Derived Demand for Energy, *The Review of Economics and Statistics,* August (1975), 259–268.

[8] J. E. Betts, *Essentials of Applied Physics*, Englewood Cliffs, NJ: Prentice-Hall, 1989.

[9] S. Chase, *The Economy of Abundance*, New York, NY: MacMillan Company, 1934.

[10] R. Costanza, R., C. Cleveland, and C. Perrings, *The Development of Ecological Economics*, Edward Elgar Publishing, Cheltenham, UK, 1997.

[11] P.A. David, The Dynamo and the Computer: An Historical Perspective on the Modern Productivity Paradox, *American Economic Review, Papers and Proceedings*, May, 1990, 355–361.

[12] A. Director, *The Economics of Technocracy*, Chicago, IL: The University of Chicago Press, 1933.

[13] R. Gordon, Does the New Economy Measure Up to the Great Inventions of the Past?. *Journal of Economic Perspectives,* **4**, 2000, 49–74.

[14] Z. Griliches, *The Discovery of the Residual: An Historical Note*, National Bureau of Economic Research, Working Paper 5348, 1995.

[15] W.S. Jevons, *The Coal Question*, London: MacMillan and Co., 1865.

[16] D.W. Jorgenson, *Energy Prices and Productivity Growth*, in S. Schurr et al. (eds) Energy, Productivity, and Economic Growth, (Cambridge, MA: Oelgeschlager, Gunn, and Hain, 1983).

[17] D.W. Jorgenson, The Role of Energy in Productivity Growth, in Kendrick, J.W. (ed.) *International Comparisons of Productivity and Causes of the Slowdown,* Cambridge MA: MIT Press, 1981.

[18] D.W. Jorgenson, and B. Fraumeni, *Relative Prices and Technical Change*, in E.R. Berndt and B Field (eds.) *Modeling and Measuring Natural Resource Substitution,* Cambridge, MA: MIT Press, 1981.

[19] D. W. Jorgenson and K. J. Stiroh. 2000. Raising the Speed Limit: U.S. Economic Growth in the Information Age, *Brookings Papers on Economic Activity:* **1**, Brookings Institution.

[20] R. Kummel, Reiner, D. Lindenberger and W. Eichorn, *The Productive Power of Energy and Economic Evolution*, University of Wurzburg Working Paper 1998.

[21] R. Kummel, J. Henn, D. Lindenberger, Capital, labor, energy and creativity: modeling innovation diffusion, *Economic Dynamics and Structural Change.* **13**, (2002) 415-433.

[22] R. Kmmel, J. Schmid and D. Lindenberger, *Why Production Theory and the Second Law of Thermodynamics Support High Energy Taxes*, Universities of Wrzburg and of Cologne (2008).

[23] D. Lloyd George, *Coal and Power*, London: Hodder and Stoughton, 1924.

[24] A. Maddison, *Growth and Slowdown in Advanced Capitalist Economies: Techniques of Quantitative Assessment*, Journal of Economic Literature, 25(2) (1987) 649–698.

[25] K. Marx, *Das Capital*, Chicago, IL: Encylcopaedia Britannica, 1867 (1991).

[26] D. E. Nye, *Electrifying America: Social Meaning of a New Technology*, Cambridge, MA: MIT Press, 1990.

[27] R. Owen, *A New View of Society and Other Writings*, London: J.M. Dent and Sons, Ltd., [1820] 1927.

[28] P.M. Romer, Crazy Explanations for the Productivity Slowdown, *NBER Macroeconomics Annual* 1987, 163–202.

[29] P.M Romer, Endogenous Technological Change, *Journal of Political Economy*, **98** (1990) s71–s102.

[30] H. Scott et al., *Introduction to Technocracy*, New York, NY: The John Day Company, 1933.

[31] A. Smith, *An Inquiry into the Nature and Causes of the Wealth of Nations*, Chicago: Encyclopaedia Britannica, 1990.

[32] F. Soddy, *Cartesian Economics, The Bearing of Physical Sciences upon State Stewardship*, London: Hendersons, 1924.

[33] R.M. Solow, The Economics of Resources or the Resources of Economics, *American Economic Review,* **64**(2) (1974) 1–14.

[34] E.O. Wilson, *Consilience, the Unity of Knowledge*, New York, NY: Vintage Books, 1998.

In: Economics of Wealth in the 21st Century
Editor: Jason M. Gonzalez

ISBN 978-1-61122-805-2
© 2011 Nova Science Publishers, Inc.

Chapter 5

A REVIEW OF MODERN THEORIES OF WEALTH INEQUALITY

Claudio Campanale
Universidad de Alicante, Spain

1. Introduction

Inequality in economic fortunes of different individuals is a popular topics both in the political debate and among academicians in different areas of the social sciences and especially in economics. Ultimately differences in individual well being will depend on the their consumption level and variability. However insofar as the availability of consumption is largely determined by the income and wealth of the households, inequality can be studied by focusing the analysis on the distribution of earnings, income and wealth in the society.

In this work I will focus my attention on one particular dimension of inequality, that is, the inequality in wealth holdings among households. More specifically I will present a summary of the work done in the field of quantitative models that have attempted to explain the distribution of wealth that is observed in the data. Most literature in this field belongs to the class of incomplete market models sometimes referred to as Bewley models, from the author of the seminal work. [1] In these models agents face a stream of random earnings. Due to market incompleteness, earnings fluctuations cannot be insured so that accumulation of an asset is used to smooth consumption. Taking the process for earnings as exogenous these models analyze the endogenous response of wealth accumulation and wealth inequality. Prototypical examples are the models presented in Aiyagari (1994) which is cast in a dynastic framework and Huggett (1996) which is instead formulated in a life-cycle setting. These models have been able to generate the empirically observed relationship between consumption, earnings and wealth inequality; however they did so only in qualitative terms while quantitatively they grossly underestimate wealth concentration, especially at the top of the distribution. This failure has prompted a substantial amount of research that has extended the basic model to include features like heterogeneity in discount factors, bequest motives and entrepreneurial activity. The new features improved the ability of the model to match the data. Still explaining the large fortunes at the very top of the wealth distribution

---

[1] See Bewley (1977) for the original work or Ljungqvist and Sargent (2000) for a textbook treatment.

remains a hard task to accomplish. This work will review the main theories that have been proposed to explain wealth concentration.

The interest of studying wealth inequality arises from several factors. One is the key role that wealth plays as a resource that the household can use to finance its consumption. As such wealth inequality is a source of welfare inequality and for this reason considerations of equity make it an interesting topics to study. Beside that, several tax policies have effects on capital formation. In a world where capital is so unequally distributed, such effects are better analyzed if we have models that correctly capture the reasons for savings especially of the very wealthy. Finally, although most macroeconomics is currently based on representative agent models, there are many issues where heterogeneity is important for the aggregate behavior of the economy and once again models that capture this heterogeneity are needed to improve our understanding of macroeconomic phenomena. The final section of this essay will present some applications of models of wealth inequality to these issues.

The essay is organized as follows. In section 2 I will briefly present the empirical evidence. In section 3 I will lay out the analytical framework of the incomplete market models, presenting the dynastic version and the life-cycle version of the model as well as some intermediate approaches that show features of both. In section 4 I will present the extensions to the basic layout that have been put forth in order to better match the wealth concentration observed in the data. In section 5 I present some alternative approaches. Finally in section 6 I present some applications of the models presented in the previous sections.

2. Data

The largest body of evidence about wealth inequality comes from the U.S. and is based on two main datasets, that is, the Survey of Consumer Finances or SCF and the Panel Study of Income Dynamics or PSID. The SCF is a survey that has been conducted every three years, starting in 1983 by the Federal Reserve Board. The survey is a repeated cross-section and includes a random sub-sample plus a second sub-sample that is selected using tax report data. This sub-sample is specifically selected to over-sample the wealthier households. The survey reports demographic characteristics plus information on different sources of income and a detailed representation of households' balance sheets. The very accurate information about households' assets and liabilities plus the over-sampling of the rich make the SCF the best, hence also most frequently used dataset when studying the wealth distribution.

The PSID is a survey that has been conducted annually starting from 1968. It collects demographic and income variables in every year and starting from 1984 it has a wealth supplement which collects some information about households assets and liabilities. The supplement though is issued only every five years. Unlike the SCF, the PSID has a panel dimension that allows the researcher to follow the same household over time. The information about assets, though is less detailed and it does not oversample the rich so that it is less suited to study the top of the wealth distribution. Due to its panel structure it can be used to study mobility across the distribution of wealth.[2]

---

[2]Curtin et al. (1989) show that total net worth implied by the SCF matches quite well the aggregate wealth

Table 1. The size distribution of wealth

Year	\multicolumn{6}{c}{Percentage share of wealth held by:}
	0-40	40-80	80-90	90-95	95-99	99-100
1989	-0.7	17.1	13.0	11.6	21.6	37.4
1995	0.2	15.9	12.1	11.5	21.8	38.5
2001	0.3	15.2	12.9	12.3	25.8	33.4
2007	0.2	14.9	12.0	11.2	27.3	34.6

To get an idea of the main features of the wealth distribution in the U.S. we report in table 1 the share of wealth held by some key percentiles of that distribution in selected years. The data are taken from Wolff (2010) and are based on the SCF. Net worth is the difference between household assets and liabilities. In turn assets include the gross value of owner-occupied housing, other real estate owned by the household, deposits and money market accounts, bonds, the cash value of life-insurance and pension plans — including IRAs, Keogh and 401(k) plans — corporate stock and mutual funds and equity in private firms and trust funds. Liabilities include mortgage debt, consumer debt, including auto loans and various other forms of debt. Totals are corrected to make the aggregate values from the survey consistent with flow of funds data. [3]

The key fact that emerges from the table is the substantial degree of wealth concentration. In all the years considered the 1 percent wealthiest American households held more than a third of national wealth, with a peak of 38.5 percent in 1995. The next 4 percent group held between about 21 and 28 percent of wealth. Summing the two groups we see that 5 percent of the U.S. households have consistently held about 60 percent of total wealth over the last two decades. On the contrary the 40 percent poorest households held less than 0.5 percent of national wealth in all of the surveys and the next 40 percent households in the wealth distribution still held between 14.9 percent of total wealth in 2007 and 17.1 percent in 1989. Another fact that can be seen from the table is that wealth inequality has remained fairly stable over the 18 year period considered. There was a small decrease in the share of net worth held by the 1 percent wealthiest families from 37.4 percent to 34.6 percent. However this was compensated by a substantial increase in the share of the next 4 percent from 21.6 percent to 27.3 percent so that overall the share of the top 5 percent of the distribution increased by about 3 percentage points. The share of the bottom 40 percent increased by about 1 percentage point, while the share of the next forty percent declined somewhat. The overall effect was that the Gini index, that was 0.832 in 1989, was still 0.834 in 2007.

In table 2 I report the size distribution of earnings for two selected years, namely 1995 and 1998. The data are taken from Díaz-Giménez et al. (1997) and Budría Rodríguez et al. (2002) respectively and are based on the SCF. Even though this is not the focus of this review it is useful to know the main features of earnings concentration to understand the main

---

in the Flow of Funds Accounts but that the PSID tracks the distribution of net worth in the SCF only up to the top 2 % - 3 %, thus missing the wealth holdings of the richest fraction of the population.

[3] These adjustments and the exclusion of certain durable goods like cars from the definition of wealth explain the difference between the data reported below and those reported in other work like Kennickell (2003), Budría Rodríguez et al. (2002) and Díaz-Giménez et al. (1997).

Table 2. The size distribution of earnings

Year	\multicolumn{6}{c}{Percentage share of earnings held by:}
	0-40	40-80	80-90	90-95	95-99	99-100
1995	2.8	35.8	17.9	12.4	16.4	14.8
1998	3.8	35.9	17.3	11.8	15.8	15.3

challenge of models of the wealth distribution. As it can be seen from the table earnings are very concentrated in the U.S. For example the top 1 percent earners accounted for about 15 percent of total earnings and the top 5 percent accounted for about 31 percent. At the same time the bottom 40 percent households earned only between 3 and 4 percent of total earnings and the next 40 percent group earned about 36 percent. A quick comparison at the figures reported in the two tables shows that even though unequal, the earnings distribution is substantially less so than the wealth distribution.

This observation sets the stage for the analysis of the quantitative literature about wealth inequality. The typical model in that literature assumes an exogenous process for earnings. The main challenge is that of embedding in the models savings mechanisms that enable them to magnify the inequality that is fed in through the earnings process so that they are able to match the much larger concentration that is observed in the wealth distribution.

3. The Basic Model with Random Earnings

Almost all the models that have been used to account for the quantitative properties of the wealth distribution are stochastic versions of the neoclassical growth model. They typically feature no aggregate uncertainty so that they can be solved for stationary equilibria. At the same time they display individual level uncertainty by introducing features of Bewley type of models. This is obtained by assuming that agents, who are ex-ante identical, face a stochastic process for earnings. Due to market incompleteness agents cannot fully insure earnings fluctuations. They have to rely on self-insurance by saving in a single asset to smooth consumption. This generates ex-post inequality in asset holdings because different agents will have faced different histories of realized earnings shocks. In the next subsections I will describe how this general framework translates into different models depending on the assumptions about the agents' planning horizon and how the resulting models fare in terms of matching the empirical wealth distribution.

3.1. The Dynastic Model

The key assumption of the dynastic model is that agents are assumed to be infinitely lived. There is a continuum of agents with identical preferences that are represented by a standard CRRA utility index. Agents do not value leisure so that they maximize the following objective function:

$$E\left\{\sum_{t=1}^{\infty} \beta^t u(c_t)\right\} \tag{1}$$

where β is the subjective discount factor. Agents receive a stochastic endowment of labor efficiency units that is typically described by a first order Markov process and they can use a single asset to smooth consumption over time. Their optimal consumption-saving problem can be represented by the following dynamic programming program:

$$V(a,z) = \max_{c,a'} \left\{ u(c) + \beta E\left[V(a',z')\right] \right\} \qquad (2)$$

subject to

$$c + a' \leq (1+r)a + zw \qquad (3)$$

$$a' \geq \underline{a} \qquad (4)$$

$$z' = \Gamma(z) \qquad (5)$$

In the equations above a prime denotes next period variables. Equation 2 is a standard Bellman equation. The value function V is defined over two state variables: current assets a and the shock z to labor efficiency units. The maximization is performed with respect to consumption c and the amount of assets a' to carry into the next period. The expectation on the right-hand side of the Bellman equation is taken with respect to the distribution of z' conditional on the current value of z represented by the first order Markov process in equation 5. The maximization is performed under the standard budget constraint given in equation 3 and a borrowing limit $\underline{a}$ applies. The production sector is competitive and can be represented by a constant return to scale production function $Y = F(K, L)$ that converts capital K and labor L into output. Rental rates r for capital and w for labor efficiency units are determined by standard marginal conditions.

At every point in time the economy can be described by a measure of households $x^*(A, Z)$ over asset holdings and labor efficiency units. A stationary equilibrium for this economy is a value function and decision rules for consumption and savings, rental rates for capital and labor, aggregate capital and labor and an invariant measure of agents such that:

- Given prices the value function and the decision rules solve the household's optimal problem described above.

- Factor prices are determined by marginal productivity:
    - $r = F_K(K, L) - \delta$
    - $w = F_L(K, L)$

  where aggregate capital and labor are obtained by summing over individual holdings using the stationary measure x^*, that is, $K = \int_{A,Z} a dx^*$ and $L = \int_{A,Z} z dx^*$

- The constant measure of households x^* is the one induced by the law of motions of the system, that is by the exogenous earnings process Γ and the endogenous policy functions of the households

The prototypical example of these types of models is the one in Aiyagari. [4] The model is solved using a labor earnings process calibrated from micro-data. The implications of

---
[4] Huggett (1993) solves a similar model but without capital where the only asset is a bond in zero net supply.

Table 3. The distribution of earnings and wealth in Aiyagari's model

	Gini	\multicolumn{5}{c}{Percentage share of earnings held by:}
		0-40	80-100	90-95	95-99	99-100
Baseline	0.10	32.5	26.0	6.5	5.8	1.7
High variability	0.23	25.6	32.8	8.2	8.1	2.8
		\multicolumn{5}{c}{Percentage share of wealth held by:}
		0-40	80-100	90-95	95-99	99-100
Baseline	0.38	14.9	41.0	10.5	9.9	3.2
High variability	0.41	13.1	44.6	10.9	11.6	4.0

the model for wealth inequality are reported in table 3 which is taken from the survey by Quadrini and Ríos-Rull 1997. Two notable things emerge from the table. First, the model generates endogenously a distribution of wealth that is more concentrated than the exogenous distribution of earnings. For example in the baseline case the Gini index for earnings is 0.10 while the one for wealth is 0.38. The share of the bottom 40 percent and top 1 percent earners are 32.5 and 1.7 percent respectively, while the corresponding figures for wealth are 14.9 and 3.2 percent. Second, comparing the data in table 3 with those in table 1 we can easily see that wealth is substantially less concentrated than in the data. The data show a Gini index of about 0.83 and the share of the bottom 40 percent and top 1 percent households in the wealth distribution are less than 1 percent and between 33 and 37 percent respectively.

In these type of models agents save to insure against random earnings fluctuations. Agents are ex-ante identical; however when agents receive a string of favorable earnings shocks they build up a stock of wealth, when they receive a string of low earnings realizations they deplete the accumulated assets. Ex-post at any point in time there will be agents with different earnings history, hence with different levels of wealth. As the table shows this mechanism is able to generate more heterogeneity in wealth than in the underlying earning process but not as much as in the data. The explanation for the latter fact is that agents in this model behave as buffer-stock savers as discussed in Carroll (1997): agents target a certain level of wealth for self-insurance purposes. Once this level of wealth is reached they don't save any more, which prevents the model to explain the large fortunes that we observe in the data. Increasing labor earnings risk helps increasing wealth inequality as shown by the line labeled "high variability" in the bottom panel of table 3 but not enough to match the inequality observed in the data.

3.2. The Life-Cycle Model

The other polar approach to modeling economies with heterogeneous agents to study quantitatively the wealth distribution is that of life-cycle agents. In this case it is assumed that households have finite lives, they work during the first part of life and then retire. In the most pure form it is assumed that no intergenerational links exist, neither in the form of bequests nor in the form of inheritance of human capital. In order to make the model consistent with the empirical evidence it is also assumed that agents face a hump shaped profile of earnings during working life and that during retirement they receive a pension benefits that replaces only a fraction of their pre-retirement income. These assumptions create a further motive for saving, namely that of smoothing consumption over the life-cycle in the face of a nonconstant profile of income.

In what follows I will describe the basic model which was formulated in Huggett (1996). In the model in each period a continuum of agents is born. Agents can live up to a maximum age T and in each period face a probability of surviving one more year p_t. All agents have the same preferences and upon entry in the model maximize the following objective:

$$E\left\{\sum_{t=1}^{T}\beta^t\left(\prod_{j=1}^{t}p_t\right)u(c_t)\right\} \quad (6)$$

where $u(c_t)$ is the constant relative risk aversion utility from consumption and β is the subjective discount factor. During working life agents receive a stochastic endowment of labor efficiency units $e(z,t)$ where z follows a first order Markov process $\Gamma(z)$. During retirement agents receive a fixed pension benefit. It is assumed that there are no annuity markets and unspent balances at the end of life are confiscated by the government and redistributed equally among living agents. In the model then households save to insure against earnings and mortality risk and to prepare for retirement. The production sector of the economy is assumed to be competitive and is represented by a standard constant returns to scale function that turns aggregate capital and labor into output.

The household's recursive problem can then be written as:

$$V(a_t, z_t, t) = \max_{c_t, a_{t+1}}\left\{u(c_t) + \beta p_{t+1}E\left[V(a_{t+1}, z_{t+1}, t+1)\right]\right\} \quad (7)$$

subject to

$$c_t + a_{t+1} \leq (1+r)a_t + e(z,t)w + B + y_t^{ss} \quad (8)$$

$$a_{t+1} \geq \underline{a} \quad \text{and} \quad \underline{a} = 0 \quad if \quad t = T \quad (9)$$

$$z_{t+1} = \Gamma(z_t) \quad (10)$$

In the equations above a are asset holdings, c is consumption, B are the transfers received from the redistribution of accidental bequests operated by the government, r is the interest rate and w is the wage rate. Finally y_t^{ss} is the social security benefit which is received after the agent retires.

The model economy is solved for stationary equilibria. In a stationary equilibrium the economy can be described by a measure of agents defined over asset holdings, labor earnings shocks and age and this measure is constant over time. A stationary equilibrium will be a value function, decision rules, prices and a constant measure of agents such that:

- Given prices the value function and the decision rules solve the household's optimal problem described above.

- Factor prices are determined by marginal productivity:
  - $r = F_K(K, L) - \delta$
  - $w = F_L(K, L)$

Table 4. The distribution of wealth in Huggett's life-cycle model

Credit limit	Gini	% wealth ≤ 0	Percentage of wealth held by: 80-100	95-99	99-100
$\underline{a} = 0$	0.69	17.0	70.0	22.0	10.9
$\underline{a} < 0$	0.76	24.0	75.5	23.8	11.8

where aggregate capital and labor are obtained by summing over individual holdings using the stationary measure.

- The constant measure of households is the one induced by the law of motions of the system, that is by the exogenous earnings process Γ, by mortality and by the endogenous policy function of the households.

Huggett calibrates the labor earnings process using micro-data, then solves it and studies its implications for the wealth distribution. These are reported in table 4. As it can be seen the model gets substantially closer to the data in terms of Gini index. This overall measure of inequality is 0.76 in the model and it is about 0.82 in the data reported by Wolff (2010). On the other hand though, the model cannot match the share of wealth held by the top 1 percent of the distribution by a large amount. This share is 11.8 percent in the model while it is above 33 percent in the data. The model generates a fraction of households with zero or negative wealth that is 17 percent when no borrowing is allowed and it is 24 percent when borrowing is allowed. According to what reported in Huggett (1996) the figure for agents with no or negative wealth in the U.S. data was between 5.8 and 15.0 percent. This implies that the ability of the life-cycle model to match the Gini index of wealth results from two balancing errors, that is, an excess of agents with no wealth balances out the small share of wealth held at the top of the distribution. Moreover in Huggett's model all agents with zero wealth are concentrated among the youngest group of the population while in the data they are more evenly distributed over the life-cycle.

In order to interpret the failure to reproduce the top of the wealth distribution one can start by observing that in the first part of life households behave like buffer-stock savers. Once an initial amount of assets is accumulated, they then move to life-cycle behavior.[5] This means that they will accumulate wealth to smooth consumption in the remaining part of their life-cycle. Furthermore, absent bequest motives, finiteness of the lifespan will induce agents to run down wealth as they age. For these reasons differences in wealth will reflect differences in lifetime earnings, hence they won't be sufficient to match the large accumulated fortunes that we observe in the data for the top of the wealth distribution, especially the top 1 percent.

---

[5]This result was established by structural estimations presented in Gourinchas and Parker (2002). They find that the change between buffer-stock and life-cycle behavior occurs around age 40. Their estimated parameters are quite close to the ones used in the literature considered here.

3.3. Intermediate Approaches

Several intermediate approaches between the pure life-cycle model and the pure dynastic model are possible. Here I will cite two works that follow an intermediate approach and that are especially relevant for this section since they are otherwise models purely based on uninsurable random earnings.

The first approach is the one pursued by Castañeda et al. (2003). The authors construct a dynastic model in which the process for random earnings is represented by a transition matrix with the following structure:

$$\Gamma = \begin{pmatrix} \Gamma_{\varepsilon,\varepsilon} & \Gamma_{\varepsilon,R} \\ \Gamma_{R,\varepsilon} & \Gamma_{R,R} \end{pmatrix}$$

Transitions within $\Gamma_{\varepsilon,\varepsilon}$ are interpreted as standard transitions between different realizations of the labor earnings process, transitions in $\Gamma_{\varepsilon,R}$ are interpreted as transitions between working and retirement, transitions in $\Gamma_{R,\varepsilon}$ represent death and replacement with a new member in the dynasty. Finally transitions in $\Gamma_{R,R}$ are ruled out since they would represent the substitution of a dying agent with a retired one. This particular transition matrix allows the authors to construct a model that, even though is mathematically identical to a pure dynastic model with random earnings shocks, still it has sufficient flexibility to capture some elements of the life-cycle. The model in fact displays a path of income over time that mimics working life followed by retirement. Moreover, by suitably calibrating the sub-matrix $\Gamma_{R,\varepsilon}$ it is possible to get an increasing profile of earnings during working life and some elements of intergenerational transmission of ability. Castañeda and co-authors calibrate the model to jointly match the Gini index and the share of earnings and wealth of selected percentiles of the two distributions including the top 1 percent. As table 5 shows they go a long way towards achieving their goal. The reason for their success is the huge amount of risk implied by their labor earnings process. In fact this features four shocks, with the highest one being about 1000 times larger than the smallest one and the transition probability from the former to the latter is about 10 percent. Facing this risk, agents with the highest labor productivity save at very high rates to self-insure, thus build a huge stock of wealth. The importance of their result lies in the fact that they show that provided earnings risk is sufficiently high, a standard dynastic incomplete markets model can explain the observed wealth concentration. Whether there is empirical support for a labor earnings process with such a high risk has not been investigated and confirmed.

The second approach, followed in De Nardi (2004) is closer to the life-cycle model. De Nardi (2004) constructs an overlapping generations model where agents go through the stages of working age and retirement. Like in the standard life-cycle model agents face a hump-shaped profile of earnings hit by idiosyncratic shocks during working life and then a fixed pension benefit during retirement. There are no annuity markets and agents face a probability of dying in each period. Given these assumptions they save for retirement and to insure against earnings risk and the risk of late death. The model departs from the pure life-cycle framework in two assumptions. First it is assumed that agents are linked to their descendants by inheritances of parental productivity in the labor force. Second it is assumed that agents are altruistic according to the "joy of giving" model of Andreoni (1989), that is, they value leaving an estate to their descendants but they receive utility from the amount

Table 5. The distribution of earnings and wealth in mixed models

Castañeda et al. (2004)	Gini	\multicolumn{5}{c}{Percentage share held by:}
		0-40	80-100	90-95	95-99	99-100
Earnings	0.63	3.74	65.7	15.2	17.7	14.9
Wealth	0.79	1.42	82.0	17.0	18.2	29.9
De Nardi (2004)		\multicolumn{5}{c}{Percentage share held by:}
		0-40	80-100	90-95	95-99	99-100
Earnings	0.44	13.0	50.0	15.0	na	na
Wealth	0.76	0.0	79.0	na	24.0	18.0

bequeathed rather than caring about the utility of their offspring. The author uses estimates from Zimmerman (1992) for the intergenerational transmission of earnings ability. She chooses a parsimonious two-parameter specification for the utility of leaving an estate and calibrates it so as to match the first moment of the bequest distribution and the fraction of capital due to intergenerational transfers reported in Kotlikoff and Summers (1981). The resulting model, when both intergenerational links are active, improves substantially on the life-cycle model in its ability to match the wealth distribution. As it can be seen in table 5 the Gini index in the model is 0.76, the share of wealth held by the top 20 percent is 79 percent, the one held by the top 1 percent is 18 percent and the one held by the next 4 percent is 24 percent. Comparing these figures with the ones in table 1 we see that the model replicates quite well the share of the top 20 percent and of the 95 to 99 percentiles. The share of the top 1 percent is just a little above half the one in the data, still it is quite larger than the 11 percent figure of the pure life-cycle model.

To understand the success of this model in replicating the wealth distribution observe that because of the bequest motive agents do not run down their assets as they get older. The most productive agents will have higher lifetime incomes, accumulate a larger amount of wealth and then pass it to the next member of the family line. In turn, because of the intergenerational correlation in individual productivity the descendant will tend to have higher than average lifetime income. Higher income and inherited wealth will lead to further increase in asset holding. The intergenerational linkages thus allow some agents in the model to accumulate large estates over several generations thus producing the large concentration of wealth that we observe at the top of the distribution.

4. Extensions

As we saw in the previous section the basic precautionary saving model fails to account for the wealth distribution observed in the data, essentially by over-estimating the share of wealth held by the poorest households and under-estimating the share held by the richest ones. This failure has prompted the search for alternative saving mechanisms that can potentially close the gap between model and data. Some of these efforts are described in the next three subsections.

4.1. Heterogeneous Investment Opportunities

A common feature of the models considered so far is the fact that agents can only save in a single asset that is the same for all households in the economy. This implies that all agents face the same return on their savings. This fact is contradicted by the empirical evidence. As it is well known households portfolios are composed by a large number of asset classes that include liquid accounts, bonds, stocks, housing — both owner occupied and other residential property — and business assets. The literature that has documented the composition of household balance sheets in the U.S. is large and includes work by Bertaut and Starr-McCluer (2000), Kennickell, Starr-McCluer and Surette (2000), Heaton and Lucas (2000) and Samwick (2000).[6] The empirical work has documented systematic patterns of assets holdings by which higher return and risk assets like equity in private firms and stocks compose a much larger share of the portfolio of wealthy households than of the portfolio of poorer households. This suggests that wealthy households may face higher returns on their assets. This would lead to faster accumulation of wealth and if substitution effects prevail also to higher saving rates for the rich thus helping to create the elongated right tail of the wealth distribution.

The possibility that higher rates of return might help explain the large estates at the top of the distribution was first explored by considering the role of entrepreneurs. Empirical research by Gentry and Hubbard (2004) and Quadrini (1999) showed that entrepreneurs represent only slightly less than 10 percent of the population, yet they hold about 40 percent of total wealth, about 40 percent of which is invested in equity in the business they run. While they also have incomes that are greater than average, their contribution to national wealth exceeds that of income and is reflected in wealth-income ratios that are higher than those of the general population by a significant amount.[7] These facts suggested that entrepreneurial activity might have an important role in the concentration of wealth at the top of the distribution. The idea was formally modeled and quantitatively analyzed in the works by Quadrini (2000) and Cagetti and De Nardi (2006).

Quadrini (2000) constructs a purely dynastic model where agents can choose between working for pay and becoming an entrepreneur. Three features characterize entrepreneurial activity. First income for the entrepreneurs is more volatile than for workers boosting precautionary savings. Second business firms come in fixed size and the entrepreneur must commit funds in the firm. Agents then need to save to start up a business or to increase its size. Third, the interest rate on borrowed funds is higher than the return on the market. This gives entrepreneurs a further incentive to save and invest funds in their private firm. By suitably calibrating the distribution of firm size Quadrini (2000) is able to give a substantial boost to concentration at the top of the wealth distribution, getting close to matching the data. He can also reproduce statistics concerning mobility across the wealth distribution.

Cagetti and De Nardi (2006) build a model that mixes features of the dynastic and of the life-cycle framework along the lines of Castañeda et al. (2003) but where agents can choose between paid-employment and entrepreneurial activity. The distinctive feature of

---

[6] For a general survey on the data, theory and estimation of portfolio choice models see the book edited by Guiso, Haliassos and Jappelli (2001) which also presents data about portfolio composition in countries other than the U.S.

[7] Their findings are based on SCF and PSID data from the 1980s. More recent work by De Nardi et al. (2007) has confirmed those findings up to the 2004 edition of the SCF.

their approach is the assumption that contracts are imperfectly enforceable. As in Albuquerque and Hopenhayn (2004) entrepreneurs can borrow to finance their activity, however they cannot be forced to repay. Assets will then act as a collateral. At the individual level the amount of borrowing will depend on wealth, hence in the aggregate the level of debt and entrepreneurial activity will be determined endogenously in the equilibrium of the economy and depend on the distribution of assets. Also, under these assumptions firm size may be suboptimal, hence the return to investing savings in the firm may be higher than market returns. The authors also allow for various degrees of intergenerational altruism. The quantitative analysis of the model shows that it gets very close to match the observed concentration with a Gini index of wealth of 0.8 and a share of wealth held by the top 1 percent of the distribution of 31 percent. Both entrepreneurial activity and altruism are key in determining this result.

A different approach was followed by Campanale (2007). Observing that that there is a systematic pattern of portfolio composition by which the share of high return assets increases with the amount of assets held, the author uses SCF data on asset holdings and historical measures of returns by asset category to construct an empirical return function that relates wealth to the return that it pays. He then constructs a life-cycle model with altruistic bequests where the usual assumption that all agents face the same return on their asset holdings is dropped and is replaced by the more realistic assumption that the return grows with wealth. The assumption of increasing returns on savings leads to a significant increase in wealth concentration and the model is able to reproduce the share of wealth held up to the top 0.5 percentile of the wealth distribution.

4.2. Alternative Preferences

The standard precautionary saving model used to explore quantitatively the wealth distribution assumes homothetic preferences that are of the constant relative risk aversion type. It also assumes that all agents have the same preferences. Several deviations from these assumptions have been considered so far.

Firstly, Krusell and Smith (1998) and Hendricks (2007) retain the assumption that the utility function is of the CRRA type and explore the role of heterogeneity in preferences. Krusell and Smith (1998) consider a standard dynastic precautionary saving model *à la* Aiyagari but assume that the agents' subjective discount factor randomly changes over time with an expected duration of each spell approximately equal to the length of a generation. In the cross-section then agents display different degrees of patience. Under this assumption the most patient agents determine the interest rate and the aggregate stock of capital. The remaining agents discount the future more heavily than the return on capital, hence they will save very little. The result is a substantial increase in the cross-sectional dispersion of wealth: The Gini index takes a value of 0.82 and the share of wealth held by the top 1 and 5 percent of the distribution become 24 and 55 percent respectively, compa red with 0.25, 3 percent and 11 percent for the same model with homogeneous preferences. Hendricks (2007) explores again the role of heterogeneous preferences but he does that in the context of a life-cycle model with altruistic bequests. Contrary to Krusell and Smith (1998) who calibrate the heterogeneity of discount factors to generate the desired concentration of wealth, Hendricks constrains the amount of heterogeneity in preferences to be consistent with the evolution of wealth inequality over the life-cycle. The author shows that in this case wealth inequality rises to the point that it is possible to match the Gini index, however the share of wealth held by the 1 percent wealthiest agents still falls short of what is observed in the data by 10 percentage points, casting doubts about the ability of this mechanism to account for the data.

The alternative route of preserving homogeneity of preferences but moving to an alternative formulation of the utility function has been pursued by Díaz, Pijoan-Mas and Ríos-Rull (2003) and Carroll (1998). Díaz et al. (2003) introduce habit formation preferences in a dynastic version of the standard incomplete markets model used to study the wealth distribution. More specifically they introduce what are known as "internal"habit, that is, preferences where the marginal utility of individual current consumption depends on the level of individual past consumption.[8] Under this specification agents not only dislike fluctuations in the level of consumption but also in its change. The authors reasoned that this would bring an increase in precautionary saving but that its effect on wealth concentration is more difficult to predict and would depend on asymmetric effects at different levels of asset holdings. The quantitative analysis of the model confirmed that the aggregate capital stock increases compared to a model with standard preferences even when the IES is kept constant. On the other hand wealth inequality is reduced. Both effects turn out to be stronger when the habit process is more persistent.

Carroll (1998) suggests a "capitalist spirit"model of wealth accumulation to explain the huge estates that we find at the top of the distribution. Based on anecdotal evidence about a number of famous very rich people in American history he suggests that wealth may be sought either because it directly provides a flow of services or because it is an instrument for achieving other goals like power or social status. In either case wealth directly enters agents' utility function. He proposes a simple two parameter specification of the direct contribution of wealth to utility that makes it a luxury good. Finally he shows with a simple two-period model that this formulation is able to generate savings rates that increase with lifetime income, a feature that can be found in the data and that is needed to explain wealth concentration at the top of the distribution. Unfortunately he does not solve a general equilibrium model to check the extent to which th is assumption can help match the empirical wealth distribution. This contribution, although valuable, is likely difficult to achieve because of the problems in pinpointing the value of the parameters of the wealth component of the utility function from independent sources.

4.3. Social Programs

As we saw the standard incomplete markets model fails to match the wealth distribution at both ends. In the previous sections I focused on the research efforts that were mainly prompted by the desire to explain the large concentration of wealth in the right tail of the distribution. In this section I will focus instead on the research that has been carried out to explain the very low savings, hence wealth holdings, in the left tail of the distribution. In this

---

[8]This type of preferences has a long tradition in asset pricing where it gives an important contribution to the explanation of the equity premium and risk-free rate puzzles. See Abel (1990) and Constantinides (1990) for the exchange economies and Jermann (2000) and Boldrin, Christiano and Fisher (2001) for the production economies.

second line of research the main focus has been on social insurance programs. The reason can be easily understood by considering that precautionary saving occurs to insure against random earnings fluctuations. To the extent that social programs are aimed at insuring income levels in the face of negative outcomes in the labor market or negative health shocks they act as a substitute for individual household savings. Similarly, a key reason for savings in life-cycle models is saving for retirement. If, as it is the case in the US and in the other developed countries, replacement ratios of pension benefits are progressive, the incentives to save will be stronger for households with higher lifetime incomes than for households with lower lifetime income potentially leading to more wealth inequality.

An early work along this line is the research by Hubbard, Skinner and Zeldes (1995). The authors consider a model with labor earnings risk during working life and with medical expenses risk later in life. They also introduce in the model an asset based means-tested welfare program that insures a consumption floor in case of bad luck. In practice they assume that households receive a transfer from the government that is equal to the difference between the sum of the consumption floor and medical expenditure minus the sum of earnings and assets, if this difference is positive and it is zero otherwise. This formulation, that captures in a simplified way the working of programs like food stamps and Medicaid, acts as a 100 percent tax on savings at very low levels of assets, since close to the insured consumption level the transfer is reduced on a one-to-one basis in the face of increased savings. The authors solve the households' optimal consumption-saving problem. They calibrate earn ings and medical expense risk to mimic those faced by households without and with high school and with a college degree in the data. They find that the model with the social program in place is able to reproduce better the relative life-cycle wealth accumulation path of the three groups, moreover it can correctly predict the existence of an important group of agents with low lifetime resources that hold no wealth at all. More recently Dynan, Skinner and Zeldes (2004) have explored empirically the relationship between lifetime income and saving rates. They observe that this relationship is strongly positive and test a number of theories that could explain it, concluding that such a theory should include a combination of uncertainty in — potentially large — medical expenditures coupled with social insurance programs and a bequest motive. Both works thus point to the role of social insurance programs in shaping the wealth distribution. Unfortunately none of them explicitly solves a general equilibrium model to quantify the impact of those programs on the wealth distribution.

The role of social security was explored first in Huggett and Ventura (2000). The two authors constructed a standard life-cycle model with uninsured idiosyncratic risk and added to it a careful representation of the U.S. social security system in particular with reference to the formula that fixes replacement ratios as a function of cumulated past earnings. Their model can generate the positive relationship between saving rates and income that we observe in the data; however the features of the social security system are not key to this result. A progressive formula to compute pension benefits though, turns out to be important to generate the positive relationship between income and saving rates also conditional on age, which suggests that this feature might help improving the ability of the model to match the wealth distribution. However they do not provide statistics about the wealth concentration generated by their model.

The task of fully analyzing the role of the social security system in shaping the wealth distribution was undertaken by Domeij and Klein (2002) with reference to the Swedish economy. They choose the Swedish economy because Sweden is a country with a substantial degree of wealth inequality as represented by a Gini index of 0.79 but where this inequality is largely determined by the low wealth holdings at the left corner of the distribution with almost a quarter of the households having zero or negative wealth. At the same time Sweden has a very progressive social security system with a generous fixed component of pension benefits and a low level of earnings beyond which further increases in earnings do not generate an increase in the variable component of the benefit. The two authors construct a careful life-cycle model that features both earnings risk and shocks to family structure and analyze two different model economies, one without social security and one with the structure of the Swedish social security system. The quantitative analysis of the model shows that the very progressive pension benefit scheme is responsible for the large wealth inequality observed in the data and can rationalize the large proportion of agents with zero or negative wealth. The intuition is that the very high replacement ratios for agents with low lifetime earnings frees them from the need to save.

5. Other Approaches

The models considered thus far are based on the standard incomplete markets model and as such share one common feature that is the uninsurable earnings risk. There have been attempts to construct models that try to explain the wealth concentration that we observe in the data but that abstract from this feature. The current section will briefly address that literature.

One of these contributions is Laitner (2001). The author constructs a model with no earnings risk and with perfect annuity markets so that all bequests are voluntary. Agents are altruistic, that is, they care about the utility of their descendants but they may care less than they care about their own utility. He also assumes that agents are characterized by permanent earnings differences and that these differences are partially inherited with the intergenerational correlation of ability taken from Solon (1992). The two assumptions create a new motive for saving, that is, insuring against the offspring ability risk: agents of high ability will save to bequeath a large amount of wealth since they expect their offspring to be of lower ability while the reverse happens with agents with low ability. The author is mainly interested in testing if the American economy resembles more closely to a dynastic or to a life-cycle economy and for this reason particular care is taken in the calibration to fix the strength of the altruistic motive and the aversion to intertemporal substitution. The model though has implications for the wealth distribution and under the best calibration it generates a degree of concentration that is reasonably close to the empirical one with a model Gini index of 0.75 and shares of wealth for the top 1 percent and 5 percent of the distribution that are 25 and 43.4 percent respectively.

Suen (2010) considers a model with heterogeneous subjective discount factors and endogenous human capital formation. He also includes wealth in the utility function to capture a demand for status as suggested in Cole, Mailath and Postlewaite (1992). The model is dynastic and abstracts from labor income risk. The author shows that under a reasonable parametrization it can generate an amount of income and wealth inequality that are close to the data. In his baseline model the Gini index for wealth is 0.713 and the share of wealth held by the top 1 and 5 percent of the distribution are 56.8 and 34.4 percent respectively.

Finally Gokhale, Kotlikoff, Sefton and Weale (2001) consider an overlapping-generation model with random death and fertility, assortative mating, heterogeneous and inheritable human capital, progressive income taxation and social security. There are neither annuity markets nor intergenerational altruism so that all bequests are involuntary. They use the model to study wealth inequality at retirement and find that the joint operation of inheritances and social security is important to explain the data. The reason is that social security provides for consumption in the old age of low and middle-income people but constitutes a much smaller fraction of the wealth of high income households who therefore need to save to insure against the risk of a long life. In a different context this result confirms for the U.S. the findings of Domeij and Klein (2002) for Sweden. Their models also gets reasonable results in terms of wealth immobility with inheritance of skills and marital sorting pla ying the most important role in determining this result.

6. Applications

There is now some literature that has tried to apply some of the models described above to a number of issues. Most studied has been the impact of tax policies in models that capture the wealth inequality observed in the data. One of those is Díaz-Giménez and Pijoan-Mas (2006) who study the impact of a flat-tax reform that is revenue neutral in the framework of Castañeda et al. (2003). They analyze its impact on aggregate output and income inequality and find that the result depends very much on the progressiveness of the tax: in a less progressive reform output increases and so does after-tax income, in a more progressive reform the reverse occurs. In both flat-tax reforms the income poor households pay less income tax and enjoy a gain in welfare. Meh (2005) studies the effects of a constant revenue fiscal reform that implies switching from a progressive to a proportional income tax. He constructs two models, one is the model with entrepreneurs used by Quadrini (2000), the second without entrepreneurs, follows the lines of Castañeda et al. (2003). The two models are chosen precisely because of their ability to match the wealth distribution. He then simulates both economies with a progressive and with a proportional tax system. He finds that the impact on wealth inequality of moving from the former to the latter is much smaller in the economy with entrepreneurs. In both models wealth inequality increases when moving to proportional taxes since this increases the after tax income of the very rich. When entrepreneurs are present, though the increase in wealth inequality is smaller because the higher after-tax income of the entrepreneurs increases their savings and investment, hence leads to higher wages for the poorer non-entrepreneurs. Another application to tax reform is the research by Cagetti and De Nardi (2009). In this case the two authors study the effect of abolishing the estate tax in a model with entrepreneurs that resembles very closely the one in Cagetti and De Nardi (2006) that proved capable of matching quite well the wealth distribution. They find that abolishing estate taxation would not increase wealth concentration by much and in some cases would increase aggregate capital and output. However if government revenues were kept constant through an increase of consumption or income taxes the welfare of the vast majority of agents would decrease and that of the very rich would increase.

Applications to the effect that seriously considering the heterogeneity in wealth has on the aggregate behavior of the macroeconomy have been tried in the area of asset pricing. The first research in this area was carried out by Krusell and Smith (1997) who used their model with heterogeneous subjective discount factor to study the equity premium puzzle. They find that adding a reasonable amount of heterogeneity does not lead to any significant improvement towards solving the puzzle: the model still does not produce enough volatility of the excess return and can increase the market price of risk only under the most severe borrowing constraints. Storesletten, Telmer and Yaron (2007) repeat the exercise in a life-cycle model with counter-cyclical volatility of earnings and a random depreciation rate of capital that allows them to get a realistic volatility of capital returns. Their model gets reasonably closer to matching the equity premium, however the actual amount of wealth inequality that is implied by the model is not reported.

References

[1] Abel, Andrew. (1990). "Asset prices under habit formation and catching up with the Joneses."*American Economic Review*. **89**(2): 38-42.

[2] Aiyagari, S.Rao. (1994). "Uninsured idiosyncratic risk and aggregate saving."*Quarterly Journal of Economics*. **109**(3): 659-684.

[3] Albuquerque, Rui and Hugo Hopenhayn. (2004). "Optimal lending contracts and firm dynamics."*Review of Economic Studies*. **71**(2): 285-315.

[4] Andreoni, James. (1989)."Giving with impure altruism: Application to charity and ricardian equivalence."*Journal of Political Economy*. **97**(6): 1447-1458.

[5] Bertaut, Carol and Martha Starr-McCluer. (2000). "Household portfolios in the United States."*Federal Reserve Board of Governors. Finance and Economics Discussion Paper*: 26 (April).

[6] Bewley, Truman S. (1977). "The permanent income hypothesis: A theoretical formulation."*Journal of Economic Theory*. **16** (2): 252-292.

[7] Boldrin Michele, Lawrence Christiano and Jonas Fisher. (2001). "Habit persistence, asset returns, and the business cycle. ". *American Economic Review*. **91**(1): 149166.

[8] Budría-Rodríguez, Santiago, Javier Díaz-Giménez, Vincenzo Quadrini and José V. Ríos-Rull. (2002). "Updated facts on the U.S. distributions of earnings, income and wealth."*Federal Reserve Bank of Minneapolis Quarterly Review*. **26** (Summer): 2-35.

[9] Cagetti, Marco and Mariacristina De Nardi. (2006). "Entrepreneurship, frictions and wealth."*Journal of Political Economy*. **114**(5): 835-870.

[10] Cagetti, Marco and Mariacristina De Nardi. (2009). "Estate taxation, entrepreneurship, and wealth."*American Economic Review*. **99** (1): 85-111.

[11] Campanale, Claudio. (2007). "Increasing returns to savings and wealth inequality."*Review of Economic Dynamics*. **10**(4): 646-675.

[12] Carroll, Christopher D. (1997). "Buffer stock saving and the life-cycle/permanent income hypothesis."*Quarterly Journal of Economics*. **112**(1): 1-55.

[13] Carroll, Christopher D. (1998). "Why do the rich save so much?"In Joel B. Slemrod, editor, "Does Atlas shrug? The economic consequences of taxing the rich. "Harvard University Press 2000.

[14] Castañeda, Ana, Javier Dìaz-Giménez and José V. Ríos-Rull. (2003). "Accounting for earnings and wealth inequality."*Journal of Political Economy*. **111**(4): 818-857.

[15] Cole, Harold L., George Mailath and Andrew Postlewaite. (1992). "Social norms, savings behavior and growth."*Journal of Political Economy*. **100**(6): 1092-1125.

[16] Constantinides, George. (1990). "Habit formation: a resolution of the equity premium puzzle."*Journal of Political Economy*. **98**(3): 519-543.

[17] Curtin, Richard T., Thomas F. Juster and James N. Morgan. (1989) "Survey estimates of wealth: An assessment of quality."In: Lipsey, Robert E. and Helen Stone Tice, editors. "The measurement of saving, investment and wealth". Chicago, IL: University of Chicago Press.

[18] De Nardi, Mariacristina. (2004). "Wealth inequality and intergenerational links."*Review of Economic Studies*. **71**: 743-768.

[19] De Nardi, Mariacristina, Phil Doctor and Spencer D. Krane (2007), "Evidence on entrepreneurs in the United States: Data from the 1989-2004 Survey of Consumer Finances,"*Federal Reserve Bank of Chicago Economic Perspectives*.

[20] Díaz-Giménez, Javier and Josep Pijoan-Mas. (2006). "Flat tax reforms in the U.S.: A boon for the income poor."Working paper.

[21] Díaz-Giménez, Javier, Vincenzo Quadrini and José V. Ríos-Rull. (1997). "Dimensions of inequality: Facts on the U.S. distribution of earnings, income and wealth." *Federal Reserve Bank of Minneapolis Quarterly Review*, **21**, (Spring): 3-21.

[22] Domeij, David and Paul Klein. (2002). "Public pensions: To what extent do they account for Swedish wealth inequality ?"*Review of Economic Dynamics*. **5**(3): 503-534.

[23] Dynan, Karen E., Jonathan Skinner and Stephen P. Zeldes. (2004). "Do the rich save more?"*Journal of Political Economy*. **112**(2): 397-444

[24] Gentry, William M. and R. Glenn Hubbard. (2004). "Entrepreneurship and household savings."*Advances in Economic Analysis & Policy*, **4**, (1), Article 8.

[25] Gokhale, Jagadeesh, Laurence J. Kotlikoff, James Sefton and Martin Weale. (2001). "Simulating the transmission of wealth inequality via bequests." *Journal of Public Economics* **79**(1): 93-128.

[26] Gourinchas, Pierre O. and Jonathan Parker. (2002). "Consumption over the life-cycle."*Econometrica*. **70** (1): 47-89.

[27] Guiso, Luigi, Michael Haliassos and Tullio Jappelli eds. (2002). "Household portfolios."Cambridge and London: MIT press.

[28] Heaton, John and Deborah Lucas. (2000) "Portfolio choice and asset prices: The importance of entrepreneurial Risk."*Journal of Finance*. **55**(3): pp. 1163-1198.

[29] Hendricks, Lutz. (2007). "How important is discount rate heterogeneity for wealth inequality ?"*Journal of Economic Dynamics and Control*. **31**: 3042-3068.

[30] Hubbard, Glenn, Jonathan Skinner and Stephen Zeldes. (1995). "Precautionary saving and social insurance."*Journal of Political Economy*. **103**(2): 360-399.

[31] Huggett, Mark. (1993). "The risk free rate in heterogeneous agent, incomplete insurance economies."*Journal of Economic Dynamics and Control*. **17**(5-6):953-969.

[32] Huggett, Mark. (1996). "Wealth distribution in life-cycle economies." *Journal of Monetary Economics*. **38**(3):469-494.

[33] Huggett, Mark and Gustavo Ventura. (2000). "Understanding why high income households save more than low income households."*Journal of Monetary Economics*. **45**: 361-397.

[34] Jermann, Urban J. "Asset pricing in production economies."*Journal of Monetary Economics*. **41**(2): 257-275.

[35] Kennickell, Arthur B. (2003). "A Rolling tide: Changes in the distribution of wealth in the U.S., 1989-2001."Working Paper.

[36] Kennickell, Arthur. B., Martha Starr-McCluer and Brian J. Surette. (2000). "Recent changes in U.S. family finances: results from the 1998 Survey of Consumer Finances."*Federal Reserve Bulletin*, (January): 1-29.

[37] Kotlikoff, Laurence J. and Lawrence H. Summers. (1981). "The role of intergenerational transfers in aggregate capital accumulation."*Journal of Political Economy*. **89**(4): 706-732.

[38] Krusell, Per and Anthony J. Smith. (1998). "Income and wealth heterogeneity in the macroeconomy."*Journal of Political Economy*. **106** (5): 867-896.

[39] Krusell, Per and Anthony J. Smith. (1997). "Income and wealth heterogeneity, portfolio choice and equilibrium asset returns." *Macroeconomic Dynamics*. **1** (2): 387-422.

[40] Laitner, John. (2001). "Wealth accumulation in the U.S.: Do inheritances and bequests play a significant role?"Working paper.

[41] Ljungqvist, Lars and Thomas J. Sargent. (2000). *Recursive Macroeconomic Theory*. Cambridge, Massachussets, MIT press.

[42] Meh, Césaire A. (2005). "Entrepreneurship, wealth inequality, and taxation."*Review of Economic Dynamics*. **8**(3): 688-719.

[43] Quadrini, Vincenzo. (1999). "The importance of entrepreneurship for wealth concentration and mobility."*Review of Income and Wealth*. **45**,(1): 1-19.

[44] Quadrini, Vincenzo. (2000). "Entrepreneurship, saving and social mobility." *Review of Economic Dynamics*. **3**(1): 1-40.

[45] Quadrini, Vincenzo and José V. Ríos-Rull. (1997). "Understanding the U.S. distribution of wealth."*Federal Reserve Bank of Minneapolis Quarterly Review*. **21**, (Spring): 22-36.

[46] Samwick, Andrew A. (2000). "Portfolio responses to taxation: Evidence from the end of the rainbow."In: J. B. Slemrod, (Ed). "Does Atlas shrug? The economic consequences of taxing the rich". Cambridge, MA: Harvard University Press.

[47] Solon, Gary. (1992). "Intergenerational income mobility in the United States."*American Economic Review*. **82** (3): 393-408.

[48] Suen, Richard M.H. (2010). "Time preference and the distributions of wealth and income."Working paper.

[49] Storesletten, Kjetil, Christopher I. Telmer and Amir Yaron. (2007). "Asset pricing with idiosyncratic risk and overlapping generations." *Review of Economic Dynamics* **10**(4): 519-548.

[50] Wolff, Edward N. (2010). "Recent trends in household wealth in the United States: Rising debt and the middle-class squeeze — An update to 2007."WP No. 589. The Levy Economics Institute of Bard College.

[51] Zimmermann, David J. (1992). "Regression towards mediocrity in economic Stature."*American Economic Review*. **82** (3): 409-429.

In: Economics of Wealth in the 21st Century
Editor: Jason M. Gonzalez

ISBN 978-1-61122-805-2
© 2011 Nova Science Publishers, Inc.

Chapter 6

WEALTH MANAGEMENT

Klaus Hellwig[*]
Faculty of Mathematics and Economics,
University of Ulm, 89069 Ulm, Germany

JEL: G11

1. Introduction

Maximizing expected utility is the standard approach for the solution of multiperiod portfolio selection problems. However, the applicability of the approach is limited:

- It requires a multi-period utility function that reflects the time and risk preferences of the investor. Such a utility function can hardly be found.

- It requires a probability distribution of the multi-period portfolio cash flows which is difficult, if not impossible, to determine.

- The solution can be inefficient in the sense that the optimal portfolio may enable arbitrage (e.g., Copeland et al., 2004, pp. 66).

- It is assumed that that the utility function does not depend upon the menu over which choice is being made. This, for example, has been criticized by Sen (1997).

As an alternative Hellwig (2004), Hellwig et al (2000), Korn (2000) and Selinka (2005) proposed a different approach where a portfolio is determined based on two conditions. First, the portfolio is required to be (intertemporal) efficient. Second, the valuation of the portfolio cash flows is required to support the growth preferences of the investor concerning the portfolio value. It is shown that under reasonable assumptions a portfolio exists where both conditions are satisfied. However, the approach poses a number of problems. First, the portfolio value is defined as discounted consumption after present consumption is realized. This excludes cases where present consumption is part of the decision problem. Second, the

---
[*]E-mail address: hellwig@mathematik.uni-ulm.de

approach rests on the assumption of a given multiperiod probability distribution that hardly can be found. Finally, the solution does not exclude consumption to be negative. How to handle such situations remains open.

The aim of this paper is to solve these problems. In the next two sections the case is treated where the portfolio value is defined as discounted consumption before present consumption is realized (which will be denoted as ex ante valuation) while section four treats the case, where the portfolio value is defined as discounted consumption after present consumption has been realized (which will be denoted as ex post valuation). For both cases it is shown that a solution with a non negative consumption vector exists under reasonable assumptions. Finally, in section five it is shown that under relaxed growth conditions a solution exists under less restrictive assumptions.

2. The Portfolio Model

The following analysis is based on a finite-state, discrete-time approach. Uncertainty is modelled by an event-tree with a finite set of events (nodes). $S = \{0, \ldots, n\}$ denotes the set of nodes, S_t the set of nodes at time t where $t = 0, \ldots, T$ and $S_0 = \{0\}$, $N(s)$ the set of nodes succeeding s, $F(s)$ the set of nodes that immediately follow s and s^- the immediate predecessor of s where it is assumed that s^- is unique for every s.

It is assumed that the investor is endowed with a node dependent income vector $b = (b_0, \ldots, b_n)'$ and can choose in every node s from a set of investment and financing opportunities. This set can be different for every s. $x = (x_1, \ldots, x_m)'$ denotes the activity level of all opportunities where $x \in X = \{x \mid 0 \leq x_i \leq x_i^u, i = 1, \ldots, m\}$. x_i^u is assumed to be finite for every i.

Let $A \in \mathbb{R}^{(n+1) \times m}$ denote the payoff matrix. Then Ax is the cash flow if the activity level is x. Let $c = (c_0, \ldots, c_n)'$ be the vector of consumption (withdrawals). c is called feasible if $c \in C = \{c \mid c = Ax + b \text{ for some } x \in X\}$.

Assume $c \in C$ and denote by $p = (p_0, \ldots, p_n) > 0$ the price vector. Then the ex ante portfolio value in node s will be defined as

$$V_s = V_s(c, p) = c_s + \sum_{k \in N(s)} \frac{p_k}{p_s} c_k = c_s + \sum_{k \in F(s)} \frac{p_k}{p_s} V_k. \tag{1}$$

It will be assumed that the desired price vector $\bar{p}$ and the desired consumption vector $\bar{c}$ are endogenously determined such that the following conditions are met.

Given $\bar{p} > 0$, $\bar{c} \in C$ should maximize the present portfolio value:

(C1) (Efficiency) $\bar{c}$ is an optimal solution of $V_0(\bar{c}, \bar{p}) = \max\{V_0(c, \bar{p}) \mid c \in C\}$.

Given $\bar{c} \in C$, $\bar{p}$ should support the desired increase of the portfolio value:

(C2) (Compatibility) $V_s(\bar{c}, \bar{p}) = (1 + g_s)V_{s^-}(\bar{c}, \bar{p})$, $s = 1, \ldots, n$

where g_s is the required growth rate of the portfolio value between nodes s^- and s.

Definition: $\bar{c}$ is called ex ante growth-oriented (with respect to $g_1, \ldots, g_n$), if a price vector $\bar{p} > 0$ exists such that (C1) and (C2) are satisfied.

Contrary to the expected utility maximizing approach the concept of a growth-oriented consumption vector neither requires a utility function nor a probability distribution. Furthermore, efficiency is guaranteed by (C1). Finally, the concept is not independent of the menu over which the choice is made. A growth-oriented consumption vector in principle may be found by expected utility maximization. However - contrary to the standard approach - if C is changed, then expected utility maximization with the same utility function may not lead to a growth-oriented consumption vector with respect to the same growth rates (Hellwig, 2002).

3. Ex Ante Valuation

What are the consequences of the growth requirements for consumption? Assume $c \in C$ and $p > 0$. Combining (1) with (C2) yields

$$c_s = (1 - \sum_{k \in F(s)} \frac{p_k}{p_s}(1+g_k))V_s = (1 - \sum_{k \in F(s)} \frac{p_k}{p_s}(1+g_k))\Pi_{\tau \in T(0,s)}(1+g_\tau)V_0 \quad (2)$$

where $T(0, s)$ denotes the set of nodes between 0 and s (excluding 0 and including s) and V_0 is the optimal present portfolio value given p.

Let $\hat{p} > 0$ be an arbitrary price vector and $c^{su}(\hat{p})$ an optimal solution of $\max\{V_0(c, \hat{p}) \mid c \in C\}$. $c^{su}(\hat{p})$ can be understood as consumption vector supplied by $\hat{p}$. Similarly, $c^d(\hat{p})$ given by (2) can be understood as consumption vector that is demanded by $\hat{p}$. Clearly, if "excess demand" $z(\hat{p}) := c^d(\hat{p}) - c^{su}(\hat{p})$ is zero, $c^d(\hat{p}) = c^{su}(\hat{p})$ is an ex ante growth-oriented consumption vector.

Suppose that $z(\hat{p}) \neq 0$. Then a new price vector may be chosen, for example, as an optimal solution $p(z)$ of $\max\{\sum_{s=0}^{n} z_s(\hat{p})p_s \mid p \in P\}$ where P is a suitable set of price vectors. This means that prices should be increased if demand exceeds supply and decreased if supply exceeds demand. Performing $z(p) : P \to Z$ where Z denotes the image of z und thereafter $p(z) : Z \to P$ leads to a multivalued mapping $\varphi = p(z(p)) : P \to P$. In the appendix it is shown that φ has a fixed-point $\bar{p} > 0$ such that that $z(\bar{p}) = 0$ if the following assumptions hold:

(A1) In every node $s \notin S_T$ funds can be invested for one period with a return r_{1k} in node k for all $k \in F(s)$.

(A2) Between two arbitrary succeeding nodes s and $k \in F(s)$ funds can be borrowed at a rate r_{2k}.

(A3) There exists a consumption vector $c^* \in C$ such that $c^* \geq 0$, $c^* \neq 0$.

(A4) $-1 \leq g_k \leq r_{1k}$ $(k = 1, \ldots, n)$.

The opportunities in (A1) and (A2) have to be upper bounded. These bounds are chosen such that they never become active.

Finally, in Lemma 4 it is proved that $\bar{c} \geq 0$ for every ex-ante growth oriented consumption vector $\bar{c}$ if (A4) holds.

This establishes the following theorem.

Theorem 1: Given (A1) - (A4) an ex ante growth-oriented consumption vector $\bar{c} \geq 0$ exists.

4. Ex Post Valuation

In the last section, the portfolio value V_s was defined as discounted consumption before consumption in node s is realized. Alternatively, the portfolio value in node s can be understood as discounted consumption after consumption in node s has been realized, i.e.

$$W_s = \sum_{k \in N(s)} \frac{p_k}{p_s} c_k = \sum_{k \in F(s)} \frac{p_k}{p_s} (c_k + W_k). \tag{3}$$

Two problems have to be considered.

First, by definition, $W_s = 0$ for every $s \in S_T$ which may be inconsistent with the growth requirements. To solve this problem c_s will be substituted by $c_s + W_s$ ($s \in S_T$), where c_s is the amount that is actually consumed and W_s the the terminal portfolio value that remains according to the growth requirements.

Second, c_0 has to be fixed a priori because it is not included in W_0. In what follows, $c_0 \equiv 0$.

With these changes a consumption sequence $\bar{c}$ will be called ex post growth-oriented if (C1) and (C2) are satisfied after substitution of V by W.

As an example let $C = \{c = (c_0, c_1) \mid x + c_0 = 110,\ 1.1x - c_1 = 0,\ x \geq 0\}$ be the feasible set underlying the ex ante valuation. For $g_1 = 0$ the ex ante growth-oriented consumption vector is $\bar{c} = (10, 110)$ where $V_0 = V_1 = 110$.

In case of an ex post valuation $C = \{c_1 \mid x = 110,\ 1.1x - c_1 = W_1,\ x \geq 0\}$. For $g_1 = 0$ the ex post growth-oriented consumption vector is $\bar{c} = (0, 11)$ where $W_0 = W_1 = 110$.

The example illustrates the difference between the ex ante and the ex post valuation. Using the ex ante valuation implies that the present value of the economic profit ($\frac{0.1 \cdot 110}{1.1} = 10$) is consumed at $t = 0$. Using the ex post valuation implies that the economic profit ($0.1 \cdot 110 = 11$) is consumed at $t = 1$. The ex post valuation complies with the usual procedure where profit is paid out only after it is realized. On the other hand, the ex ante valuation may be appropriate if, for example, an investor wants to determine the maximum amount that he presently can consume without being worse off in the future.

The existence of an ex post growth-oriented consumption vector can be proved similar to the case of an ex ante valuation. A solution is found by determining some $p \in P$ such that excess demand $z(p) = c^d(p) - c^{su}(p) = 0$ where $c^{su}(p)$ is an optimal solution of (C1) after V is substituted by W and $c^d(p)$ is determined as follows. p_s/p_{s^-} ($p > 0$) can be written as

$$\frac{p_s}{p_{s^-}} = \frac{\pi_s}{1+r_{1s}} = \frac{\pi'_s}{1+r'_{1s}} \qquad (4)$$

where

$$\pi'_s := \frac{\pi_s}{\sum_{\tau \in F(s^-)} \pi_\tau} \text{ and } 1 + r'_{1s} := \frac{1+r_s}{\sum_{\tau \in F(s^-)} \pi_\tau}.$$

π'_s are uniquely determined for every $s \in S_t$, $t = 1, \ldots, T$, and can be understood as (pseudo-) probability of node s after node s^- has been realized.

Using (4), W_s can be written as

$$W_s = \sum_{\tau \in F(s)} \frac{(W_\tau + c_\tau)\pi_\tau}{1+r_{1\tau}} = \sum_{\tau \in F(s)} \frac{(W_\tau + c_\tau)\pi'_\tau}{1+r'_{1\tau}}, \ s \in S_t, \ t = 1, \ldots, T-1. \qquad (5)$$

(5) is satisfied if

$$W_{s^-} = \frac{W_s + c_s}{1+r'_{1s}}. \qquad (6)$$

Combining (6) and the growth requirements $W_s = (1+g_s)W_{s^-}$, $s \in S_t$, $t = 1, \ldots, T$, yields

$$c_s = (r'_{1s} - g_s)W_{s^-} = (r'_{1s} - g_s) \Pi_{\tau \in T(0,s^-)} (1+g_\tau) W_0 \qquad (7)$$

for $s = 1, \ldots, n$.

(7) is a condition for a consumption vector to be ex post growth-oriented. Therefore such a consumption vector can be understood as a consumption vector $c^d(p)$ that is demanded by p.

Similar to the proof of Theorem 1 in Lemma 5 the following theorem is proved in the appendix.

Theorem 2: Given (A1) - (A4) an ex post growth oriented consumption sequence $\bar{c} \geq 0$ exists.

5. Weakening the Growth Requirements

The existence of an (ex ante or ex post) growth-oriented consumption sequence requires the possibility of borrowing between arbitrary succeeding nodes. Clearly this assumption is quite restrictive. Fortunately, it can be dropped if (C2) is weakened to

(C2') $V_s(\bar{c}, \bar{p}) \geq (1+g_s)V_{s^-}(\bar{c}, \bar{p})$, $s = 1, \ldots, n$.

Theorem 3: Given (A1), (A3) and (A4) an (ex ante or ex post) growth-oriented consumption vector $\bar{c} \geq 0$ with respect to growth rates $g'_s \geq g_s$, $s = 1, \ldots, n$, exists.

This can be shown as follows. Let $\bar{c}$ be an ex post growth-oriented consumption sequence with respect to the growth rates $g'_s = r'_{1s}$, $s = 1, \ldots, n$, and $\bar{p}$ the price vector that supports $\bar{c}$. Then (2) and (4) imply $\bar{c}_s = 0$ if $s \notin S_T$. Because $\bar{c}$ is efficient a componentwise increasing and concave utility function that only depends upon consumption in T exists such that $\bar{c}$ maximizes utility subject to $c \in C$. Choose r_{2k} sufficiently large so that the borrowing activities according to (A2) are not contained in the optimal solution. In Lemma 4 it is shown that $r'_{1s} \geq r_{1s}$. Thus $g'_s = r'_{1s} \geq r_{1s} \geq g_s$ and the assertion follows.

Appendix

Lemma 1: Let $P := \{p \mid p_0 = 1, p^l_s \leq \frac{p_s}{p_{s-}}(s \notin S_0), 1 - \frac{1}{p_s}\sum_{k \in F(s)} p_k(1 + \bar{r}_{1k}) \geq 0 \ (s \notin S_T)\}$ where $0 < \bar{r}_{1k} < r_{1k}$ and $p^l_s > 0$ are chosen such that $P \neq \emptyset$. Then φ has a fixed-point.

Proof: P is compact, non-void and convex where $p > 0$ for every $p \in P$. $c^{su}(\hat{p})$ is upper-semicontinuous and $V_0 = V_0(c(\hat{p}), \hat{p})$ (and conse- quently V_s for $s = 1, \ldots, n$) continuous (e.g., Luenberger, 1995, pp. 467). $c^d(\hat{p})$ is continuous. Therefore $z(\hat{p})$ is upper-semicontinuous. Because P is compact and non-void, $p(z)$ is upper-semicontinuous (Luenberger, 1995, p. 468). This implies that φ (as a combination of two upper-semicontinuous mappings) is upper-semicontinuous. φ is convex, because the set of optimal solutions of a convex optimization problem is convex. Therefore (applying Kakutani's fixed point theorem, Kakutani, 1948), a fixed point exists.

□

Lemma 2: $z(\hat{p}) = 0$ for every fixed point $\hat{p}$ of φ if the following conditions hold:

(B1) $p \in P$, $1 - \frac{1}{p_s}\sum_{k \in F(s)} p_k(1 + \bar{r}_{1k}) = 0 \Rightarrow z_s(p) \geq 0 \ (s \notin S_T)$.

(B2) $p \in P$, $\frac{p_s}{p_{s-}} = p^l_s \Rightarrow z_s(p) \geq 0 \ (s \notin S_0)$.

Proof: Since $\hat{p}$ is a fixed point of φ, $\max\{\sum_s z_s(\hat{p})p_s \mid p \in P\} = \sum_s z_s(\hat{p})\hat{p}_s$. Furthermore $\sum_{s=0}^n c^d_s(\hat{p}_s)\hat{p}_s = \sum_{s=0}^n V_s\hat{p}_s - \sum_{s \notin S_T}\sum_{k \in F(s)} \hat{p}_k(1 + g_k)V_s = \sum_{s=0}^n V_s\hat{p}_s - \sum_{s \notin S_T}\sum_{k \in F(s)} V_k\hat{p}_k = V_0$. Because $\sum_{s=0}^n c^{su}_s(\hat{p}_s)\hat{p}_s = V_0$ this implies $\sum_{s=0}^n z_s(\hat{p})\hat{p}_s = 0$.

The dual of $\max\{\sum_{s=0}^n z_s(\hat{p})p_s \mid p \in P\}$ is $\min y_0$ subject to

$$\sum_{k \in F(0)} p^l_k v_k - w_0 + y_0 \geq z_0(\hat{p}) \tag{8}$$

$$-v_s + \sum_{k \in F(s)} p^l_k v_k - w_s + (1 + \bar{r}_{1s})w_s \geq z_s(\hat{p}) \quad (s \notin S_0, S_T) \tag{9}$$

$$-v_s + (1+\bar{r}_{1s})w_{s-} \geq z_s(\hat{p}) \quad (s \in S_T) \tag{10}$$

$$v_s \geq 0 \quad (s \notin S_0), w_s \geq 0 \quad (s \notin S_T), y_0 \in \mathbb{R}.$$

Since $\hat{p} > 0$, (8), (9) and (10) hold as equalities for every optimal solution $\bar{v}_s$ $(s \notin S_0)$, $\bar{w}_s$ $(s \notin S_T)$, $\bar{y}_0$ where $\bar{y}_0 = 0$. Therefore $z_s(\hat{p}) < 0$ implies $\bar{v}_s > 0$ and/or $\bar{w}_s > 0$. By complementary slackness $\frac{\hat{p}_s}{\hat{p}_{s-}} = p_s^l$ and/or $\sum_{k \in F(s)} \hat{p}_k(1 + \bar{r}_{1k}) = \hat{p}_s$ which contradicts (B1) and (B2). Thus $z_s(\hat{p}) \geq 0$. Noting $\sum_s z_s(\hat{p}_s)\hat{p}_s = 0$ and $\hat{p} > 0$ completes the proof. □

Lemma 3: (B1) and (B2) follow from (A1) and (A2).

Proof: Assume, that (A1) holds. Choose $\hat{p} \in P$ such that $\sum_{k \in F(0)} \hat{p}_k(1 + \bar{r}_{1k}) = 1$. Then the net present value of investing one unit according to (A1) in $t = 0$ is $-1 + \sum_{k \in F(0)} \hat{p}_k(1 + r_{1k}) > -1 + \sum_{k \in F(0)} \hat{p}_k(1 + \bar{r}_{1k}) = 0$. Value maximization therefore requires to invest as much as possible. As a result $c_0(\hat{p})$ strictly decreases with the amount invested. On the other hand $c^d(\hat{p}) = (1 - \sum_{k \in F(0)} \hat{p}_k(1 + g_k))V_0 = 0$. Thus $z_0(\hat{p}) > 0$ if the investment is increased sufficiently. A similar argumentation applies to all nodes $s \in S_1$ and subsequently to all nodes $s \in S_t$, $t = 2, \ldots, T-1$. This proves (B1).

Now assume that (A2) holds. For $k \in F(0)$ choose p_k^l such that $p_k^l < (1 + r_{2k})^{-1}$ and $\hat{p} \in P$ such that $\frac{\hat{p}_k}{\hat{p}_0} = p_k^l$. Then the time zero value of borrowing one unit between nodes $s = 0$ and k is $1 - \hat{p}_k(1 + r_{2k}) = 1 - p_k^l(1 + r_{2k}) > 0$. Therefore as much as possible should be borrowed and $c_k(\hat{p})$ strictly decreases with the amount borrowed. On the other hand $c_k^d(\hat{p}) = (1 - \frac{1}{\hat{p}_k}\sum_{\tau \in F(k)} \hat{p}_\tau(1 + g_\tau))V_0 \geq 0$ since $\hat{p} \in P$ and $V_0 \geq 0$ by (A3). Thus $z_k(\hat{p}) > 0$ if the upper bound for borrowing is chosen sufficiently high. A similar argumentation subsequently applies to the succeeding nodes. This proves (B2). □

Lemma 4: Given (A1) - (A4). Then $\bar{c} \geq 0$ for every ex ante growth-oriented consumption sequence $\bar{c}$.

Proof: Let $\bar{c}$ and $\bar{p}$ satisfy (C1) and (C2). (A3) and (A4) imply $V_s \geq 0$ for $s = 1, \ldots, n$. Inserting (4) into (2) yields $c_s = (1 - \sum_{k \in F(s)} \frac{p_k}{p_s}(1 + g_k))V_s = c_s = (1 - \sum_{k \in F(s)} \frac{\pi_k'}{1+r_{1k}'}(1 + g_k))V_s$. Furthermore $-1 + \sum_{k \in F(s)} \frac{\pi_k(1+r_{1k})}{1+r_{1k}} \leq 0$ that is $\sum_{k \in F(s)} \pi_k \leq 1$. Thus $r_{1k}' \geq r_{1k} \geq g_k$ for all $k \in F(s)$ which implies $c_s \geq 0$.

□

Proof of Theorem 2:

Under the ex post valuation $c^d(p)$ is given by (7). Lemma 1 remains valid. Lemma 2 remains valid because

$$\sum_{s=0}^{n} c_s^d(\hat{p}_s)\hat{p}_s = 0 = \sum_{s=1}^{n}(r_{1s}' - g_s)W_s \hat{p}_s + \sum_{s \in S_T} W_{s-}\hat{p}_s$$

$$= \sum_{s=1}^{n}(1 + r_{1s}')W_{s-}\hat{p}_s - \sum_{s=1}^{n}(1 + g_s)W_{s-}\hat{p}_s + \sum_{s \in S_T} W_s\hat{p}_s$$

$$= \sum_{s=1}^{n}(1+r'_{1s})\frac{\hat{p}_s - \pi'_s}{1+r'_{1s}}W_{s-} - \sum_{s=1}^{n} W_s\hat{p}_s + \sum_{s \in S_T} W_s\hat{p}_s$$

$$= \sum_{s=1}^{n} \pi'_s \hat{p}_{s-} W_{s-} - \sum_{s \notin S_0, S_T} W_s \hat{p}_s = W_0$$

Lemma 3 remains valid because, using $W_{s-} \geq 0$ and $r'_{1s} \geq g_s$, $c_s^d = (r'_{1s} - g_s) W_{s-} \geq 0$.

□

References

Copeland, T.E; Weston, J.F. and Shastri, K. (2005). *Financial Theory and Corporate Policy (4th ed.)*, Addison-Wesley Series in Finance.

Hellwig, K.; Speckbacher, G. and Wentges, P. (2000). Utility maximization under capital growth constraints, *Journal of Mathematical Economics,* **33**, pp. 1-22.

Hellwig, K. (2002). Growth and utility maximization, *Economics Letters,* **77**, pp. 377-380.

Hellwig, K. (2004). Portfolio selection subject to growth objectives, *Journal of Economic Dynamics and Control* **28**, pp. 2119-2128.

Kakutani, S. (1948). A generalization of Brower's fixed point theorem, *Duke Mathematical Journal* **8**, pp. 457-459.

Korn, R. (2000). Value preserving strategies and a general framework for local approaches to optimal portfolios, *Mathematical Finance,* **10**, pp. 227-241.

Luenberger, D.C.(1995). *Microeconomic Theory*. Mc Graw-Hill.

Selinka, M. (2005). Ein Ansatz zur wertorientierten *Portfolioplanung mit nichtnegativen Konsumentnahmen*, Logos Verlag.

Sen, A, (1997). Maximization and the act of choice, *Econometrica,* **65**, pp. 745-780.

In: Economics of Wealth in the 21st Century
Editor: Jason M. Gonzalez

ISBN: 978-1-61122-805-2
©2011 Nova Science Publishers, Inc.

Chapter 7

THE DISTRIBUTION OF WEALTH IN THE UNITED STATES FROM 1983 TO 2004: INEQUALITY AND POLARIZATION[1]

Conchita D'Ambrosio[*,a], *Davide Fiaschi*[≠,b] *and Edward N. Wolff*[‡,c]
aUniversità di Milano-Bicocca, and DIW Berlin, Italy
bUniversità di Pisa, Italy
bNew York University and the Levy Institute of Bard College, USA

ABSTRACT

Recent work has documented a rising degree of wealth inequality in the United States between 1983 and 1989 but little change from 1989 to 2004. In this paper, we compare the increase in the spread of the distribution with another dimension, polarization. Using alternative approaches proposed in the literature, we examine whether a similar pattern exists with regard to trends in wealth polarization over this period. Perhaps, our most notable finding is the huge increase in wealth polarization that occurred in the U.S. from 1983 to 2004, particularly from 1998 to 2004. In contrast, the Gini coefficient for household wealth shows an increase in wealth inequality from 1983 to 1989 but almost no change thereafter.

Keywords: polarization, inequality, wealth distribution

JEL-codes: I30, D31

---

[1] This paper was originally prepared for the workshop "Income Polarization: Measurement, Determinants and Implications", May 26-28 2008, Israel. We thank Philippe Van Kerm, and workshop participants for comments.
* conchita.dambrosio@unibocconi.it
≠ dfiaschi@ec.unipi.it
‡ Edward.wolff@nyu.edu

1. INTRODUCTION

Recent work has documented a rising degree of and income inequality in the United States during the 1980s and the 1990s and into the first decade of the twenty-first century (see, for example, Piketty and Saez, 2003; Autor, Katz, and Kearny, 2005; and Wolff, 2006a, 2007). Our own calculations from the Survey of Consumer Finances show the Gini coefficient for household income rising from 0.48 in 1983 to 0.52 in 1989, 0.53 in 1998, 0.56 in 2001, and then to 0.54 in 2004.

While the sharp rise in income inequality in the U.S. starting in the 1980s and lasting through at least the first decade of the twenty-first century is well known, the time trend in wealth inequality is less widely known. As reported in a series of papers over the years by one of us (see Wolff, 1994, 1998, 2006b, 2007, and forthcoming), wealth inequality rose sharply during the 1980s but then flattened out during the 1990s and into the first decade of the twenty-first century. In particular, as we report below on the basis of the Survey of Consumer Finances, the Gini coefficient for household wealth rose from 0.80 in 1983 to 0.83 in 1989 and basically remained at this level through 2004.[2]

The finding of little change in wealth inequality during the 1990s and 2000s constitutes a "puzzle." The reason is that in Wolff (2002a) two factors were identified that seem to underlay much of the change in wealth inequality. The first is the change in underlying income inequality and the second is the change in the ratio of stock prices to housing prices. In a simple regression of the share of the top one percent of the wealth distribution on these two factors, both variables proved statistically significant and the goodness of the fit of the equation was quite high.[3] Over the period from 1989 to 1998, income inequality, as measured by the share of the top five percent increased by 2.8 percentage points, and the ratio of share prices to housing prices surged by a factor of 2.5. Extrapolating on the basis of the regression estimates, we would have expected a *9.9* percentage point increase in the share of the top one percent between 1989 and 1998, compared to its actual gain of 0.7 percentage points. Perhaps, instead of showing up in terms of rising wealth inequality, the rise in income inequality and the ratio of stock to house prices will lead, instead, to rising wealth polarization.

Increasing dispersion in a distribution can take different forms and it is of interest to understand its generating process. Of particular importance for social stability and economic growth is monitoring the movements of the middle class (see Pressman, 2007, for a discussion on the importance of the middle class). Regarding the distribution of income, some earlier work has reported that the increasing dispersion was due to the shrinkage of the middle class. In particular, Burkhauser et al. (1999) found that the effect of the business cycle during

---

[2] The time trend found by Kopczuk and E. Saez (2004) is rather similar, though they did not find as sharp a rise in wealth inequality during the 1980s. Using estate tax data, they reported that the share of personal wealth held by the top one percent rose from 21.1 percent in 1983 to 22.0 percent in 1989 and then generally leveled off, dipping slightly to 21.7 percent in 1998.

[3] A regression of a wealth inequality index, measured by the share of marketable wealth held by the top 1 percent of households (WLTH) on income inequality, measured by the share of income received by the top 5 percent of families (INC), and the ratio of stock prices (the Standard and Poor index) to housing prices (RATIO), with twenty-one data readings between 1922 and 1998, yields: WLTH = 5.10 + 1.27 INC + 0.26 RATIO, R2 = 0.64, N = 21 (0.9) (4.2) (2.5) with t-ratios shown in parentheses. Both variables are statistically significant (INC at the 1 percent level and RATIO at the 5 percent level) and with the expected (positive) sign. Also, the fit is quite good, even for this simple model.

the 1980s was such that while economic growth benefited all groups, the gains were not evenly distributed and the great majority of the middle class became richer. In contrast, Blank and Card (1993), in an even earlier study, reported an increase in the mass in the lower tail of the income distribution with increasing poverty rates.

The aim of our paper is to investigate changes in the entire distribution of wealth and to investigate what happened to its middle-class. Using techniques developed by Esteban and Ray (1994) and by Wolfson (1994), we examine whether the trend in wealth inequality is mirrored that of polarization over the two decades. At the same time, we are interested in understanding how the distribution of wealth evolved for alternative partitions of the population into social groups. For this aim we apply standard decomposition of inequality measures in between- and within-group components as well as hybrid polarization measures developed by D'Ambrosio (2001) and Zhang and Kanbur (2001). We examine inequality and polarization patterns and their change over time with regard to a number of household dimensions. The first is by race, between whites and non-whites; the second is age group, between the elderly and non-elderly; the third is by family type, between female headed and male headed households; the fourth is by education, between college graduates and all others; the fifth is by tenancy, between home owners and renters; and the sixth is by income class, between the top 20 percent and the bottom 80 percent.

The wealth concept used in this paper is marketable wealth (or net worth), which is defined as the current value of all marketable or fungible assets less the current value of debts (see Section 2 for details). The results show that there was a sizeable increase in wealth polarization that occurred in the U.S. from 1983 to 2004, though particularly over the period from 1998 to 2004. In contrast, the Gini coefficient showed an increase in wealth inequality from 1983 to 1989 and little change thereafter, while the Generalized Entropy index (with parameter 2) showed an increased from 1983 to 1989 followed by a decline from 1989 to 2004 and a net decrease over the whole 1983 to 2004 period.

When focusing on population groups, the polarization indices often give mixed results for the whole 1983 to 2004 period; however, they do show a sizeable increase in polarization by race, gender, education, home ownership status, and income between 1998 and 2004. (The exception is by age group).

The rest of the paper is organized as follows: the next section (Section 2) contains a description of the data sources. Section 3 introduces the methods used to estimate the wealth densities and the indices used to summarize the observed movements. Sections 4 to 6 present basic data on trends in household wealth, wealth inequality and polarization, and disparities between groups from 1983 to 2004 in the U.S. Conclusions are drawn in Section 7.

2. DATA SOURCES

The data sources used for this study are the 1983, 1989, 1998, and 2004 Survey of Consumer Finances (SCF) conducted by the Federal Reserve Board. Each survey consists of a core representative sample combined with a high-income supplement. In 1983, for example, the supplement was drawn from the Internal Revenue Service's Statistics of Income data file. For the 1983 SCF, an income cut-off of $100,000 of adjusted gross income was used as the criterion for inclusion in the supplemental sample. Individuals were randomly selected for the sample within pre-designated income strata. In later years, the high income supplement was selected as a list sample from statistical records (the Individual Tax File) derived from tax data by the Statistics of Income Division of the Internal Revenue Service (SOI). This second sample was designed to disproportionately select families that were likely to be relatively wealthy (see, for example, Kennickell, 2001, for a more extended discussion of the design of the list sample in the 2001 SCF). The advantage of the high-income supplement is that it provides a much 'richer' sample of high income and therefore potentially very wealthy families. However, the presence of a high-income supplement creates some complications, because weights must be constructed to meld the high-income supplement with the core sample.[4]

The wealth concept used here is marketable wealth (or net worth), which is defined as the current value of all marketable or fungible assets less the current value of debts. Net worth is thus the difference in value between total assets and total liabilities or debt. Total assets are defined as the sum of: (1) the gross value of owner-occupied housing; (2) other real estate owned by the household; (3) cash and demand deposits; (4) time and savings deposits, certificates of deposit, and money market accounts; (5) government bonds, corporate bonds, foreign bonds, and other financial securities; (6) the cash surrender value of life insurance plans; (7) the cash surrender value of pension plans, including IRAs, Keogh, and 401(k) plans; (8) corporate stock and mutual funds; (9) net equity in unincorporated businesses; and (10) equity in trust funds. Total liabilities are the sum of: (1) mortgage debt, (2) consumer debt, including auto loans, and (3) other debt.

This measure reflects wealth as a store of value and therefore a source of potential consumption. We believe that this is the concept that best reflects the level of well-being associated with a family's holdings. Thus, only assets that can be readily converted to cash (that is, 'fungible' ones) are included. As a result, consumer durables such as automobiles, televisions, furniture, household appliances, and the like, are excluded here, since these items are not easily marketed or their resale value typically far understates the value of their consumption services to the household. Also excluded is the value of future social security benefits the family may receive upon retirement (usually referred to as 'social security wealth'), as well as the value of retirement benefits from private pension plans ('pension wealth'). Even though these funds are a source of future income to families, they are not in their direct control and cannot be marketed.[5]

3. METHODOLOGY

The density estimation method we use here is optimally derived from the adaptive kernel density estimator to take into account the sample weights attached to each observation. The adaptive kernel is built with a two-stage procedure: a density is determined in the first stage in

---

[4] For a discussion of some of the issues involved in developing these weights, see Kennickell and Woodburn (1992) for the 1989 SCF and Kennickell (2001) for the 2001 SCF. We use here the Designed-Base Weights (X42000) -- a partially design-based weight constructed on the basis of original selection probabilities and frame information and adjusted for nonresponse. The 1998, 2001 and 2004 weights are actually partially Designed-Based weights (X42001), which account for the systematic deviation from the CPS estimates of homeownership rates by racial and ethnic groups.

[5] See Weller and Wolff (2005) for recent estimates of social security and pension wealth.

order to obtain the optimal bandwidth parameter; in the second stage, the final density is computed. The estimate of the density function, $\hat{f}(y)$, is determined directly from the data of the sample, $y_1, y_2,..., y_N$, without assuming its functional form a priori.

To measure inequality we use standard indices such as the Gini coefficient (henceforth G) and the Generalized Entropy index with parameter $\sigma = 2$ (henceforth $GE2$). Since wealth can be negative the Generalized Entropy index is well-defined only if $\sigma > 1$ while the Gini coefficient is always well-defined but its upper bound may be greater than one. These two inequality indices respond differently to changes in the distribution: the Gini coefficient is most sensitive to transfers around the mode of the distribution, while $GE2$ to high income values. When the population is partitioned in k groups, $k = (1,...,K)$ each with dimension n_k, $GE2$ is additively decomposable into a component summarizing inequality between groups and another which captures inequality among groups. That is:

$$GE2(y) = \sum_{k=1}^{K} w_g GE2(y_k) + GE2(\lambda_1 1^{n_1},..., \lambda_K 1^{n_K}) \qquad (1)$$

where λ_k is the mean income of each group, 1^{n_k} is a vector of 1 of dimension n_k, and $w_k = p_k^{(1-\sigma)} s_k^{\sigma}$ with $\sigma = 2$ and p_k, s_k indicating the population and the income share respectively. The first term of the r.h.s. of equation (1) is the within-group component while the second is the between-group one.

Since the upper tail in the wealth distribution deserves particular attention for the gains that took place in the time period focus of analysis, we also employ a more unusual measure of inequality: the Pareto exponent. According to Vilfredo Pareto (see Pareto, 1897) the upper tail of the distribution of wealth (and income) follows an exponential law whose cumulative distribution function is:

$$P[w > \overline{w}] \propto w^{-\alpha}, \qquad (2)$$

that is the probability to observe a wealth higher than $\overline{w}$ is proportional to $w^{-\alpha}$. Parameter α is denoted the Pareto exponent and a lower value of α means higher inequality in the upper tail of distribution. Heuristically a lower value of α means a higher probability to observe very high levels of wealth.[6]

There are two approaches to the measurement of polarization: the Wolfson approach (Wolfson, 1994) and the Esteban and Ray approach (Esteban and Ray, 1994; Duclos, Esteban and Ray, 2004). According to the first approach, polarization is shrinkage of the middle class. In contrast, in the second, the Esteban and Ray approach regards polarization as clustering around local means of the distribution, wherever these local means are located on the wealth scale. In this paper we use both approaches to measuring polarization.

---

[6] For more details see Ch.10 in Champernowne and Cowell (1998).

The two characteristics that are considered as being intrinsic to the Wolfson notion of polarization are increasing spread and increasing bipolarity. According to increasing spread, a movement of incomes from the middle position to the tails of the income distribution makes the distribution more polarized than before. In other words, as the distribution becomes more spread out from the middle position, polarization increases. On the other hand, increasing bipolarity amounts to a clustering of incomes below or above the median, which leads to a distribution more polarized than before. Equivalently, a reduction of gaps between any two incomes, above or below the median increases polarization. Thus, polarization involves both an inequality-like constituent, the increasing spread criterion, which increases both inequality and polarization, as well as an equality-like constituent, the clustering or bunching principle, which increases polarization, while decreasing any inequality measure that fulfils the Pigou-Dalton transfers principle (a requirement under which inequality is decreasing for a transfer of income from a rich to a poor person). This principle is at the heart of inequality measures consistent with the Lorenz ordering, such as G and $GE2$. Thus, polarization and inequality are two different concepts. The Wolfson index of polarization is:

$$P(y) = \frac{2(2T-G)}{m/\lambda}, \qquad (3)$$

where m is the median income, λ is the mean income and $T = 0.5 - L(0.5)$, with $L(0.5)$ being the income share of the bottom 50 per cent of the population.

Esteban and Ray (1994) introduce a model of individual attitudes in a society to measure polarization and suppose that each individual is subject to two forces: on the one hand, he identifies with those he considers to be members of his own group, $I : \mathbf{R}_+ \to \mathbf{R}_+$ represents the identification function; and on the other hand, he feels alienated from those he considers to be members of other groups, $a : \mathbf{R}_+ \to \mathbf{R}_+$ is the alienation function. An individual with wealth y_i feels alienated to a degree of $a(\delta(y_i, y_j))$ from an individual with wealth y_j. $\delta(y_i, y_j)$ is a measure of distance between the two wealth levels. For Esteban and Ray, this is simply the absolute distance $|y_i - y_j|$.[7] The joint effect of the two forces is given by the effective antagonism function, $R(I, a)$, and total polarization in the society is postulated to be the sum of all the effective antagonisms:

$$ER(\eta, y) = \sum_{i=1}^{M} \sum_{j=1}^{M} \eta_i^{1+\alpha} \eta_j R\big(I(\eta_i), a(\delta(y_i, y_j))\big)$$

where η_i represents the population associated with y_i and M is the number of distinct wealth levels. The measure that satisfies the axioms introduced by Esteban and Ray has the following expression:

---

[7] We have adapted the framework of Esteban and Ray (1994) to the distribution of wealth. Their contribution focuses on the distribution of income.

$$ER(\eta, y) = \upsilon \sum_{i=1}^{M} \sum_{j=1}^{M} \eta_i^{1+\alpha} \eta_j \delta(y_i, y_j) = \upsilon \sum_{i=1}^{M} \sum_{j=1}^{M} \eta_i^{1+\alpha} \eta_j |y_i - y_j| \quad (4)$$

for some constants $\upsilon > 0$ and $\alpha \in [1, 1.6]$ that indicates the degree of sensitivity to polarization. Duclos, Esteban and Ray (2004) extended the above to measuring polarization for continuous rather than discrete distributions. These measures (henceforth *DER*) can be viewed as continuous analogues of those introduced in the discrete setting. The only difference is that $\alpha \in [0.25, 1]$. In this paper we will compute *DER* for alternative values of the parameter α.

For understanding how the distribution of wealth evolved for alternative partitions of the population into social groups we apply hybrid polarization measures introduced by D'Ambrosio (2001) and Zhang and Kanbur (2001).

D'Ambrosio (2001) proposed a modification of (2) to compute the level of polarization within a given society for continuous distributions, and at the same time considering a characteristic, other than wealth, to generate the group partition, for example, race, age or education. Wealth polarization is hence thought to be linked to specific characteristics of the population. The polarization index has to register the moving apart of the densities classified according to some characteristics of the household that forms the groups and differences in the frequencies between the groups. Each individual identifies with those of his own group and feels alienated from those he considers to be members of other groups, as Esteban and Ray noted, but now the groups are identified by these other characteristics and not by levels of wealth. The index of polarization that Esteban and Ray proposed is modified in order to take into account the distance between the distributions of wealth of each group. The measure of distance between two distributions suggested is the Kolmogorov measure of variational distance[8] and the following polarization index obtained from (2) can be computed:

$$PK(y) = \sum_{i=1}^{K} \sum_{j=1}^{K} \pi_i^{1+\alpha} \pi_j Kov_{ij}, \quad (5)$$

where $\alpha \in [1, 1.6]$. *PK* ranges between 0 and $\left(\frac{1}{2}\right)^{1+\alpha}$. The maximum is achieved when there are only two groups of the same size with no overlapping. The index can be normalized to take values between [0, 1] by multiplying it by $2^{1+\alpha}$.

Zhang and Kanbur (2001) propose an hybrid polarization measure based on the ratio of the between- and within-group inequality components of (1). "As income differences within

---

[8] The Kolmogorov measures of variational distance between distributions i and j, $Kov_{ij} = \frac{1}{2} \int |f_i(y) - f_j(y)| dy$, captures the lack of overlapping between them. In particular, Kovij = 0 if the densities coincide for all values of y; it reaches the maximum, Kovij = 1, if the densities do not overlap. The distance is sensitive to changes of the distributions only when both take positive values, being insensitive to changes whenever one of them is zero. It will not change if the distributions move apart, provided either that there is no overlapping between them or that the overlapping part remains unchanged.

Table 1. Mean and Median Wealth and Income, 1983-2004 (In thousands, 2004 dollars)

Wealth Concept	1983	1989	1998	2004	1983-1989	1989-1998	1998-2004	1983-2004
A. Net Worth								
1. Median	63.3	67.7	70.3	77.9	7.0	3.8	10.8	23.1
2. Mean	246.4	282.3	313.2	430.5	14.6	11.0	37.4	74.7
3. Percent with net worth								
a. Zero or negative	15.5	17.9	18.0	17.0				
b. Less Than $5,000[a]	25.4	27.6	27.2	26.8				
c. Less Than $10,000[a]	29.7	31.8	30.3	29.9				
B. Income[b]								
1. Median	39.6	44.0	45.1	42.0	11.2	2.3	-6.8	6.0
2. Mean	48.2	55.6	60.1	68.8	15.5	8.0	14.4	42.7

Source: own computations from the 1983, 1989, 1998, and 2004 Survey of Consumer Finances.
a. Constant 1995 Dollars.
b. Source for household income data: U.S. Census of the Bureau, Current Populations Surveys, available on the Internet.

group diminish, that is as the groups become more homogeneous internally, differences across groups are, relatively speaking, magnified and 'polarisation' is higher. Similarly, for given within group differences, as the groups means drift apart, polarisation increases." (Zhang and Kanbur, 2001, p.96). Formally,

$$ZK(y) = \frac{GE2(\lambda_1 1^{n_1},...,\lambda_K 1^{n_K})}{\sum_{k=1}^{K} w_g GE2(y_k)} \tag{6}$$

4. WEALTH TRENDS: SUMMARY STATISTICS AND DENSITY FUNCTIONS

Table 1 documents a robust growth in wealth during the early 2000s. Median wealth was 11 percent greater in 2004 than in 1989.[9] After rising by 7 percent between 1983 and 1989, median wealth increased by 4 percent from 1989 to 1998 and then rose by 11 percent from 1998 to 2004, its fastest growth over the entire period.

Moreover, as shown in the third row of Panel A, the percentage of households with zero or negative net worth increased from 15.5 percent in 1983 to 17.9 percent in 1989, remained essentially at this level in 1998, and then slightly decreased to 17.0 percent in 2004. The share of household with net worth less than $5,000 and less than $10,000 (both in 1995 dollars) also declined somewhat between 1989 and 2004.

Mean net worth also showed a sharp increase from 1983 to 1989 followed by a slightly slower growth from 1989 to 1998 and then, buoyed largely by rising stock prices, another surge in 2004. Overall, it was 75 percent higher in 2004 than in 1983 and 53 percent larger than in 1989. Mean wealth grew quite a bit faster between 1989 and 2004, at 5.3 percent per year, than from 1983 to 1998, at 1.6 percent per year. Moreover, mean wealth grew more than three times as fast as the median between 1983 and 2004, indicating widening inequality of wealth over these years.

For comparison, we also show statistics on household income (based on Current Population Survey data). Median household income, after gaining 11 percent between 1983 and 1989, grew by only 2.3 percent from 1989 to 1998 and then nosedived by almost 7 percent between 1998 and 2004, for a net change of only 6 percent from 1983 to 2004. In contrast, mean income rose by 16 percent from 1983 to 1989, by another 8 percent from 1989 to 1998, and again by 14 percent from 1998 to 2004, for a total change of 43 percent from 1983 to 2004. Between 1983 and 2004, mean income grew less than mean net worth, and median income grew at a much slower pace than median wealth.

In sum, while household income virtually stagnated for the average American household over the period from 1983 to 2004, median net worth grew strongly over this period.

The estimated density functions of net worth are plot in Figure 1. We observe over time a constant decrease in the mass over the interval [0,100000] accompanied by an increase over negative values of wealth and on the right tail of the distributions.

---

[9] All figures are deflated to 2004 dollars on the basis of the Consumer Price Index series CPI-U.

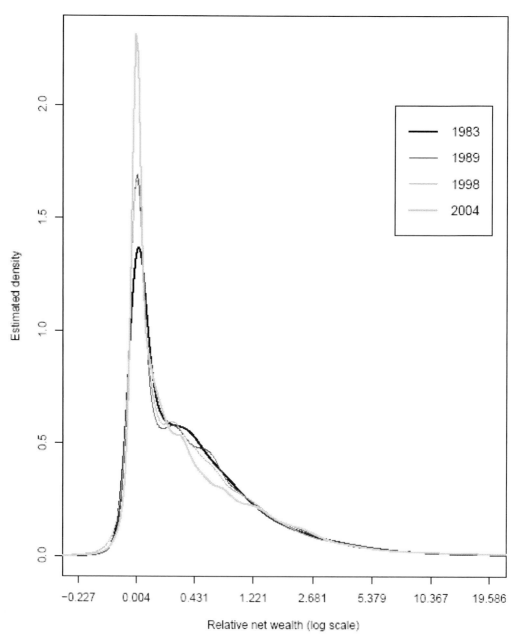

Source: own estimations from the 1983, 1989, 1998, and 2004 SCF.

Figure 1. Wealth Densities, 1983 – 2004.

Table 2. The Size Distribution of Net Worth, 1983-2004

Percentage Share of Wealth or Income held by:

Year	Gini Coefficient	GE2	Top 1%	Next 4%	Next 5%	Next 10%	Top 20%	4th 20%	3rd 20%	Bottom 40%	All
1983	0.8015 (0.0165)	18.279 (11.6113)	33.8	22.3	12.1	13.1	81.3	12.6	5.2	0.9	100
1989	0.8286 (0.0412)	21.6439 (16.3739)	37.4	21.6	11.6	13	83.5	12.3	4.8	-0.7	100
1998	0.8213 (0.0156)	21.6044 (28.8025)	38.1	21.3	11.5	12.5	83.4	11.9	4.5	0.2	100
2004	0.8292 (0.0058)	17.2602 (7.2105)	34.3	24.6	12.3	13.4	84.7	11.3	3.8	0.2	100

Memo: Mean Wealth by Quantile ($2004)

	Top 1%	Next 4%	Next 5%	Next 10%	Top 20%	4th 20%	3rd 20%	Bottom 40%	All
1983	7,170	1,050	410.2	183.9	762.9	66	14.2	-3.7	167.2
2004	13,485	2,132	767.9	369.7	1,477.40	116.9	19.9	-8.7	319.4
% change	88.1	103	87.2	101.1	93.6	77	39.7	135.6	91
% of gain	41.5	28.4	11.8	12.2	93.9	6.7	0.7	-1.3	100

Source: own computations from the 1983, 1989, 1998, and 2004 SCF.
Standard errors in parenthesis.

5. TRENDS IN WEALTH INEQUALITY AND POLARIZATION

Table 2 shows that wealth inequality, measured by the Gini coefficient, after rising from 0.802 in 1983 to 0.829 in 1989, remained virtually unchanged from 1989 to 2004. In contrast, according to Generalized Entropy measure with parameter equal to 2 wealth inequality showed a sharp rise from 1983 to 1989 and then an even sharper drop from 1989 to 2004.[10] On net, there was a slight reduction in wealth inequality between 1983 and 2004.

The change in wealth shares seems to conform more to movements in the Gini coefficient than in *GE2*. The share of wealth held by the top 1 percent rose by 3.6 percentage points from 1983 to 1989. Between 1989 and 2004, the share of the top percentile actually declined sharply, from 37.4 to 34.3 percent, though this was almost exactly compensated for by an increase in the share of the next four percentiles. As a result, the share of the top five percent remained at 58.9 percent in the two years, while the share of the top quintile rose from 83.5 to 84.7 percent. The share of the fourth and middle quintiles also each declined by a percentage point, while that of the bottom 40 percent increased by almost one percentage point.

The Memo in Table 2 shows the absolute changes in wealth and income between 1983 and 2004. The results are even more striking. Over this period, the largest gains in relative terms were made by the wealthiest households. The top one percent saw their average wealth (in 2004 dollars) rise by over 6 million dollars or by 78 percent. The remaining part of the top quintile experienced increases from 78 to 92 percent and the fourth quintile by 57 percent. While the middle quintile gained 27 percent, the poorest 40 percent lost 59 percent! By 2004, their average wealth had fallen to $2,200.

Another way of viewing this phenomenon is afforded by calculating the proportion of the total increase in real household wealth between 1983 and 2004 accruing to different wealth groups. This is computed by dividing the increase in total wealth of each percentile group by the total increase in household wealth, while holding constant the number of households in that group. If a group's wealth share remains constant over time, then the percentage of the total wealth growth received by that group will equal its share of total wealth. If a group's share of total wealth increases (decreases) over time, then it will receive a percentage of the total wealth gain greater (less) than its share in either year. However, it should be noted that in these calculations, the households found in each group (say the top quintile) may be different in the two years.

The results indicate that the richest one percent received over one third of the total gain in marketable wealth over the period from 1983 to 2004. The next 4 percent received over a quarter of the total gain, as did the next 15 percent, so that the top quintile collectively accounted for 89 percent of the total growth in wealth, while the bottom 80 percent received only 11 percent.

These results indicate rather dramatically that despite the relative stability of inequality of net worth from 1989 to 2004, the growth in the economy during the period from 1983 to 2004 was concentrated in a surprisingly small part of the population -- the top 20 percent and particularly the top one percent.

---

[10] For a discussion on the appropriateness of the use of inequality measures when comparing wealth distributions see Jenkins and Jäntti (2005).

Figure 2 reports the log of cumulative density of the top 5% U.S. households (y-axis) against the log of normalized net wealth (x-axis), and two linear regressions for 1983 and 2004.[11] The fit of the linear regressions is very high, supporting the claim that the upper tail of the U.S. distribution of wealth follows the Pareto law reported in Eq. (5).[12] The slope of the regressions corresponds to Pareto exponent α in Eq. (2). In Figure 2 we do not consider the top 0.5% since the extreme top tail appears to be underrepresented in the SCF sample and this could bias upward the estimate of α.[13] Indeed, in order to respect the privacy of the richest U.S. households, SCF does not explicitly consider the 400 wealthiest people included in the Forbes list; the total wealth of the latter account for 1.5% in 1989 and 2.2% in 2001 of total U.S. wealth (see Kennickell, 2003). For the wealthiest people we refer to Klass et al. (2006), who show how the distribution of wealth for the people in the Forbes list follows a Pareto distribution, whose Pareto exponent α decreased from 1.6 in 1988 to 1.2 in 2003 (see also Castaldi and Milakovic, 2006).

Table 6 reports the estimates of Pareto exponent, $\hat{\alpha}$, of the top 5% U.S. households for all the four years by using the Hill's Estimator and their standard errors.[14] Table 6 shows the decrease in the estimate of Pareto exponent $\hat{\alpha}$ from 1.31 in 1983 to 1.16 in 2004; however, this decrease is only slightly statistically significant given the high standard errors of estimates.[15] These findings confirm Klass et al. (2006)'s results and suggest that inequality in the upper tail of the distribution increased from 1983 to 2004. Finally, a comparison between Tables 2 and 7 highlights the inverse relationship between α and the size of the upper tail of distribution: a decline in α from 1.31 in 1983 to 1.16 in 2004 correspond an increase in the share of top 5% from 0.561 in 1983 to 0.589 in 2004.

Polarization measured by the Wolfson index increased constantly over the four years (see Table 3). Looking at the wealth densities, plotted in Figure 1, we observe that both phenomena which characterize polarization in the Wolfson approach took place. Median wealth increased over time from 63,300 to 77,900. "Spreadoutness" around the median also increased because of increasing bimodality and increasing spread. The first occurred due to clustering of wealth on the distribution to the left of the median, while increasing spread took place on both tails, particularly the increasing wealth among top wealth groups, as reported above. However, what is particularly notable is that the Wolfson index shows by far the largest increase between 1998 and 2004 (a change of 0.315). In contrast, between 1983 and 1998, the index rose by only 0.113.

DER with the polarization sensitivity parameter equal to .25 is consistent with Wolfson's results, showing an increase in polarization for all four years. However, once again, the increase is quite moderate between 1983 and 1998 (0.0049) and very sharp from 1998 to 2004 (.0397). *DER* with the other specifications of this parameter also indicates very little change

---

[11] In order to control for the growth of average net wealth the net wealth of households is normalized with respect to the average net wealth of the period.

[12] The Adjusted R² is equal to 0.99 for both regressions.

[13] Comparable results are obtained by excluding the top 0.1% of the upper tail. We choose to exclude the top 0.5% of the upper tail because the resulting regression has a higher adjusted R².

[14] See Embrechts et al. (1997) for more details on the estimate of the Pareto exponent and its asymptotic properties. We use a more general formula of the estimator than the one reported in Embrechts et al. (1997), which allows for weighted observations. Hill's plots show that the estimate of α is convergent for all years.

[15] Test of equality of α in 1983 and in 2004 is rejected at 15% significance level, while tests of equality of α in 1983 and in 1989 and 1998 cannot be rejected at 15% significance level. Hypothesis testing follows the bootstrap procedure described in Efrom and Tibshirani (1993), p. 221.

in polarization between 1983 and 1998 (in two cases, an actual decline), followed by a large jump between 1998 and 2004. The spike in polarization between 1998 and 2004 may be tied into the rising debt burden over these years (see Wolff, forthcoming, for example).[16]

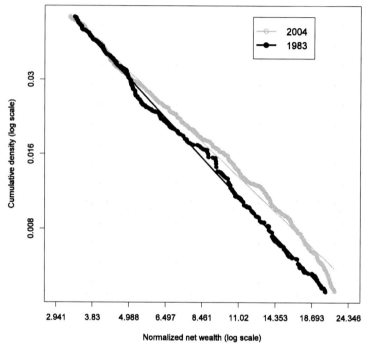

Source: own estimations from the 1983 and 2004 SCF.

Figure 2. The upper tail of the U.S. distribution of wealth in 1983 and 2004.

Table 3. Polarization in the Distribution of Net Worth, 1983-2004

Year	Wolfson	DER Alpha=.25	DER Alpha=.5	DER Alpha=.75	DER Alpha=1
1983	1.1254	0.4689	0.3548	0.2886	0.2403
	(0.0471)	(0.0088)	(0.0154)	(0.0220)	(0.0277)
1989	1.1926	0.4707	0.3469	0.2729	0.2191
	(0.0520)	(0.0207)	(0.0203)	(0.0282)	(0.0334)
1998	1.2385	0.4738	0.3569	0.2883	0.2381
	(0.0400)	(0.0123)	(0.0198)	(0.0258)	(0.0311)
2004	1.5534	0.5135	0.4324	0.3995	0.3822
	(0.0296)	(0.0064)	(0.0117)	(0.0192)	(0.0287)

Source: own computations from the 1983, 1989, 1998, and 2004 SCF.
Standard errors in parenthesis.

---

[16] For example, according to Wolff (forthcoming), the ratio of total debt to household income from mushroomed from 68 percent in 1983 to 115 percent in 2004.

6. Wealth Disparities between Groups

We now turn to analyze how the distribution of wealth evolved for alternative partitions of the population into social groups. We examine differences in densities, inequality and polarization patterns and their change over time with regard to a number of household dimensions. The first is by race, between whites and non-whites; the second is by age group, between the elderly and non-elderly; the third is by family type, between female headed and male headed households; the fourth is by education, between college graduates and all others; the fifth is by tenancy, between home owners and renters; and the sixth is by income class, between the top 20 percent and the bottom 80 percent. Results are contained in Tables 4 and 5.

The Kolmogorov measures of variational distance between distributions are reported in the last column of Table 4. This measure captures the degree of overlapping between the distributions in which we have partitioned the population. In particular, $Kov_{ij} = 0$ if the densities coincide for all values of wealth; it reaches the maximum, $Kov_{ij} = 1$, if the densities do not overlap. An increasing value of *Kov* thus indicates widening distance between the two groups, and conversely.

Its highest value is found when the partition of the population is performed according to tenancy since owner-occupied housing was the most important asset among American households (see Wolff, forthcoming, for details). Hence the wealth distributions of home-owners and renters show a very low level of overlapping. *Kov* between home owners and renters started with a value of 0.63 in 1983 but fell to 0.50 in the last year of our sample, with a big drop from 1983 to 1989 followed by a sharp rise from 1989 to 1998. Income class is another partition that gave rise to high differences in wealth holdings, confirming that wealth is positively associated with income. For income we observe a pattern over time that mimics the one reported for tenancy except for 1989. *Kov* between the top 20 percent and the bottom 80 percent started with a value of 0.65 in 1983 but then fell to 0.55 in the last year of our sample after declining in 1989 and then rising slightly in 1998.

A higher degree of overlapping is found for racial and educational groups. In the case of racial differences, we observe a sharp decline from 1983 to 1989, a more modest decline from 1989 to 1998, and then a slight increase in 2004. In 2004, *Kov* equaled only 0.26. In the case of educational groups, the distributions of net worth reached their greatest distance in 1983, at a value of 0.41, declined sharply in 1989 and 1998 but then increased in 2004. Family type and age group partitions present the highest degree of overlapping, with *Kov* in the range of 0.15 to 0.33. When we partition the population according to family type the *Kov* index showed a small decline from 1983 to 1989, a huge drop in 1998, and then a very sharp increase in 2004. Its value in 2004 was greater than in 1983. In somewhat similar fashion, for age classes, the *Kov* index showed a sharp decline from 1983 to 1998 and then a modest increase in 2004, though the 2004 value was well below the 1983 value of the index.

In the other columns of Table 4, we report the means and medians of the distributions. Striking differences are found in the wealth holdings of different racial and ethnic groups. In Panel A of Table 4, households are divided into two groups: (i) African-Americans and Hispanics, and (ii) non-Hispanic whites, Asians, and others. In 2004, the ratio of mean wealth holdings between the two groups was 0.27 and the ratio of median wealth was 0.11. Over

Table 4. Household Wealth by Selected Groups, 1983-2004 (In thousands, 2004 dollars)

Year	Population Percentage First Group	Population Percentage Second Group	Mean Values First Group	Mean Values Second Group	Ratio	Median Values First Group	Median Values Second Group	Ratio	KOV	Standard errors KOV
A. Non-whites versus Whites[a]										
1983	18.2	82	67.7	287.2	0.24	7.3	81.6	0.09	0.4744	0.0719
1989	24.9	75	104.7	341	0.31	4.6	99.3	0.05	0.2893	0.1675
1998	22.3	78	108.2	375.1	0.29	12	96.1	0.13	0.2585	0.1512
2004	26.4	74	141.9	534	0.27	13	118.3	0.11	0.2643	0.1115
B. Elderly versus Non-elderly[b]										
1983	19.1	81	397.6	211.6	1.88	109	52.9	2.06	0.316	0.1896
1989	21.5	79	413.7	246	1.68	117	57.8	2.02	0.2489	0.1426
1998	21.5	79	446.1	280	1.59	155	50.6	3.06	0.1457	0.1554
2004	21	79	594	386.9	1.54	165	59.1	2.79	0.1998	0.1377
C. Female-headed versus Male-headed households[c]										
1983	31.7	68	117	307.5	0.38	28	81.7	0.34	0.3254	0.1361
1989	28.6	71	116	348.5	0.33	18	89.4	0.2	0.3174	0.1285
1998	27.1	73	138.6	381.6	0.36	31	89.5	0.34	0.1135	0.1533
2004	27.3	73	161.1	531.6	0.3	26	114.9	0.23	0.3597	0.046
D. Less educated versus College graduates[d]										
1983	78.9	21	153.2	599.6	0.26	48	159.3	0.3	0.4075	0.1185
1989	80.8	19	176.5	727.5	0.24	54	221	0.24	0.3398	0.1357
1998	71.9	28	175.4	675	0.26	49	174.2	0.28	0.2062	0.1382
2004	67.9	32	203.1	911.6	0.22	45	235.9	0.19	0.3104	0.0929
E. Renters versus Home owners										
1983	36.9	63	42.7	367	0.12	1.5	124.4	0.01	0.626	0.0877
1989	37.2	63	76.5	403.9	0.19	0.7	144.2	0.01	0.3506	0.1448
1998	33.8	66	43.2	454.5	0.09	0.4	140.6	0	0.5101	0.0867
2004	30.9	69	46.5	602.5	0.08	0.1	167.2	0	0.4954	0.0908
F. Bottom 80 percent versus Top 20 percent of the income distribution										
1983	80	20	103	825.4	0.12	38	258.7	0.15	0.6546	0.0505
1989	80	20	123.1	919.3	0.13	41	302.1	0.13	0.5676	0.0762
1998	80	20	126.1	1,076.30	0.12	40	340.7	0.12	0.5762	0.05
2004	80	20	170.2	1,481.40	0.11	45	474.7	0.09	0.5458	0.0256

Source: own computations from the 1983, 1989, 1998, and 2004 SCF.

a. "Whites" are defined as non-Hispanic whites. "Non-whites" include African-Americans and Hispanics.
b. "Elderly" refers to households whose head is age 65 or over.
c. "Male-headed" households include married couples and single males; "female-headed" are all others.
d. Households are classified by the education of the household head.

Table 5. Polarization and Inequality among Population Groups in the Distribution of Net Worth, 1983-2004

PK alpha=1	Race	Age	Gender	Education	Home	Income
1983	0.0707	0.0489	0.0704	0.0677	0.1458	0.1046
	(0.0107)	(0.0294)	(0.0294)	(0.0197)	(0.0204)	(0.0081)
1989	0.0542	0.042	0.0647	0.0526	0.0819	0.0907
	(0.0314)	(0.0241)	(0.0262)	(0.021)	(0.0338)	(0.0122)
1998	0.0448	0.0246	0.0224	0.0416	0.1141	0.092
	(0.0262)	(0.0262)	(0.0303)	(0.0279)	(0.0194)	(0.008)
2004	0.0513	0.0332	0.0714	0.0676	0.1059	0.0868
	(0.0217)	(0.0229)	(0.0091)	(0.0202)	(0.0194)	(0.0041)
PK alpha=1.3	Race	Age	Gender	Education	Home	Income
1983	0.0622	0.0428	0.0587	0.0587	0.12	0.0912
	(0.0094)	(0.0257)	(0.0245)	(0.0171)	(0.0168)	(0.007)
1989	0.0462	0.0364	0.0545	0.0461	0.0674	0.0791
	(0.0268)	(0.0208)	(0.0221)	(0.0184)	(0.0278)	(0.0106)
1998	0.0386	0.0213	0.019	0.0351	0.0946	0.0802
	(0.0226)	(0.0227)	(0.0256)	(0.0235)	(0.0161)	(0.007)
2004	0.0436	0.0288	0.0604	0.0563	0.0885	0.0757
	(0.0184)	(0.0199)	(0.0077)	(0.0169)	(0.0162)	(0.0035)
PK alpha=1.6	Race	Age	Gender	Education	Home	Income
1983	0.0559	0.0383	0.0495	0.052	0.0994	0.0812
	(0.0085)	(0.023)	(0.0207)	(0.0151)	(0.0139)	(0.0063)
1989	0.0401	0.0321	0.0465	0.0412	0.0557	0.0704
	(0.0232)	(0.0184)	(0.0188)	(0.0164)	(0.023)	(0.0095)
1998	0.034	0.0188	0.0163	0.03	0.0791	0.0714
	(0.0199)	(0.02)	(0.022)	(0.0201)	(0.0134)	(0.0062)
2004	0.0375	0.0255	0.0518	0.0474	0.0747	0.0675
	(0.0158)	(0.0176)	(0.0066)	(0.0142)	(0.0137)	(0.0032)

Table 5 (Continued)

ZK	Race	Age	Gender	Education	Home	Income
1983	0.0032	0.0024	0.0035	0.015	0.0111	0.0388
	(0.0028)	(0.0027)	(0.0025)	(0.0098)	(0.0086)	(0.0265)
1989	0.003	0.0014	0.0032	0.0138	0.0073	0.0303
	(0.0025)	(0.0026)	(0.0023)	(0.0122)	(0.0055)	(0.02)
1998	0.0029	0.0011	0.0027	0.0118	0.0089	0.0346
	(0.0023)	(0.0017)	(0.0023)	(0.0099)	(0.0075)	(0.0218)
2004	0.0047	0.0011	0.005	0.0174	0.0104	0.0447
	(0.0017)	(0.0006)	(0.0016)	(0.0055)	(0.0041)	(0.0124)
GE Within	Race	Age	Gender	Education	Home	Income
1983	18.2202	18.2352	18.2148	18.008	18.0785	17.5969
	(12.2775)	(11.0515)	(11.5583)	(10.1188)	(11.006)	(9.9146)
1989	21.5782	21.6141	21.5746	21.3484	21.4864	21.0071
	(13.4053)	(14.8108)	(17.4702)	(12.3553)	(13.6209)	(11.3682)
1998	21.5425	21.5811	21.5458	21.3515	21.4145	20.8811
	(24.7557)	(24.8833)	(21.2188)	(18.0117)	(17.4597)	(14.8372)
2004	17.1796	17.2409	16.6518	16.9649	17.0819	16.5217
	(7.7503)	(8.1914)	(8.2114)	(5.9914)	(8.3996)	(4.9645)
GE Between	Race	Age	Gender	Education	Home	Income
1983	0.0588	0.0438	0.0642	0.271	0.2004	0.6821
	(0.0075)	(0.0393)	(0.0139)	(0.0669)	(0.0133)	(0.0593)
1989	0.0657	0.0298	0.0693	0.2955	0.1574	0.6368
	(0.0127)	(0.035)	(0.0102)	(0.0632)	(0.0168)	(0.037)
1998	0.0619	0.0233	0.0585	0.2529	0.1899	0.7233
	(0.0089)	(0.03)	(0.0142)	(0.0442)	(0.0098)	(0.0275)
2004	0.0806	0.0193	0.0835	0.2953	0.1783	0.7385
	(0.0052)	(0.0096)	(0.0031)	(0.0163)	(0.0052)	(0.0117)

Source: own computations from the 1983, 1989, 1998, and 2004 SCF.
Standard errors in parenthesis.

time, there was a slight increase in the ratios of both mean and median wealth between races. The *Kov* index, on the other hand, showed a steep decline over the 1983 to 2004 period.

Table 6. the estimate of Pareto exponent 1983-2004

Year	$\hat{\alpha}$
1983	1.31 (0.094)
1989	1.20 (0.101)
1998	1.21 (0.088)
2004	1.16 (0.037)

Source: own computations from the 1983, 1989, 1998, and 2004 SCF. Standard errors in parenthesis.

The second breakdown is between elderly and non-elderly households. The elderly were much richer than the latter. In 2004, the ratio of mean wealth between the two groups was 1.5 and the ratio of median wealth was 2.8. In terms of mean values, the wealth gap narrowed between 1983 and 2004, with the ratio falling from 1.9 to 1.5, but in terms of median wealth, the gap increased, with the ratio rising from 2.0 to 2.8. The *Kov* index declined, paralleling the time trend in the ratio of mean wealth between the two groups.

The third breakdown is between male-headed (including both married couples and single males) and female-headed households. In 2004, the mean wealth of the latter was only 30 percent of the former and the median wealth of the latter was only 23 percent. In this case, there was an unambiguous widening of the wealth gap over time, with the ratio of mean wealth falling from 0.38 in 1983 to 0.30 in 2004 and that of median wealth from 0.34 to 0.23. The *Kov* index also increased over the period, indicating an increasing wealth disparity between the two groups.

The fourth division is by the education of the household head. Households with less than a college education had only 22 percent of the mean wealth of college graduates and only 19 percent of the median wealth in 2004. Here, too, there was a clear widening of the wealth gap between 1983 and 2004, with the ratio of mean values falling from 26 to 22 percent and that of median values from 30 to 19 percent. A similar trend is evident between renters and home owners, with the ratio of mean wealth declining from 12 to 8 percent (the median wealth of renters was close to zero in all years). However, in both cases, the *Kov* index declined, indicating lessening wealth disparity between the groups.

In our last breakdown, we divide households into the top 20 percent and the bottom 80 percent according to their household income. The mean wealth of the bottom 80 percent was only 11 percent that of the top 20 percent and their median wealth only 9 percent. There was not much trend in the ratio of mean wealth over the years from 1983 through 2004 (it fell slightly, from 0.12 to 0.11) but the ratio of median wealth did decline from 0.15 to 0.09. The *Kov* index, in contrast, lessened somewhat over the period.

Results of polarization patterns and their change over time are contained in Table 5. The most polarized year for *PK* between whites and non-whites was 1983 for all the values of the parameter α. This result is due to the alienation between racial groups, as measured by the Kolmogorov measure of varational distance, reaching its maximum value in that year. It is interesting to notice that the ratio of the mean values confirms this finding but not that of the medians. Results differ when we measure polarization among races with the index proposed by Zhang and Kanbur. *ZK* decreased from 1983 to 1998 but then increased to its highest level in 2004 because of both an increase in inequality between groups and a reduction in the within group component. While PK (for all three α values) shows a substantial decline in racial polarization between 1983 and 2004, the ZK index indicates a substantial increase.

Age polarization declined continuously from 1983 to 1998 and then increased in 2004 according to PK for all values of α, mirroring Kov, since we do not observe relevant changes in the identification components captured by the population shares of the groups. Overall, between 1983 and 2004 there was a sharp decline in polarization according to the three PK measures. Likewise, ZK decreased from 1983 to 1998, with no change in 2004, because of both a decrease in inequality between groups and an increase in inequality within group. Over the entire period, the ZK index showed a sizeable decline.

When we partition the population on gender differences of the household head, PK for all values of α mirrors Kov, decreasing sharply from 1983 to 1998 and then increasing even more steeply from 1998 to 2004. Over the entire period, PK showed increasing polarization. ZK decreased continuously from 1983 until 1998 and then increased in 2004. Over the 21 years, ZK also showed a sizeable jump due to an increase in inequality between groups and a reduction in the within group component.

The two educational groups became progressively less polarized from 1983 to 1998 and then polarization increased substantially in 2004 according to PK for all values of α. PK declined from 1983 to 1998 since the overlap of the wealth distribution increased over these years and there was a relevant shift in the population shares of the two groups in 1998 with an increase in the identification component of the index. ZK also showed a decline from 1983 to 1998 followed by a sizeable jump in 2004. Over the entire period ZK also showed a substantial increase in polarization while PK showed a modest decline.

Polarization among home ownership classes showed a sharp decline from 1983 to 1989 and then generally increased from 1989 to 2004 according to PK for all values of α. The ZK index shows the same pattern. Both indices show a net decline in polarization over the full 1983 to 2004 period, though the decline was more modest according to ZK. The results by income status according to PK for all values of α show a decline from 1983 to 1989, a slight increase in 1998, and then a further decline in 2004, for an overall net decrease from 1983 to 2004. However, The ZK index indicates an increase in polarization from 1998 to 2004 and over the entire 1983 to 2004 period. The time pattern in polarization by both home ownership and income classes when measured by PK basically mirrored the time patterns of Kov.[17]

7. CONCLUSIONS

We find that wealth inequality increased from 1983 to 1989 according to the Gini coefficient but there was little change between 1989 and 2004. Over the entire period there was a net increase in inequality. The Generalized Entropy index with parameter 2 also shows an increase in wealth inequalilty from 1983 to 1989 and then a decline to 2004, for a net overall decline. According to the various polarization measures used in the paper, there was little change from 1983 to 1998 (the results were mixed on whether an increase or decline occurred) followed by a huge jump from 1998 to 2004, for an overall large increase from

---

[17] For income groups this is so by definition since the population shares are predetermined.

1983 to 2004. We speculate that the very large increase in polarization from 1998 to 2004 may be connected to the rising debt burden of US households over the period. It is also of note the difference in timing in wealth inequality trends as opposed to wealth polarization trends. The polarization indices seem to be capturing a very different dimension of disparity than inequality indices.

According to the two standard measures of inter-group differences, the ratio of mean values and the that of median values, the racial wealth gap showed a slight decline between 1983 and 2004 (that is, the ratio of wealth between non-whites and whites increased). The Kolmogorov measure of variational distance showed a large decline (also indicating a declining wealth gap), as did the *PK* index. In contrast, the *ZK* index of hybrid polarization showed a substantial rise in racial polarization between 1983 and 2004.

The wealth gap between elderly and non-elderly households narrowed in terms of mean wealth but increased in terms of median wealth. The Kolmogorv measure of variational distance likewise fell sharply, paralleling the time trend in the ratio of mean wealth between the two groups. The two polarization indices *PK* and *ZK* showed similar time trends to *KOV*.

The wealth disparity between between male-headed (including both married couples and single males) and female-headed households grew sharply between 1983 and 2004, and the *Kov* index also showed increasing polarization. Over the entire period, both *PK* and *ZK* showed increasing polarization by the gender of the head of household, though the relative increase was greater for the former than the latter.

There was a clear widening of the wealth gap between non-college-educated and college-educated households and between renters and home owners, but in both cases, the *Kov* index showed a sharp decline. The *PK* indices showed a modest decline in polarization by education and a large decline by home owner status, while *ZK* showed a fairly pronounced increase in polarization between educational groups from 1983 to 2004 and a modest drop in polarization between 1983 and 2004 by home ownership status.

The ratio of mean wealth between the bottom 80 percent and the top 20 percent of income recipients fell slightly between 1983 and 2004 but the ratio of median wealth did show a sizeable drop. In contrast, the *Kov* index declined over the period. The *PK* indices also showed a decline in polarization over the period but *ZK* indicated an overall increase.

The *PK* indices showed a spike in polarization by race, age, gender, and education between 1998 and 2004 but declines by home ownership status and income between 1998 and 2004. The ZK index showed an increase in polarization between 1998 and 2004 for all categories except age (which remained unchanged). These results seem generally consistent with the huge jump in the overall polarization measures from 1998 to 2004. It is possible that these results, as suggested above, are also due to the very large rise in indebtedness of the US population over these 6 years, particularly of the middle class (see Wolff, forthcoming, for more discussion).

On a political note, it may be that the growing political divisiveness that appears to have characterized the U.S. during the George W. Bush years in the decade of the 2000s is more of a response to the growing polarization of those years. This trend, on the other hand, does not appear to be captured by standard inequality measures. Moreover, the Wolfson polarization measure suggests a shrinkage of the middle class over those years as well.

REFERENCES

Autor, David H., Lawrence F. Katz, and Melissa S. Kearny, *"Trends in U.S. Wage Inequality: Re-Assessing the Revisionists,"* Harvard Institute of Economic Research Discussion Paper Number 2095, October 2005.

Blank, R.M. and D. Card, 1993, "Poverty, Income Distribution, and Growth: Are They Still Connected?," *Brooking Papers on Economic Activity*, 2, 285–339.

Burkhauser, R., A. Crews, M.C. Daly and S.P. Jenkins, 1999, "Testing the Significance of Income Distribution Changes over the 1980s Business Cycle: A Cross-National Comparison," *Journal of Applied Econometrics*, 14, 253–272.

Castaldi, C. and M. Milakovic, 2006, "Turnover Activity in Wealth Portfolios," *Journal of Economic Behavior and Organization*, 63, 537-552.

Champernowne, D.G. and F.A. Cowell, 1998, *Economic Inequality and Income Distribution*, Cambridge: Cambridge University Press.

D'Ambrosio, C., 2001, "Household Characteristics and the Distribution of Income in Italy: An Application of Social Distance Measures," *Review of Income and Wealth*, 47, 43–64.

Duclos, J-Y., J.M. Esteban and D. Ray, 2004, "Polarization: Concepts, Measurement, Estimation," *Econometrica*, 72, 1737–1772.

Efrom, B. and Tibshirani, R, 1993, *An introduction to the bootstrap*. London: Chapman and Hall.

Embrechts, P., C. Klueppelberg and T. Mikosch, 1997, *Modelling Extremal Events*, Berlin: Springer.

Esteban, J.M. and D. Ray, 1994, "On the Measurement of Polarization," *Econometrica*, 62, 819–851.

Jenkins, S.P. and M. Jäntti, 2005, *"Methods for Summarizing and Comparing Wealth Distributions,"* ISER Working Paper Number 2005-05.

Kennickell A., 2003, *"A Rolling Tide: Changes in the Distribution of Wealth in the U.S., 1989-2001,"* Levy Economics Institute Working Paper No. 393.

Kennickell, A.B., 2001, "Modeling Wealth with Multiple Observations of Income: Redesign of the Sample for the 2001 Survey of Consumer Finances," paper downloadable from *http://www.federalreserve.gov/pubs/oss/oss2/method.html*.

Kennickell, A.B. and R.L. Woodburn, 1992, *"Estimation of Household Net Worth Using Model-Based and Design-Based Weights: Evidence from the 1989 Survey of Consumer Finances,"* Federal Reserve Board of Washington, Unpublished paper.

Klass O., Biham O., Levy M., O. Malcai and S. Solomon, 2006, "The Forbes 400 and the Pareto wealth distribution," *Economics Letters*, 90, 290-295.

Kopczuk, W., and E. Saez, 2004, "Top Wealth Shares in the United States: 1916-2000: Evidence from estate Tax Returns," *National Tax Journal*, 57, 445-488.

Pareto, V., 1897, *Corso di Economia Politica*, Busino G., Palomba G., edn (1988), Torino: UTET.

Piketty, T. and E. Saez, 2003. "Income Inequality in the United States, 1913-1998," *Quarterly Journal of Economics*, 118, 1-39.

Pressman, S., 2007, "The Decline of the Middle Class: An International Perspective," *Journal of Economic Issues*, 41, 181-201.

Weller, C. and E.N. Wolff, 2005, *Retirement Income: The Crucial Role of Social Security*, Washington, DC: Economic Policy Institute.

Wolff, E.N., 1994, "Trends in Household Wealth in the United States, 1962-1983 and 1983-1989", *Review of Income and Wealth*, 40, 143-174.

Wolff, E.N., 1998, "Recent Trends in the Size Distribution of Household Wealth," *Journal of Economic Perspectives*, 12, 131-150.

Wolff, E.N., 2006a, *Does Education Really Help? Skill, Work, and Inequality*, New York: Oxford University Press.

Wolff, E.N., 2006b, "Changes in household wealth in the 1980s and 1990s in the U.S." in Edward N. Wolff, Editor, *International Perspectives on Household Wealth*, Cheltenham, UK: Edward Elgar Publishing Ltd., pp. 107-150.

Wolff, E.N., *"Recent Trends in Household Wealth in the United States: Rising Debt and the Middle-Class Squeeze."* Levy Institute Working Paper No. 502, June, 2007.

Wolff, E.N., forthcoming, "Recent Trends in Household Wealth in the U.S.: Rising Debt and the Middle Class Squeeze," this volume, *The Economics of Wealth in the 21st Century*.

Wolfson, M.C, 1994, "When Inequality Diverge," *American Economic Review Papers and Proceedings*, 84, 353-358.

Zhang, X. and R. Kanbur, 2001, "What Diffference Do Polarisation Measures Make? An Application to China," *Journal of Development Studies*, 37, 85-98.

INDEX

A

accession instrument, 44
accounting, 13, 30, 57, 58
activity level, 114
adjustment, 40, 41, 63
African-American, 3, 21, 24, 25
agencies, 49, 51, 52
agriculture, 74, 81
Albania, 44
alienation, 126, 139
altruism, 104, 108, 109
amines, 87
analytical framework, ix, 94
antagonism, 126
anxiety, 79
arbitrage, ix, 113
architects, 79
assessment, 45, 110
assets, vii, 1, 2, 3, 4, 6, 7, 10, 13, 14, 15, 16, 17, 18, 19, 20, 24, 28, 29, 30, 31, 34, 36, 41, 84, 94, 95, 97, 98, 100, 102, 103, 104, 106, 123, 124
attribution, 89
automation, 89
automobiles, 4, 5, 79, 124
aversion, 107

B

balance sheet, 39, 41, 94, 103
Balkans, 44
Bank of England, 80
benefits, 4, 33, 99, 106, 107, 124
bias, 5, 133
bonds, 4, 14, 15, 16, 18, 19, 28, 36, 95, 103, 124
Bosnia, 44
Bosnia-Herzegovina, 44
bounds, 116
breakdown, 13, 139
Britain, 80
business cycle, 76, 109, 122
business environment, 45

C

calibration, 107
capital accumulation, 111
capital gains, 10, 33
capitalism, 76, 88
cash, ix, 2, 4, 13, 14, 16, 17, 18, 20, 28, 95, 113, 114, 124
cash flow, ix, 113, 114
census, 2, 5, 6, 40, 128
central planning, 51
certificates of deposit, 4, 14, 19, 124
chaos, 82
chemical, 79
Chicago, 91, 110
China, 86, 143
civilization, 79
classes, 17, 21, 33, 103, 135, 140
classical mechanics, viii, 71, 74, 75, 77, 78, 82, 83, 84, 85, 90
classification, 22
clients, 51, 52
clustering, 125, 126, 133
coal, 78, 79
collateral, 104
communication, 85, 86
community, 24
competition, 52
competitors, 51
compliance, 44
complications, 4, 124
composition, 1, 3, 13, 17, 18, 29, 103, 104

computation, 9, 11
conservation, 78
consulting, 45, 46, 47, 48, 49, 50, 51, 52
Consumer Price Index, 2, 129
consumption, viii, ix, 2, 4, 14, 20, 21, 35, 36, 73, 74, 93, 94, 96, 97, 99, 100, 105, 106, 108, 113, 114, 115, 116, 117, 118, 124
Continental, 89
convention, 80
convergence, 81, 85
correlation, 68, 102, 107
cost, 46, 47, 49, 52
CPI, 5
Cuba, 74
cumulative distribution function, 125
currency, 80
Czech Republic, 59

D

data set, vii, 21, 61, 63, 64
database, 39
debts, 4, 64, 123, 124
decomposition, 123
deflate, 5
deflator, 5
democracy, 2, 88
demographic characteristics, 94
demographic factors, 65
dependent variable, 62, 64, 65, 69
deposits, 3, 4, 13, 14, 16, 17, 18, 19, 20, 28, 95, 124
depreciation, 109
destruction, 72, 80
developed countries, 106
development policy, vii, 43
deviation, 32, 39, 124
diffusion, 91
directives, 51
disclosure, 63
dispersion, 104, 122
distribution of income, 39, 40, 82, 122, 126
diversity, 84
draft, 35
drawing, 72

E

earnings, viii, 2, 93, 95, 96, 97, 98, 99, 100, 101, 102, 106, 107, 109, 110
Eastern Europe, 44, 45, 58
economic consequences, 110
economic crisis, 43

economic development, 51, 52, 88
economic downturn, 81
economic growth, viii, 43, 71, 74, 76, 81, 87, 122
economic performance, 43
economic policy, 58
ecosystem, 83, 84
education, 62, 65, 67, 68, 69, 84, 136, 139, 141
electricity, 88
empirical studies, 45
employment, 44, 103
endurance, 79
energy, 72, 73, 74, 75, 76, 78, 79, 80, 81, 82, 83, 84, 85, 86, 87, 88, 89, 90, 91
energy constraint, 74
energy consumption, 81, 86
engineering, 72, 73
entrepreneurs, 44, 51, 52, 103, 104, 108, 110
entropy, 73, 78, 82, 86
environmental protection, 44
equality, 126, 133
equilibrium, vii, 43, 44, 45, 49, 50, 52, 53, 54, 57, 58, 78, 97, 99, 104, 106, 111
equipment, 83, 85
equities, 15
equity, ix, 4, 13, 14, 15, 16, 17, 18, 19, 20, 28, 29, 35, 36, 67, 68, 69, 94, 95, 103, 105, 109, 110, 124
ethics, 80
ethnic groups, 21, 22, 26, 39, 64, 124, 135
ethnicity, 3, 25, 64
European Commission, 44, 45, 58
European Investment Bank, 44
European Union (EU), 44, 45, 59, 60
excess demand, 115, 117
exchange rate, 80
exclusion, 4, 95
expenditures, 4, 20, 21, 35, 36, 106
exports, 80, 82

F

factories, 86
family income, 5
farmers, 86
Federal Reserve Board, 3, 38, 39, 41, 94, 109, 123, 142
fertility, 108
financial resources, 46, 49, 50, 52
firm size, 103, 104
fish, 84
fluctuations, viii, 93, 96, 98, 106
formula, 5, 106, 133
foundations, 76
funding, 51, 52

G

game theory, vii, 43, 44, 52
GDP, 44
gender differences, 140
genre, 51
Germany, 83, 113
glucose, 74
goods and services, 74, 84
government revenues, 108
governments, 87, 88
Great Britain, 75, 76, 79, 80, 82
Great Depression, 81, 90
Greeks, 72
growth rate, 5, 72, 87, 88, 89, 90, 114, 115, 118

H

heterogeneity, viii, ix, 93, 94, 98, 104, 109, 111
Hispanics, 21, 22, 23, 25, 26, 135, 136
home ownership, 29, 68, 123, 140, 141
homeowners, 34, 37, 68
homogeneity, 105
hourly wage, 2
House, 38
household composition, 64
household income, 2, 6, 7, 8, 25, 35, 40, 61, 62, 65, 67, 68, 69, 122, 128, 129, 134, 139
housing, vii, 1, 2, 4, 5, 6, 7, 13, 15, 20, 29, 34, 35, 36, 95, 103, 122, 124, 135
human capital, 98, 107, 108
Human Development Report, 60
Hungary, 44, 45, 59
hybrid, 123, 127, 141
hypothesis, 110

I

idiosyncratic, 101, 106, 109, 112
image, 115
imports, 74
income distribution, 12, 40, 123, 126, 136
income inequality, 9, 10, 34, 40, 41, 108, 122
income tax, 108
increasing returns, 104
independence, 51
independent variable, 63, 64, 65, 68
India, 86
Indians, 21, 22
industrial revolution, 75, 77, 79, 81
inequality, vii, viii, ix, x, 1, 3, 7, 8, 9, 10, 11, 12, 34, 35, 37, 41, 93, 94, 95, 96, 98, 100, 105, 106, 107, 108, 109, 110, 111, 121, 122, 123, 125, 126, 127, 129, 132, 133, 135, 140, 141
inflation, 5, 29, 80
infrastructure, 44
inheritance, 26, 62, 65, 67, 68, 69, 98, 108
institutions, 44, 52, 65
integration, 72, 84
Internal Revenue Service, 3, 39, 40, 123
intervention, 43
inventions, 77
investments, 32, 45
investors, 32
Ireland, 76
iron, 79
Israel, 121
Italy, 121, 142

J

Japan, 83

K

Keynesian, 38, 81

L

labor force, 101
Latvia, 49, 58, 60
lead, 20, 34, 50, 54, 55, 56, 62, 65, 88, 102, 103, 109, 115
legislation, 44
leisure, 2, 96
lending, 109
lifetime, 100, 102, 105, 106, 107
liquid assets, 14, 15, 17, 18, 19
liquidity, 2
local government, 51

M

Macedonia, 44
machinery, 77, 78, 85
macroeconomic policy, 76
macroeconomics, ix, 94
magnitude, 13, 63, 86
majority, 6, 108, 123
management, vii, 51, 62, 85
manufacturing, 82

mapping, 115
marginal product, 82, 97, 99
marginal utility, 105
marital status, 69
market economy, 44
marriage, 62, 69
married couples, 136, 139, 141
Marx, 76, 77, 78, 92
matrix, 48, 101, 114
median, vii, 1, 2, 3, 5, 6, 7, 8, 10, 13, 20, 21, 24, 25, 26, 34, 35, 37, 126, 129, 133, 135, 139, 141
Medicaid, 106
membership, 44
metals, 14
methodology, 62, 63, 72
middle class, vii, 1, 2, 3, 6, 15, 17, 18, 19, 20, 21, 24, 33, 34, 35, 36, 122, 125, 141
middle-class families, 15
models, viii, ix, 65, 68, 71, 72, 73, 76, 80, 84, 85, 87, 88, 89, 90, 93, 94, 96, 97, 98, 101, 102, 103, 106, 107, 108
modernity, 79
molecules, 80
money income, 2
mortality risk, 99
Moses, 87, 89
multidimensional, 89

N

Nash equilibrium, 49, 50, 53, 54, 55, 56, 57, 58
national income, 88
natural sciences, 72
negative outcomes, 106
neglect, 44
nodes, 52, 53, 114, 115, 117, 119
normal distribution, 64, 65, 69
Norway, 43, 58

O

oil, 86
old age, 108
operating costs, 47, 49, 51
opportunities, 62, 114, 116
optimization, 89, 118
OSCE, 45, 59
overlap, 127, 135, 140
ownership, 2, 3, 14, 15, 16, 17, 18, 19, 20, 26, 27, 28, 29, 30, 31, 32, 33, 36, 84, 140

P

Pareto, 125, 133, 139, 142
Parliament, 59
partition, 127, 135, 140
pension plans, 4, 14, 19, 32, 36, 95, 124
percentile, 8, 9, 10, 11, 12, 16, 104, 132
permanent income hypothesis, 109
personal computers, 5
petroleum, 82
physical sciences, viii, 71, 88
physics, viii, 71, 72, 73, 75, 78, 79, 80, 81, 82, 83, 84, 85, 86, 87, 88, 89
platform, 45
Poland, 44
polarization, x, 121, 122, 123, 125, 126, 127, 133, 135, 139, 140, 141
politics, 73, 88, 89
popular support, 81
population group, 123
portfolio, ix, 1, 13, 18, 24, 26, 29, 34, 37, 103, 104, 113, 114, 115, 116
positive correlation, 68
positive relationship, 106
potential output, 76, 81
poverty, 26, 79, 123
present value, 26, 116, 119
price changes, 34
price deflator, 5
price index, 5
private firms, 51, 103
privatization, 44
probability, ix, 99, 101, 113, 114, 115, 117, 125
probability distribution, ix, 113, 114, 115
production function, 82, 83, 84, 85, 97
productivity growth, 86
profit, 49, 116
programming, 97
progressive income tax, 108
project, 51
proliferation, 88
property rights, 89
proteins, 74
public financing, 49, 51
public interest, 51
public policy, vii, 44, 61, 89

R

race, 3, 25, 64, 123, 127, 135, 141
racial differences, 135
racial minorities, 29

radicals, 88
real estate, 3, 4, 13, 14, 15, 16, 17, 18, 19, 28, 29, 35, 36, 95, 124
real income, 5, 12, 21
real numbers, 46
real property, 14
real terms, 2, 7, 13, 34
recall, 50, 52
recession, 2, 5, 35
recycling, 84
redistribution, 99
regression, 34, 63, 64, 68, 69, 122, 133
regression equation, 64
regression model, 63, 64, 68
rejection, 50
relevance, 45, 87
replacement ratios, 106, 107
requirements, 115, 117
resale, 4, 124
researchers, 61, 62, 63, 64
resolution, 110
resources, 5, 83, 84, 85, 86, 106
restructuring, 44
retirement, 4, 14, 15, 16, 18, 19, 28, 29, 30, 31, 32, 33, 99, 101, 106, 108, 124
retirement age, 29, 99
revenue, 49, 80, 108
risk aversion, 99, 104
Romania, 45, 59, 60
rules, 97, 99

S

SAPARD, 44
savings, ix, 4, 6, 14, 15, 16, 18, 19, 28, 34, 68, 75, 88, 94, 96, 97, 103, 104, 105, 106, 108, 109, 110, 124
savings account, 14
savings rate, 68, 105
scattering, 45
securities, 13, 15, 16, 17, 18, 28, 29
sensitivity, 127, 133
shape, 75, 78
shock, 79, 80, 81, 97
shortage, 74
significance level, 133
slaves, 74
small businesses, 51
social group, 123, 127, 135
social institutions, 72
social programs, 106
social sciences, viii, 93
social security, 4, 99, 106, 107, 108, 124

Social Security, 143
social status, 105
SOI, 4, 39, 40, 41, 124
Spain, 93
specialization, 75
Spring, 110, 112
standard error, 63, 133
state-owned enterprises, 44
statistics, 29, 65, 81, 103, 106, 129
stock price, 1, 6, 7, 10, 11, 15, 18, 29, 30, 31, 34, 37, 122, 129
store of value, 4, 124
subsidy, 49, 51
subsistence, 43
substitution, 5, 17, 32, 82, 101, 103, 107, 116
supervision, 73, 85, 89
supporting institutions, 45
surplus, 74, 76
survival, 51
sustainability, 51, 79, 83
Sweden, 107, 108
synthesis, 72

T

target, 50, 51, 52, 98
tax data, 4, 124
tax reform, 108, 110
tax reforms, 108, 110
tax system, 108
taxation, 108, 109, 111, 112
taxes, 88, 108
taxonomy, 83
technical assistance, 44
technological change, viii, 71, 76
technologies, 80
technology, viii, 71, 72, 75, 80, 81, 85, 87, 88, 89, 90
temperature, 78, 80
terrorism, 86
testing, 107, 133
thermodynamics, viii, 72, 73, 74, 78, 79, 80, 81, 82, 83, 84, 85, 90
time deposits, 13, 14, 19
tracks, 95
training, 84, 88
transfer payments, 49
transformation, 64, 65, 69, 80
transmission, 74, 80, 101, 102, 110
transport, 44
transportation, 81
Treasury, 80
trust fund, 4, 17, 30, 31, 32, 36, 95, 124
Turkey, 45, 59

U

U.S. Bureau of Labor Statistics, 5
U.S. economy, 79
uniform, 80
uninsured, 106
universality, 85, 86
universe, 72, 85, 90

V

valuation, ix, 113, 114, 116, 119
variables, 34, 62, 64, 65, 68, 69, 94, 122
variations, viii, 65, 71
vector, x, 114, 115, 116, 117, 118, 125
volatility, 109

W

wage rate, 99
wages, 2, 76, 78, 108
Washington, 38, 142, 143
water, 75, 84
weakness, 64
wealth distribution, viii, 64, 93, 94, 95, 96, 98, 100, 102, 103, 104, 105, 106, 107, 108, 121, 122, 125, 132, 135, 140, 142
welfare, ix, 94, 106, 108
workers, 81, 103
workplace, 29
World Bank, 44, 59, 60
World Development Report, 60
world policy, 52